KT-558-703

CULTURE AND ANARCHY

Arnold advocates literary and cultural
values as an antidote to the
progressive materialism of Victorian
society (industrial society).

— culture = liberal education.

education → liberation / freedom

mechanisation in → materialsm - does
industrialisation   not lead to classless
                         society - reinforces
                         class divisions.

MATTHEW ARNOLD

CULTURE AND ANARCHY

Edited with an introduction by
J. DOVER WILSON

CAMBRIDGE
UNIVERSITY PRESS

Published by the Press Syndicate of the University of Cambridge
The Pitt Building, Trumpington Street, Cambridge CB2 1RP
40 West 20th Street, New York, NY 10011-4211, USA
10 Stamford Road, Oakleigh, Melbourne 3166, Australia

ISBN 0 521 04061 2 hard covers
ISBN 0 521 09103 9 paperback

First published 1932
Reprinted (with corrections) 1935
Reprinted 1938 1946 1948 1950
1954 1955 1957 1960
First paperback edition 1960
Reprinted 1961 1963 1966 1969 1971 1978 1979 1981 1984 1986
1988 1990 1994 1996

Printed in Great Britain at
The University Press, Cambridge

CONTENTS

To
G. B. W.

EDITOR'S PREFACE

Culture and Anarchy was first published as a book in 1869, and has never been reprinted in its original form; for when a second edition was called for in 1875 Arnold carefully revised the whole, corrected a few misprints, added a motto from the Vulgate on the back of the title-page, inserted the now familiar titles at the heads of the chapters, reparagraphed the text at many points, and, while developing certain passages, deleted or abridged a number of others. Clearly the principal object of these deletions was to suppress or tone down personal allusions, either in order to remove grounds of offence—Arnold was ever a man of peace—or because the allusions had ceased to be topical and would no longer interest the public. But *Culture and Anarchy* is now a classic; the shrinking flesh flicked on the raw by its original "vivacities" has long been compounded with the dust; and though many of the names and allusions omitted in 1875 are ten times more forgotten in 1931, the rediscovery of them often gives point to Arnold's argument and helps us to understand the mood in which he wrote. While adopting, therefore, the improvements in phrasing and arrangement above mentioned, correcting misprints, and incorporating the sentences and passages added in 1875, together with one or two small corrections made in a third edition of 1882, this reprint in other respects follows the unexpurgated text of 1869. In a few places, as I have indicated in the Notes, textual combination has given rise to problems involving editorial authority. But on the whole the task has proved an easy one.

The restoration is by no means of purely antiquarian interest. Cambridge men, and members of King's College in particular, will be at once astonished and delighted to encounter at the very beginning of the book the familiar features of "the O.B." The future founder and first Principal of the Cambridge University Training Department for secondary teachers was an assistant master at Eton, aged 31, when he crossed the path of the prophet of secondary education by writing a rather rude review of *Schools and Universities on the Continent* in the *Quarterly* for October 1868. The anonymity of that journal did not protect him; it was obvious that the attack came from Eton, so that Arnold had little difficulty in discovering the reviewer's identity. And that he knew his Oscar Browning well is clear from the reference to "the strains of his heroic ancestor, Malvina's Oscar, as they are recorded by the family poet, Ossian." Perhaps that pretension was left behind at Eton when "the O.B." came to Cambridge; perhaps it was submerged by the tides of others. It is at any rate new to me, though I have listened to many stories at King's.

Another passage which I have enjoyed restoring throws a new light upon that Liberal Christian gentleman, the great Doctor himself. It will I think please Mr. Lytton Strachey, though if he is tempted to quote it in the next edition of his *Eminent Victorians* he will I hope make fair use of it. After dwelling upon the importance of supporting the executive "in repressing anarchy and disorder," Thomas Arnold's son continues (p. 203):

With me, indeed, this rule of conduct is hereditary. I remember my father, in one of his unpublished letters written more than forty years ago, when the political and social state of the country was gloomy and troubled, and there were riots in many places, goes on, after strongly insisting on the badness and foolishness of the government, and on the harm and dangerousness of our feudal and aristocratical constitution of society, and ends thus: "As for rioting, the old Roman way of dealing with *that* is always the right one; flog the rank and file, and fling the ringleaders from the Tarpeian Rock!"

Why Arnold cut this out in 1875 we do not know, but I suspect that the family misliked it in 1869.

Family piety of my own compels me to add a word in defence of the Alderman-Colonel of the City of London Militia, upon whom Arnold expends some of his best witticisms, and who seemed as anxious as Dogberry himself that the bills of his troops should not be stolen by the "vagrom men" of the town*. I come of London city stock, and one of the golden names on the family roll of honour is Samuel Wilson, for forty years alderman of the City and in 1838–9 Lord Mayor. There is nothing in Arnold's second edition to suggest any connexion between his antic alderman and my august relative. The reader can therefore imagine my agitation when the text of 1869 revealed the name Wilson, and my consternation when on turning up the *Times* of June, 1867, I found not only a full account of the whole notorious affair, but the Christian name, Samuel, as well. There could be no doubt of it. The great Samuel Wilson had made himself the laughing-stock of London by his route march in Hyde Park, so much so that Arnold was using him as good copy twelve months after the event. And yet a kinsman, sixty-four years later, may perhaps be allowed to plead extenuating circumstances, circumstances no doubt unknown to Arnold at the time. The "Philistine Alderman-Colonel" was seventy-five years of age in 1867; he was in fact the "Father of the City." Furthermore, he loved the militia which he commanded, much as Frederick-William I of Prussia loved his tall soldiers; he thought of them, that is to say, as a gallant spectacle, and never contemplated their being engaged in serious combat. Thus when he excused his inaction against the rioters of Hyde Park on the ground that "if he had allowed his soldiers to interfere they might have been

* *Editor's Introd.* p. xxx and below pp. 92, 205, 207.

overpowered, their rifles taken from them and used against them by the mob," the plea is to be put down not to weakness and cowardice but to an old man's fatherly affection and pride for the troops at the head of which he had marched for many years through the streets of London. That so much gallantry should be jeopardized in a scuffle with a crowd of roughs was not to be thought of, at any rate by a septuagenarian.

J. D. W.

August 1931

EDITOR'S INTRODUCTION

Matthew Arnold holds a position in the history of modern English civilisation which it requires an unusual combination of qualities and interests to appreciate. As a poet and a critic he was the most considerable literary figure of the mid-Victorian period; for though his poetry ranks third after that of Browning and Tennyson, it is a good third, and they have nothing in criticism in any way comparable with his brilliant *Essays*. As a religious thinker he produced books which had a remarkable vogue and much influence in his own day and, though at the moment a little outmoded, one of them at least, the beautiful *Literature and Dogma*, will assuredly find an enduring place as an expression, no less sincere because more liberal than that of his much-admired master Newman, of the religious genius of the English race. Lastly, as an educationalist—to use an ugly if convenient word which he himself detested—he was both in experience and insight far ahead of his contemporaries and of most of his present-day successors.

Here, in his passion for education, the passion of a life-time inherited from a father equally devoted to its service, is to be found the centre of all his work and the root even of his poetry and his religious writings. These have attracted more notice because they afforded greater scope to his gifts of expression, and because "education" is for most critics at once a dull and a technical subject. Arnold has accordingly often been ill served by those who have written upon him, for to slight or to misunderstand his educational work is to miss the heart of the man. He was indeed all of a piece. His *Essays in Criticism* cannot be fully appreciated without a study on the one hand of the Introduction to *Popular Education on the*

Continent and *A French Eton*, and on the other of *Literature and Dogma*, while a reading of the poems and the *Essays in Criticism* forms the best preparation for the understanding of his educational and religious writings. But the culmination of it all—I do not say the best thing he ever wrote but certainly his most characteristic utterance—is *Culture and Anarchy*, which is at once a masterpiece of vivacious prose, a great poet's great defence of poetry, a profoundly religious book, and the finest apology for education in the English language.

A brief account of Arnold's career up to 1869 when the volume first appeared, and of the years 1866–70, which were some of the most critical in modern English history, and to the events of which *Culture and Anarchy* makes constant reference, will help to explain how the book, here for the first time reprinted in its original entirety, came to be written.

Born in 1822, Matthew Arnold was the eldest son of Thomas Arnold, the headmaster of Rugby and the principal creator of the modern English public school system. He inherited a full share of his father's moral force, which was, however, to some extent concealed by a lively temperament and poetic gifts, both evident in boyhood. As a pupil at Rugby he also drank deep of his father's intellectual interests, and came to appreciate under the greatest teacher of the age the national significance of education and its connexion with social and political problems. Dr Arnold died a year after his son went up to Oxford, but his memory was the most abiding influence in Matthew Arnold's life, and nothing is more charming in his letters than the delight he displays at any public tribute to it. Thomas Arnold was a liberal both in theology and politics; so was Matthew, but he wore his liberalism with a difference, a difference, it cannot be doubted, due to the influence of Oxford, which during the period of his residence was in the throes of the Tractarian Movement. Matthew Arnold cared little for the ecclesiastical problems which agitated Newman, Pusey and the other tractarians, but Newman won his wholehearted respect both as a man and as a writer, and when he was made a cardinal Arnold was found among the crowd to pay him homage. Thus the spirit of the Oxford Movement, which he associated with the traditions and beauty of the city itself, "spreading her gardens to the moonlight and whispering from her towers the last enchantments of the middle ages," may be seen in everything he wrote*. And but for Newman's *Idea of a University* it is likely that *Culture and Anarchy* would never have seen the light; different as the two books are in tone and in the circumstances which produced them, their hearts beat as one. These two men then, Thomas Arnold and John Henry Newman, were Matthew Arnold's chief teachers; and when he speaks of "culture" he is thinking of the "liberal education" of which Newman writes made available for the whole of England by an indefinite multiplication of non-residential Rugby schools under state supervision.

In 1851 he was appointed H.M. Inspector of Schools, a post he continued to hold until 1886, two years before his death, and it was as an official that he learnt to look to the state as the agent of the educational reformation which he dreamed of. When he entered the public service English elementary education had been under government control for twelve years, the guiding hand for the first ten years being that of Kay-Shuttleworth, a man who regarded elementary education as missionary work on behalf of civilisation, and the inspectors he sent out as apostles of culture. Ill-health forced him to retire in 1849 so that

* Cf. pp. 61-3 below.

Arnold never served under him, but he greatly admired him and derived much from his spirit, which continued to animate the inspectorate until 1862. In that year, however, on the recommendation of the Newcastle Commission, in the supposed interests of "sound and cheap elementary instruction," and under aegis of the brilliant but commercially minded Robert Lowe, the cabinet minister then responsible for education, the notorious Revised Code was promulgated which shackled the elementary schools for a generation with the mechanical system of "payment by results," and entirely changed the character of the inspectors' duties. Hitherto Arnold had inspected schools which he entered, as the guide, philosopher and friend of the teacher; henceforward he became the examiner of children in the three R's at an annual judgment day. When he complains, as he does in his letters, of the tedium and drudgery of his official duties, all this should be remembered. The life of an inspector under the Revised Code must have been well-nigh unendurable, and Arnold endured it for twenty-four years. When again we find Lowe, with his preposterous education speeches and his glorification of the middle-classes, as one of Arnold's chief butts in *Culture and Anarchy*, we should recollect that the shafts of ridicule are directed at a man who was not merely one of "the enemies of culture" but the organiser of an educational disaster under which the inspectorate, the teachers and the children of the country groaned. In defiance of official prudence Arnold exposed and condemned the Revised Code in report after report. But the road that way was barred; and if he was to carry on the work his father had begun he must approach the enemy from another quarter.

Nevertheless, his life as an inspector taught him many things he could never have guessed at from Rugby and Oxford. Of all the nineteenth-century prophets who

pronounced upon the condition of England, Matthew
Arnold knew his England best. His work took him all over
the country, and made him intimately acquainted with
every class of society. Above all it threw him into close
contact with what used at that period to be called "the
lower middle class," the small shopkeepers and petty
employers, for the most part nonconformist in persuasion,
who were managers of the schools he inspected, and often
parents of the children attending them. For by an arrangement with the National Society church schools were at this
period reserved for clerical inspectors, and laymen were only
permitted to visit the schools of the other denominations.
Thus Arnold's whole official career was spent in that
atmosphere of "disputes, tea-meetings, openings of chapels,
sermons" which made up "the dismal and illiberal life"
of the nonconformist in the 'sixties, "a life so unlovely, so
unattractive, so incomplete, so narrow, so far removed
from a true and satisfying ideal of human perfection*,"
that he found himself compelled to write *Culture and
Anarchy* for its sweetening and enlightening.

   It is idle to say, with Professor Saintsbury, that "to
derive an idea of England from the English Dissenter is
and was absurd†." After the rise of Methodism in the
18th century, nonconformists formed the majority of the
English people; and after the second Reform Bill of 1867
they came to form the majority of the English electorate.
The future of the country, as Arnold very well knew, was
in their hands. Were they not indeed already remaking and
rebuilding the country according to their "dismal and
illiberal" vision, inasmuch as the bulk of the new industrial magnates were drawn from their ranks? It is
equally idle to say, as nonconformists of to-day will be

* *v.* below, p. 58.
† *Matthew Arnold* ("Modern English Writers"), p. 127.

inclined to say, that Arnold was unfair, that a man of his temperament and upbringing could not help being unfair, to those outside the pale of the Established Church. It is beyond question that the atmosphere of most nonconformist homes in the mid-nineteenth century was inexpressibly dreary and stuffy, so stuffy that a modern nonconformist would find it insufferable. What has happened in the meantime? The nonconformists have been saved in the only way that, as Arnold pointed out, they could be saved. In 1869 they lived in Arnold's phrase a "hole-and-corner" existence with an entirely provincial outlook. To-day they are "of the centre," they take part freely in all departments of the national life, they give us leaders of art movements, heads of colleges, prime ministers of conservative governments, they even have their great public schools. And the main agency of this remarkable transformation has been the spread of secondary and university education, the necessity for which was the whole burden of Arnold's writings*.

Moreover, though the Philistines were Arnold's chief preoccupation, because their need was greatest, he by no means confined his attention to them. With the Populace, for him as for most other thinking men in 1868 an unknown quantity, he could do little directly. But he saw their filthy and ragged children daily in the schools— "children eaten up with disease, half-sized, half-fed, half-clothed, neglected by their parents, without health, without home, without hope†"—he had to thread his way through

* Two reforms of the "Liberal practitioners" whom Arnold so distrusted, carried through within three years of the publication of *Culture and Anarchy*, greatly assisted this process: (i) the substitution of open competition for patronage as the gateway to the Civil Service in 1871, thus making it possible to recruit the public administration from all classes and denominations; (ii) the Universities Tests Act of 1871 which likewise threw open all posts in the older universities to nonconformists.

† v. below, p. 194.

their squalid streets and past their unsanitary hovels as he went to his work, and he knew all too well what a foul canker of poverty lay beneath the smiling prosperity of the middle classes. As for the upper classes, he kept his eye, with its irrepressible twinkle, constantly open for their excesses, and reserved some of his best "vivacities" for their follies and their purely "external culture." His father had begun taking the Barbarians in hand, but there was much, very much, still to do.

By the time *Culture and Anarchy* came to be written Arnold had not only studied England to some purpose, he had also won for himself a position in the very first rank of English poets and critics. This is not the place to speak of his verse, except in so far as it throws light upon his general standpoint. He defined literature as "a criticism of life," and much of his own is criticism both of life and letters. Above all it expresses better than any other poetry of the age the strange malaise which beneath all the glitter and pretentiousness of industrial success afflicted the heart of the country. In 1851, the year Arnold became an inspector, the new industrial order, with the "hungry forties" now behind it and a vista of unlimited progress before it, had celebrated high festival in the Great Exhibition; and the next quarter of a century was a period of immense commercial prosperity—and immense self-complacency. Science was at the same time opening up new and unexpected horizons; the *Origin of Species* appeared in 1859, and Huxley the champion of Evolution had met and routed the magnificent but specious Bishop Wilberforce in open debate at Oxford. Everywhere the forces of materialism seemed triumphant, everywhere the old creeds, the old institutions, the old traditions with all their beauty and historic associations were in retreat. Arnold was no blind opponent of change; in many ways he welcomed the new

tendencies*. Yet at the same time he shuddered as he
noted how uncivilised the English were, how lacking in the
foundations of culture, how self-satisfied and provincial,
how utterly unprepared for the readjustment which the
time demanded. "I see a wave," he writes in 1848, "of
more than American vulgarity, moral, intellectual and
social, preparing to break over us†"; and in the concluding
lines of *Dover Beach* this constantly recurring thought
finds other expression.

> The Sea of Faith
> Was once, too, at the full, and round earth's shore
> Lay like the folds of a bright girdle furl'd.
> But now I only hear
> Its melancholy, long, withdrawing roar,
> Retreating, to the breath
> Of the night-wind, down the vast edges drear
> And naked shingles of the world.
>
> Ah, love, let us be true
> To one another! for the world, which seems
> To lie before us like a land of dreams,
> So various, so beautiful, so new,
> Hath really neither joy, nor love, nor light,
> Nor certitude, nor peace, nor help for pain;
> And we are here as on a darkling plain
> Swept with confused alarms of struggle and flight,
> Where ignorant armies clash by night.

In these last three lines the whole country traversed in
Culture and Anarchy is revealed as in a lightning flash.

Arnold's two recipes for the rawness and provinciality of
his countrymen were the organisation of higher education
under state control and the disinterested criticism of ideas
and political nostrums, which involves a study of "the best
that is known and thought in the world" and "a free play
of the mind on all subjects which it touches‡." And in both

---

* *v.* pp. 45–6, 97, 197 below and *Essays in Criticism*, I, pp. 17–18, 159–60.
† *Letters*, I, p. 4.   ‡ *Essays in Criticism*, I, pp. 18–19.

instances he went abroad for his illustrations. Being that rare thing, an Englishman who had at command not only the classical languages but also French and German, he was found useful as a foreign agent by his department which sent him to the continent in 1859 to report on popular education in France, Holland and Switzerland for the Newcastle Commission, and again in 1865 to report on higher education abroad for the Taunton Commission. The fruit of these journeys were *Popular Education on the Continent* (1861), *A French Eton, or middle-class education and the state* (1864), and *Schools and Universities on the Continent* (1868). In all three books he urged again and yet again that the real need of England was an organised system of secondary schools for the education of the middle classes, that it was idle to look for such provision to any other body but the state, and that all progressive nations on the continent had long ago discovered this and acted upon it. The Taunton Commission itself reported very much on these lines, but its sole legislative result, the Endowed Schools Act of 1869, concerned itself merely with the question of endowments and their redistribution, an important matter but falling very far short of what Arnold had recommended and hoped for. Once again his frontal attack had failed.

It remained to try the weapon of ridicule, in the use of which he was past master, and a flanking movement under cover of literary criticism. In 1857 Arnold had been appointed Professor of Poetry at Oxford, and retained the chair, according to the usual custom, for ten years. The more important of his lectures appeared in 1865 as *Essays in Criticism* (First Series), in which following the lead of his friend and idol, the great contemporary French critic Sainte-Beuve, he set himself with brilliant success to break new ground in English criticism. For Arnold, however, there was never any frontier between life and letters, and the central principles of *Culture and Anarchy* are already explicit in the essay on "The Function of Criticism at the Present Time," seeing that the disinterested criticism advocated is the very core of the "culture" he speaks of later. As for the other essays, their subjects are chosen with exquisite tact to illustrate the study of perfection which is the true aim of culture. There is much about Goethe, who exemplified the ideal in the highest possible measure; but Arnold devotes no essay to him. Rather he turns to Heine, still comparatively neglected in England in 1865, and to quite unknown people like the de Guérins and Joubert, as if to mark the fact that on the continent "sweetness and light," so much to seek in England, were possible to the obscure and the second-rate. They were possible too—a very important point—to persons holding religious opinions quite different from those entertained by the Hebraising Englishman, opinions indeed which he would repudiate with horror as "heathenish superstitions." The heroes of *Essays in Criticism* are French Catholics, two Jews, an Italian saint, Marcus Aurelius and Sophocles. It was as if before setting his hand "to pull out a few more stops in that powerful but at present narrow-toned organ, the modern Englishman*," Arnold wished to show what sweetness and range of harmony could be extracted from instruments of foreign manufacture.

In *Essays in Criticism* Arnold makes an open declaration of war against the Philistines, and the campaign developed quickly. The publication of the book in Feb. 1865 was immediately followed by a rejoinder in the *Saturday Review* entitled "Mr Arnold and his Countrymen" which took him solemnly to task for his attitude towards England. Such an attack in a Benthamite periodical, "expressly

---

* *Essays in Criticism*, i, p. vii.

aiming, to use Arnold's words, "at an immunity from the common newspaper spirit, aiming at being a sort of organ of reason*," and numbering writers like Fitzjames Stephen, E. A. Freeman, and J. R. Green among its contributors, gave him just the opening he required. He was abroad most of 1865 collecting material for the Taunton Commission, but at the beginning of 1866 a long article on "My Countrymen" appeared over Arnold's signature in the *Cornhill Magazine*. This article, exceedingly entertaining in itself, is the germ of the wittiest of all Arnold's books, *Friendship's Garland* and *Culture and Anarchy*. Both, like many other Victorian masterpieces, were written in serial form, *Friendship's Garland* appearing as two letter sequences in the *Pall Mall Gazette*, the first written between July 1866 and April 1867 and the second between June 1869 and November 1870, while *Culture and Anarchy* saw light in the intervening period, its opening section (now comprising the Introduction and "Sweetness and Light") being appropriately enough Arnold's concluding lecture as Professor of Poetry at Oxford, which lecture was given in May 1867 under the title of "Culture and its Enemies." Two months later this was published in the *Cornhill*, and was succeeded by five other articles, under the title of "Anarchy and Authority," which were printed by the same magazine in January, February, June, July and September 1868. The six articles, which provoked the liveliest discussion as they came out, were then revised slightly, brought together in one volume and published in January, 1869, with a long preface written during the Christmas holidays, as *Culture and Anarchy: an essay in political and social criticism*, by Smith, Elder and Co., who also issued *Friendship's Garland*.

The close connexion between the two books is note-

* *Essays in Criticism*, i, p. 67.

worthy. They are the product of the same impulse, full of
the same allusions and personalities, and couched in the
same happy vein of irony, so that if either is to be rightly
appreciated both must be read. Yet there is a difference in
their function. *Friendship's Garland*, which purports to be
an account in letter form of a visit to England of a very
outspoken young Prussian savant named Arminius, whom
Arnold invents as the mouthpiece of his entertaining
sallies upon British self-complacency, is written throughout
in a vein of high-spirited raillery, and lacks the impassioned
seriousness which lies beneath the surface levity of *Culture
and Anarchy*. Disposed as it were on the flanks of the
attacking force, the two letter-series in the *Pall Mall* were
like light cavalry sent forward to harass the enemy with
the shafts of ridicule while the main onslaught was
launched from the centre.

The two books reflect minutely the occurrences, the
hopes and the fears of the time in which they were written.
The years 1866–70 represent a great turning-point in the
history both of Europe and of England. The outstanding
event was, of course, the sudden and dramatic rise of
Prussia to a position of ascendancy on the continent, first
by the victory over Austria in 1866 and then by the crush-
ing defeat of France in 1870. But though there is much
about this in the second half of *Friendship's Garland* the
writing of *Culture and Anarchy* was practically complete
two years before Sedan. The earlier book is therefore
mainly concerned with internal affairs, the chief of these
being the passing of the Second Reform Act of 1867, the
immense discussion and agitation, together with rioting,
which preceded this, and the spate of radical legislation
which threatened to follow.

The Reform Act of 1832 had enfranchised half the
middle class of the country, leaving the other half and the

whole of the working class outside the pale. In 1865 Palmerston, the old Whig statesman who had kept the country from dwelling overmuch upon internal affairs by brilliant if risky adventures in foreign policy, died, leaving arrears of domestic legislation and a very different man from himself, named Gladstone, to carry them out. One of Gladstone's first acts was to introduce a franchise reform bill in March, 1866. It was a moderate measure, but it went too far for some of the Whigs of his own party, and a revolt in the House of Commons led by Robert Lowe who idolised the middle classes and dreaded any opening of the door to classes lower in the scale, enabled the conservatives to defeat the Russell ministry in which Gladstone held office and to form a government of their own with Lord Derby as prime minister, though really under the leadership of Disraeli. Lowe's secession group was wittily dubbed the Cave of Adullam by John Bright, the Quaker radical who led the left wing of Gladstone's forces, and in the course of the debates on the bill Lowe made the most famous speech of his life, one passage of which stirred the country to its depth, and which he was never allowed to forget. "You have had the opportunity," he declared to his fellow representatives, "of knowing some of the constituencies of this country; and I ask, if you want venality, if you want ignorance, if you want drunkenness and facility for being intimidated; or if, on the other hand, you want impulsive, unreflecting, and violent people, where do you look for them in the constituencies? Do you go to the top or to the bottom?" John Bright made capital out of these words in every speech he delivered in the campaign that followed in the country; they were printed on leaflets, distributed broadcast among the working classes, and even posted up in factories and workshops. Without a doubt they did more, by inflaming the country, to make the Reform

Act of 1867 inevitable than any action of the Reform party itself. Yet they were true. As he spoke them, Lowe had in mind a rough handling by a mob at Kidderminster in which he had barely escaped with his life, an experience which he well knew could be paralleled more or less by most members of parliament.

The fact is that at this period the great mass of the people were in a condition of ignorance, squalor and brutality which in our happier age it is almost impossible to imagine. It is therefore to Arnold's credit that though he clearly fears the advent of "this vast residuum" to political power he yet retains his faith in their possibilities of perfection and does not, like Lowe, give way to the shrieking of panic, or like Carlyle turn in despair to the upper classes and implore them to effect a *coup d'état* and rule the country from the House of Lords. Indeed, nothing can give a better idea of the essential liberalism of Arnold's attitude than a comparison of *Culture and Anarchy* with an article published by Carlyle in *Macmillan's Magazine* for Aug. 1867 and significantly entitled "Shooting Niagara: and After?" Arnold retorts by asking how our aristocrats can govern when they are entirely devoid of ideas*. Moreover, though Carlyle was the son of a working man, he understood the working classes less than did the Oxford professor of poetry who visited their schools. Both were convinced of the necessity of order and authority in the state—who that thinks about politics at all is not? But while Carlyle persuaded himself that no order could be had except through a discipline exerted by an aristocracy, Arnold "a true apostle of equality"† believed that order could only be ultimately secure when the whole people learnt self-discipline through culture, culture which "seeks to do

---

* *v.* below, pp. 83–5.
† *v.* p. 70.

away with classes, to make the best that has been thought and known in the world current everywhere*." Moreover, he was alive to the fact that in 1867 there was already a large and growing "respectable" section of the working-class, trades unionists and others, such as the admirable George Odger, a London shoemaker and a well-known public speaker, whom Arnold singles out as standing "for the beautiful and virtuous mean of our present working class†." It is true that the trades unions had acquired an undesirable notoriety in 1866 through certain excesses, mostly in the Sheffield area, and that in the following year a decision in the courts had seemed to deprive them of their legal rights. But the larger unions, confident in their integrity, thereupon demanded a commission of enquiry. The commission was granted and sat from 1867 to 1869, issuing a report largely inspired by Frederic Harrison, which eventually led to legislation satisfactory to the workers. Harrison, at this time a young barrister, an ardent supporter of working-class causes and already a leader of the English disciples of Comte, is often referred to in the pages that follow, sometimes in irony but always with respect. Arnold is careful to draw a very clear distinction between such a man, much as he might disagree with him, and violent people like Charles Bradlaugh, who seemed to him a mere demagogue of a dangerous kind.

The defeat of the Reform Bill of 1866 and of the Liberal government was followed by demonstrations all over the country. Ten thousand persons assembled in Trafalgar Square on June 29, marched to Gladstone's house to cheer, to the Carlton Club to hoot, and then quietly dispersed. Three weeks later a more serious affair took place in Hyde Park. A body known as the Reform League, under the leadership of a lawyer named Edmond

* v. p. 70.   † v. p. 94.

Beales, a certain Colonel Dickson, G. J. Holyoake the co-operator and secularist, and Charles Bradlaugh, then known chiefly as an extreme radical and violent agitator, marched in processions converging from different quarters upon Hyde Park with the intention of holding a meeting there. The Park was at this time regarded by middle-class Londoners as a pleasure garden set aside for themselves and their families to take the air, and the notion of mass meetings being held there filled them with disgust and alarm. The Home Secretary therefore ordered the gates to be closed, and after a formal demand for entrance the leaders of the procession retired in an orderly fashion to hold their meeting in Trafalgar Square. They left behind them, however, a huge and miscellaneous crowd, which had collected en route. The rougher portions of this assemblage thereupon proceeded to pull down the railings, burst into the Park, and trample down the flower-beds, all very much to the terror of well-to-do citizens but little to the harm of any human being. The Hyde Park riots, as they were called, continued for some days, and produced an immense effect upon public opinion. It is scarcely too much to say that the fall of the Park railings did for England in July 1866 what the fall of the Bastille did for France in July 1789. The shooting of Niagara was seen to be inevitable.

Meanwhile John Bright began his campaign in the provinces at which he addressed enormous meetings in city after city. "The order of the day was a mass meeting, on some moor outside the town, of 150,000 to 200,000 citizens, a march past of the Trades Unions and Trades Societies before Bright, and in the evening one of his orations delivered in the largest hall of the city to as many as could find room therein. On the next day all England would be reading admirable reports of his speeches*."

* G. M. Trevelyan, *Life of Bright*, p. 362.

Bright with "a foot in both worlds, the world of middle-
class liberalism and the world of democracy"* seemed a
shallow person to Arnold. *Culture and Anarchy* is full of
quotations from his speeches, and the context is almost
always unfavourable. Professor George Trevelyan,
Bright's biographer, explains the dislike as that of a man of
Oxford culture for a self-taught industrialist and a non-
conformist†. I think the truer explanation is that in 1866
Bright was a portent rather than a man; his real greatness
had not made itself evident; and Arnold distrusted what
he stood for and for passages in his speeches which
flattered the pride of the unenfranchised middle and lower
classes. Moreover, he dealt in "clap-trap" and believed in
"machinery"; instead of employing his great powers in
grappling with "pauperism and ignorance and all the
questions which are called social . . . he still goes on with his
glorifying of the great towns"‡ and with his liberal
nostrums like the disestablishment of the Irish Church and
the Deceased Wife's Sister Bill. Arnold found him lacking in
a sense of real values: he seemed a blind leader of the blind.
He was one of those thinkers who had learnt "to call the
desires of the ordinary self . . . of the community edicts of
the national mind and laws of human progress and to give
them a general, a philosophic, and an imposing expression."
Not that he was a conscious hypocrite; "a generous statesman may honestly soon unlearn any disposition to put his
tongue in his cheek in advocating these desires, and may
advocate them with fervour and impulsiveness §."

The upshot of Bright's campaign is known to all.
Parliament met in Feb. 1867, and before six months were
out the wily Disraeli, seeing that Reform was sooner or

* *v.* below, p. 64.　　　　　† *Life of Bright*, p. 289.
‡ *v.* below, p. 18.　　　　　§ *v.* below, pp. 34-5.

later inevitable, had "dished the Whigs" by passing an Act far more radical and sweeping than that introduced by Gladstone the previous year. As so often happens in English history, it was only when the conservative party found a "leap in the dark" necessary that the nation took the plunge. The state of England in 1867 did not encourage hopefulness of success in the adventure; and not a few agreed with Carlyle that the country was shooting the rapids leading to anarchy. Serious disturbances took place in Sheffield on June 12 among trade unionists*. It was a year too of Fenian outrages organised in different parts of England by the party of revolutionary republican Irishmen, many of whom had returned from taking part in the American Civil War. On Feb. 11 Fenians attempted to seize the arms and ammunition at Chester castle. This was followed by disorders elsewhere, and on Sept. 18 armed Fenians rescued two men under arrest in the streets of Manchester and shot the sergeant in charge, while a little later an attempt to rescue prisoners in London took the form of blowing up with gunpowder the walls of Clerkenwell gaol in which they were incarcerated. The explosion failed in its object, but succeeded in killing a dozen innocent people living in the locality and injuring some hundred and twenty more. Concern was felt in certain circles for the Irishmen arrested in connexion with the affair at Manchester, some of whom were clearly innocent of murder, and a group of English sympathisers actually forced their way into the office of the Home Secretary with a demand for pardon, an incident to which Arnold refers on p. 77. But Arnold makes light of Fenianism; it was the natural product of "centuries of ill-usage†." Much more serious in his view, because symptomatic of the anarchical tendencies in English society, were

v. Annual Register.   † *v*. pp. 79–80.

the counter-antics of a certain Mr Murphy which enlivened the Midlands in the summer of 1867 and the spring of 1868. This person, who described himself as "an agent of the London Protestant Electoral Union," after causing riots in Wolverhampton and the neighbourhood by injudicious language concerning Roman Catholicism uttered on public platforms, announced a course of lectures on "The Errors of the Roman Church" to be delivered in Birmingham, beginning on June 16. He had applied to the Mayor for the use of the town hall, an application which was wisely refused. He therefore caused to be built, with the assistance of his local Protestant supporters, an enormous wooden "tabernacle" to hold 3000 people, which was packed at the first lecture. His lectures and speeches by his friends, sentences from which Arnold quotes (v. pp. 77–8, 91), were of a highly inflamatory character, and were followed by a series of disgraceful riots in the streets of Birmingham, which continued for days, and which the police were found unable to cope with, though they charged the crowds repeatedly with drawn cutlasses. Nothing abashed, Murphy repeated his exploits in Ashton under Lyne (May 1868) and again in Manchester (Sept. 1868), on both occasions causing bloodshed*.

Such events, following on the Hyde Park riots of 1866, filled all lovers of order with grave foreboding. Nor did the executive appear to be upholding authority with the firmness that might be expected. The Home Secretary, Spencer Walpole, handled the Hyde Park affair with such culpable gentleness, in the opinion of many Londoners, that he was forced to resign, and it was even rumoured, no doubt quite falsely, that on one occasion in pleading with

* v. *Annual Register*, June 16, 1867; May 10, 1868; Sept. 1868 and *Times*, June 17–21, 1867.

a deputation of the Reform League he had actually shed tears*. Something which looked very like an attempt to mob his successor, as we have seen, took place in connexion with the Fenian outrage, while a week before the Murphy riots Hyde Park again attracted public attention on account of a curious incident which still further shook the confidence of Londoners in those responsible for the preservation of law and order, and gave Arnold yet another instance of "the relaxed habits of government†." Alderman Samuel Wilson, Colonel of the Royal London Militia, a regiment belonging to the Corporation of London and long since disbanded, on Monday, June 10, took his men for a route march into Hyde Park, whither he was followed by a number of roughs, who knocked off people's hats as they went along and generally made a nuisance of themselves without any interference on the part of the gallant colonel and his troops. Great indignation was felt at the affair. Questions were asked in Parliament about the conduct of the colonel, and he attempted to justify it in a letter to the *Times* on June 12 and at a meeting of the Court of Aldermen reported on June 19. He did not improve his case by alleging that he was proud of his men and that he feared they might lose their rifles had they meddled with the roughs‡.

Meanwhile the Parliament elected in the time of Palmerston was nearing the end of its days. It dragged on through most of 1868, with Disraeli as premier but with Gladstone as its dominant personality. The General Election which came in November under the reformed franchise was a foregone conclusion; the new House of Commons was found to be predominantly liberal if not radical in colour, and while Arnold was busy writing his

* *v.* p. 205.   † *v.* p. 79.
‡ *v.* p. 92; for the colonel's defence, *v. Ed. Preface*, pp. ix–x.

Preface, Gladstone was making up his cabinet, in which for the first time in history a nonconformist, John Bright, was to hold office. *Culture and Anarchy* appeared from the press in January and the new parliament got to work on Feb. 16; seldom was a book better timed. It should be remembered also that the final chapter, "Our Liberal Practitioners," appearing as it did in the *Cornhill* for July and September 1868 just before the dissolution, was almost an electioneering pamphlet. Certainly the Preface was deliberately political in intention and Arnold took pains that it should come under Disraeli's eye*. In it he once again addresses himself to the burning topic of the hour, which he had already handled in Chapter VI, namely the disestablishment of the Irish Church. This was in fact the first great measure taken in hand by the new Liberal government, Gladstone introducing the Bill on March 1, 1869 and placing it on the statute book in the following July. The other two examples of "Liberal practice" cited in Chapter VI are a Real Estate Intestacy Bill and the Deceased Wife's Sister Bill, which after Lord Lyndhurst's Act of 1835 made it definitely illegal for a man to marry his deceased wife's sister (a matter which had been in controversy among English lawyers since the Reformation), became almost a hardy annual in parliament, until the act of 1907 finally decided the question. Arnold uses the first of these measures as an illustration of Liberal muddle-headedness. His objection to the second, which will seem curious to many to-day, was more deep-seated. It was not based upon respect for the ecclesiastical table of affinity, for which he cared little. Rather it expressed "his strong sense...that the sacredness of marriage, and the customs

---

* *Letters* i, 402; ii, 1. Perhaps he hoped to interest the Jewish sphinx in his interesting plan, borrowed from Germany, of bringing all the important religious denominations within the Establishment.

that regulate it, were triumphs of culture which had been won, painfully and with effort, from the unbridled promiscuity of primitive life. To impair that sacredness, to dislocate those customs, was to take a step backwards into darkness and anarchy*." As for the Bill itself, it ministered to "that double craving so characteristic of our Philistine, and so eminently exemplified in that crowned Philistine, Henry the Eighth—the craving for forbidden fruit and the craving for legality†."

I have spent some time explaining the contemporary allusions and background of *Culture and Anarchy* in order that the reader may spend less upon them when he comes to the book itself. They are interesting for themselves, and they were important for Arnold, since his primary object was to arrest and persuade his own generation, to which end topical allusion is at all times the readiest means, and was particularly appropriate to the exciting historical moment when the book was written. Moreover, to understand exactly what was in Arnold's mind is necessary to the full appreciation of the delicious turns of irony, the urbane humour—so obviously enjoyed by the humorist—the "sunny malice" and "slim feasting smile‡" with which he handles his victims, handles them gently, almost lovingly; to the appreciation, in a word, of his comic muse. The task of unearthing the facts, which were the small change of London gossip in 1867, but which have to-day often proved difficult to come by, about the egregious Murphy, the golden Mrs Gooch, the perfect Lord Elcho, the lithe and sinewy Hepworth Dixon and his "great sexual insurrection," the feeble-kneed Alderman-Colonel Samuel Wilson and his immaculate toy militia,

* *Matthew Arnold*, by G. W. E. Russell, p. 205.
† *v.* below, p. 181.
‡ I quote from George Meredith's *Essay on Comedy*, which strangely enough makes no mention of Arnold.

together with all the other living puppets of Arnold's variety entertainment, has immensely quickened my own sense of his genius as master of a comic style all his own; and I hope that this introduction and the notes that follow may do the like for others. Yet these matters are after all by the way. What an editor has to do, if he can, with such a book as this, is—to adapt words of Arnold himself—"to labour, to divest it of all that is uncouth, difficult, transient, to make it efficient outside the circle of the author's immediate contemporaries, and a true source therefore of sweetness and light to posterity." For what keeps, and will keep, the book alive and what concerns us is its great argument. Let us then consider this argument for a moment in conclusion.

It is not to be supposed that Arnold really thought, with Carlyle, that England in 1869 was about to plunge into a whirlpool of anarchy. What he did was to use certain anarchical tendencies and lawless incidents of his own day, due to a temporary phase of intense political excitement, as illustrations of the deep-seated *spiritual* anarchy of the English people, an anarchy which expressed itself in its hideous sprawling industrial cities, its loud-voiced assertion of personal liberty, its dismal, stuffy, and cantankerous forms of Christianity, its worship of size and numbers and wealth and machinery generally, its state-blindness, and its belief in collision (collision of parties, of sects, of firms) as the only way of salvation. Were Arnold to revisit the English glimpses of the moon in 1931, he would no longer see

> a darkling plain,
> Swept with confused alarms of struggle and flight,
> Where ignorant armies clash by night.

The scene is dark enough, but the shadow is not wholly of our making, while the slough of despond into which we have tumbled for the moment is at least more salutary for

the spirit than the vanity fair of great industrial triumphs
and exhibitions through which our grandparents wandered
and with which they drugged and deluded their souls. And
as we struggle to climb out of the mire of unemployment
and economic depression we shall assuredly find ourselves
on a bank further from the city of destruction and nearer
the wicket-gate which leads to perfection. For sweetness
and light have wonderfully increased since Arnold first
preached them to a stiff-necked generation. The "ignorant
armies" still clash now and again; they have recently, as
Arnold would not fail to note, trampled an education bill
underfoot in a skirmish after the bad old nineteenth-century
fashion. But such incidents are rare, and the armies have
grown thin and ragged and discredited. Indeed, the outstanding change in England since 1869 is the decline in
religious asperity and the almost miraculous sweetening
of all the operations of national life in consequence.

Closely connected with this, and probably its main cause,
is another change which would equally rejoice Arnold's
heart, the organisation of secondary and higher education
since 1902, or rather since 1869, for the Endowed Schools
Act which so disappointed him was the beginning of it
and opened the door to women and girls. The advance,
however, has of course been mainly since 1902, and the
country has as yet hardly begun to realise the incalculable
increase of light, comparable in the spiritual with the
coming of electricity in the material sphere, brought about
by its municipal and county secondary schools, and the
developments in university education that they have
promoted. Furthermore, the progress in education, on the
lines for which he pleaded in season and out for thirty-five
years, has been accomplished by the very means which he
prescribed. Nothing would strike him more about modern
England than the ubiquity of state activity and the acqui-

escent temper of the people who rejoice to have it so. The network of local government which now covers the whole country and affects every side of human life, together with the great central departments which supervise from Whitehall the all-embracing work of local government, was unknown in his day, and has in the meanwhile created a new England. He would observe, as symptoms of all this, the cleanliness and salubrity of our streets filled with a healthier, better-mannered and better-dressed Populace than he could have dreamed possible. Arnold was no socialist; he was no -ist of any kind, for he profoundly distrusted all rigid systems of thought. But he believed in the state as the organ of the "right reason and best self" of the whole community, and the history of the last sixty years has done much to justify his faith in that and in the value of education, or rather the ripe fruit of education, which is culture.

It has been said that Arnold's conception of culture, despite his disclaimers, was too bookish, too academic, too aloof. One of the shrewdest of his contemporary critics, Henry Sidgwick, uttered a pregnant comment upon it:

If any culture really has what Mr Arnold in his finest mood calls its noblest element, the passion for propagating itself, for making itself prevail, then let it learn "to call nothing common or unclean." It can only propagate itself by shedding the light of its sympathy liberally; by learning to love common people and common things, to feel common interests. Make people feel that their own poor life is ever so little beautiful and poetical; then they will begin to turn and seek after the treasures of beauty and poetry outside and above it*.

There is indeed another kind of culture than that derived from "the best that has been known and thought in the world," as we are coming more and more to realise. It is

* *The Prophet of Culture* (Miscellaneous Essays and Addresses, p. 53), cf. note, p. 148.

the culture that springs from the common life of the people, the culture which means cultivation of the ordinary soil of the human spirit, which sanctifies the work that men do with their hands and makes significant and beautiful the labour wherewith they earn their bread. Perhaps Arnold was a shade lacking in human sympathy, a little too much of the don to see this. Perhaps he lived just too early to catch a glimpse of this great possibility in "the vast residuum" which, "raw and half-developed, had long lain half-hidden amidst its poverty and squalor, and was then issuing from its hiding-place to assert an Englishman's heaven-born privilege of doing as he likes*." Certainly the first to see it clearly in this country was William Morris, born twelve years later than Arnold, and his *Hopes and Fears for Art*, which appeared in 1882, supplied what was missing in *Culture and Anarchy*. It supplies too the basic principles for the next step in civilisation which the nation, hesitatingly, doubtingly, and yet perforcedly, is about to take. This step is the provision of schooling for all young persons who do not now find their way into secondary schools, that is to say for those who are destined to enter industrial and commercial rather than professional life. Such provision will, in the long run, result in a new kind of education and a new kind of industry; for it will bring face to face for the first time labour and culture and effect a marriage between them. What the offspring of this marriage will be we can only guess. But Morris's words: "If art which is now sick is to live and not die, it must in the future be of the people, for the people, by the people; it must understand all and be understood by all," may set us dreaming. One thing we know, that nothing but good can come from the union for both parties, since what is wrong with labour to-day is not so much low wages and long hours

* *v.* p. 105.

as its lack of social meaning in the eyes of the worker, and what is wrong with our culture is its divorce from the crafts of common life. Yet though Arnold did not or could not see all this, it in no sense runs counter to his message. On the contrary, it fulfils and completes it. It gives a larger and deeper meaning to his great conclusion: "This is the *social* idea and the men of culture are the true apostles of equality*."

Nor is his own view of culture in any way out of date; it can never be, since its relevance is eternal. And despite all the changes above spoken of, it needs reiterating to-day just as much as when Arnold first gave utterance to it. We are only at the beginning of the developments he foresaw in education, and if he could look into our class-rooms —university, secondary, elementary—and examine our curricula, he would, while acknowledging much improvement, find the instruction still far too rigid and too specialist to effect the "harmonious expansion of *all* the powers which make the beauty and worth of human nature†," and too external and mechanical to create that "inward condition of the mind and spirit"‡ from which perfection alone can proceed. "Repent, for the kingdom of Heaven is within you" was his message to his own generation. And how much we are still in need of this message let every teacher enquire of himself. Above all as regards religion, the schools, at last free or almost free from the disastrous war between the sects, find themselves drawing the breath of liberty in a desert where no water is. Thomas Arnold knew that religion was the heart of education and worship the centre of school life, and his son did no less, though his religion was different in emphasis from that preached in Rugby Chapel. No reader of *Culture and Anarchy* can fail to see that what its author cares about most is religion,

---

* *v.* p. 70.   † *v.* p. 48.   ‡ *v.* p. 48.

a religion which would embrace the best of Hellenism and the best of Hebraism. And here once again time has worked with him, for the modern doctrine of absolute values—the values of Beauty, Truth and Goodness—which goes back to Plato and has become a commonplace of popular philosophy and religious thought, is implicit in all that Arnold writes about "an inward spiritual activity, having for its character increased sweetness, increased light, increased life, increased sympathy*." The writings of Clutton-Brock, Dean Inge and Baron von Hügel would have interested him beyond measure, for he would have found in them his own ideas developed, articulated and clarified. He would have assuredly perceived also that here was a common ground upon which all denominations might meet and from which an undenominational religious education might proceed. "The State," he wrote, "is of the religion of all its citizens without the fanaticism of any of them†." If the future makes such a religion possible in our state schools, the credit will be partly his.

But points of contact between Arnold and the problems of to-day are innumerable. Let us be content with one more. Though the shadow of domestic anarchy under which his book was written has to some extent passed away, if it be not too bold to say this within five years of the Great Strike, a huger shadow has taken its place, that of a world-anarchy which threatens to bring the whole structure of civilisation toppling to the ground. Never in the history of the race was there greater demand for sweetness and light in human affairs, for a true Hellenic clarity of vision, for a "disinterested play of consciousness upon stock notions and habits," in a word for men of culture determined "to make reason and the will of God prevail." And this need is not one that affects Geneva or our public men alone. It

*v. p. 64.   †v. p. 166.

knocks at the door of every home; it intimately concerns the schools and the teachers, as Professor Zimmern's wise little book, *Learning and Leadership*, has recently reminded us.

And so we come back again, as is fitting, to the children. It is part of the artistry of *Culture and Anarchy* that it leads us, by a cunning route, through the back alleys of the Deceased Wife's Sister Bill and Free Trade, to the little ones in the East End, and there—but for a brief "conclusion" —leaves us. Arnold might be deficient in sympathy for the crude and the uncultivated among adults, but he loved children, his own passionately, and all tenderly. Everything he wrote about education he dedicated to them, and what would delight him most of all in the world to-day is that, gigantic and terrifying as are the problems that press upon their parents for solution, the children at any rate have entered or are entering the promised land. Like the leader of the Israelites of old he could see that land in vision but was not permitted to pass its frontier himself. Arnold had a good life and a full life, and he died as most men would wish to die, suddenly, without pain, and at the height of his powers. Yet there is something wistful about him, the wistfulness of a man who could see what ought to be done, knew that in the end men would follow his behest, and yet knew too that he would long be dead before they did it. The thought recurs again and again in his writings. Let me conclude by quoting one expression of it, a passage which is itself the conclusion of one of his most beautiful, though less well-known books, *A French Eton*.

Children of the future, whose day has not yet dawned, you, when that day arrives, will hardly believe what obstructions were long suffered to prevent its coming! You who, with all your faults, have neither the aridity of aristocracies, nor the narrow-mindedness of middle classes, you, whose power of simple enthusiasm is your great gift, will not comprehend how progress towards man's best perfection—the adorning and ennobling of his spirit—should have been reluctantly undertaken; how it should have been for years and years retarded by barren commonplaces, by worn-out clap-traps. You will wonder at the labour of its friends in proving the self-proving; you will know nothing of the doubts, the fears, the prejudices they had to dispel; nothing of the outcry they had to encounter; of the fierce protestations of life from policies which were dead and did not know it, and the shrill querulous upbraiding from publicists in their dotage. But you, in your turn, with difficulties of your own, will then be mounting some new step in the arduous ladder whereby man climbs towards his perfection; towards that unattainable but irresistible lode-star, gazed after with earnest longing, and invoked with bitter tears; the longing of thousands of hearts, the tears of many generations.

CULTURE AND ANARCHY

AN ESSAY
IN
POLITICAL & SOCIAL CRITICISM

Estote ergo vos perfecti!

PREFACE

My foremost design in writing this Preface is to address a word of exhortation to the Society for Promoting Christian Knowledge. In the essay which follows, the reader will often find Bishop Wilson quoted. To me and to the members of the Society for Promoting Christian Knowledge his name and writings are still, no doubt, familiar. But the world is fast going away from old-fashioned people of his sort, and I learnt with consternation lately from a brilliant and distinguished votary of the natural sciences, that he had never so much as heard of Bishop Wilson, and that he imagined me to have invented him. At a moment when the Courts of Law have just taken off the embargo from the recreative religion furnished on Sundays by my gifted acquaintance and others, and when St. Martin's Hall and the Alhambra will soon be beginning again to resound with their pulpit-eloquence, it distresses one to think that the new lights should not only have, in general, a very low opinion of the preachers of the old religion, but that they should have it without knowing the best that these preachers can do. And that they are in this case is owing in part, certainly, to the negligence of the Christian Knowledge Society. In the old times they used to print and spread abroad Bishop Wilson's *Maxims of Piety and Christianity*. The copy of this work which I use is one of their publications, bearing their imprint, and bound in the well-known brown calf which they made familiar to our childhood; but the date of my copy is 1812. I know of no copy besides, and I believe the work is no longer one of those printed and circulated by the Society. Hence the error, flattering, I own, to me personally, yet in itself to be regretted, of the distinguished physicist already mentioned.

But Bishop Wilson's *Maxims* deserve to be circulated as a religious book, not only by comparison with the cartloads of rubbish circulated at present under this designation, but for their own sake, and even by comparison with the other works of the same author. Over the far better known *Sacra Privata* they have this advantage, that they were prepared by him for his own private use, while the *Sacra Privata* were prepared by him for the use of the public. The *Maxims* were never meant to be printed, and have on that account, like a work of, doubtless, far deeper emotion and power, the *Meditations* of Marcus Aurelius, something peculiarly sincere and first-hand about them. Some of the best things from the *Maxims* have passed into the *Sacra Privata*. Still, in the *Maxims*, we have them as they first arose; and whereas, too, in the *Sacra Privata* the writer speaks very often as one of the clergy, and as addressing the clergy, in the *Maxims* he almost always speaks solely as a man. I am not saying a word against the *Sacra Privata*, for which I have the highest respect; only the *Maxims* seem to me a better and a more edifying book still. They should be read, as Joubert says Nicole should be read, with a direct aim at practice. The reader will leave on one side things which, from the change of time and from the changed point of view which the change of time inevitably brings with it, no longer suit him; enough will remain to serve as a sample of the very best, perhaps, which our nation and race can do in the way of religious writing. M. Michelet makes it a reproach to us that, in all the doubt as to the real author of the *Imitation*, no one has ever dreamed of ascribing that work to an Englishman. It is true, the *Imitation* could not well have been written by an Englishman; the religious delicacy and the profound asceticism of that admirable book are hardly in our nature. This would be more of a reproach to us if in poetry, which requires, no less than religion, a true delicacy of spiritual perception, our race had not done great things; and if the *Imitation*, exquisite as it is, did not, as I have elsewhere remarked, belong to a class of works in which the perfect balance of human nature is lost, and which have therefore, as spiritual productions, in their contents something excessive and morbid, in their form something not thoroughly sound. On a lower range than the *Imitation*, and awakening in our nature chords less poetical and delicate, the *Maxims* of Bishop Wilson are, as a religious work, far more solid. To the most sincere ardour and unction, Bishop Wilson unites, in these *Maxims*, that downright honesty and plain good sense which our English race has so powerfully applied to the divine impossibilities of religion; by which it has brought religion so much into practical life, and has done its allotted part in promoting upon earth the kingdom of God.

With ardour and unction religion, as we all know, may still be fanatical; with honesty and good sense, it may still be prosaic; and the fruit of honesty and good sense united with ardour and unction is often only a prosaic religion held fanatically. Bishop Wilson's excellence lies in a balance of the four qualities, and in a fulness and perfection of them, which makes this untoward result impossible. His unction is so perfect, and in such happy alliance with his good sense, that it becomes tenderness and fervent charity. His good sense is so perfect, and in such happy alliance with his unction, that it becomes moderation and insight. While, therefore, the type of religion exhibited in his *Maxims* is English, it is yet a type of a far higher kind than is in general reached by Bishop Wilson's countrymen; and yet, being English, it is possible and attainable for them. And so I conclude as I began, by saying that a work of this sort is one which the Society for

Promoting Christian Knowledge should not suffer to remain out of print and out of currency.

And now to pass to the matters canvassed in the following essay. The whole scope of the essay is to recommend culture as the great help out of our present difficulties; culture being a pursuit of our total perfection by means of getting to know, on all the matters which most concern us, the best which has been thought and said in the world; and through this knowledge, turning a stream of fresh and free thought upon our stock notions and habits, which we now follow staunchly but mechanically, vainly imagining that there is a virtue in following them staunchly which makes up for the mischief of following them mechanically. This, and this alone, is the scope of the following essay. I say again here, what I have said in the pages which follow, that from the faults and weaknesses of bookmen a notion of something bookish, pedantic, and futile has got itself more or less connected with the word culture, and that it is a pity we cannot use a word more perfectly free from all shadow of reproach. And yet, futile as are many bookmen, and helpless as books and reading often prove for bringing nearer to perfection those who use them, one must, I think, be struck more and more, the longer one lives, to find how much, in our present society, a man's life of each day depends for its solidity and value on whether he reads during that day, and, far more still, on what he reads during it. More and more he who examines himself will find the difference it makes to him, at the end of any given day, whether or no he has pursued his avocations throughout it without reading at all; and whether or no, having read something, he has read the newspapers only. This, however, is a matter for each man's private conscience and experience. If a man without books or reading, or reading nothing but his letters and the newspapers, gets nevertheless a fresh and free play of the best thoughts upon his stock notions and habits, he has got culture. He has got that for which we prize and recommend culture; he has got that which at the present moment we seek culture that it may give us. This inward operation is the very life and essence of culture, as we conceive it. Nevertheless, it is not easy so to frame one's discourse concerning the operation of culture, as to avoid giving frequent occasion to a misunderstanding whereby the essential inwardness of the operation is lost sight of.

We are often supposed, when we criticise by the help of culture some imperfect doing or other, to have in our eye some well-known rival plan of doing, which we want to serve and recommend. Thus, for instance, because we have freely pointed out the dangers and inconveniences to which our literature is exposed in the absence of any centre of taste and authority like the French Academy, it is constantly said that we want to introduce here in England an institution like the French Academy. We have indeed expressly declared that we wanted no such thing; but let us notice how it is just our worship of machinery, and of external doing, which leads to this charge being brought; and how the inwardness of culture makes us seize, for watching and cure, the faults to which our want of an Academy inclines us, and yet prevents us from trusting to an arm of flesh, as the Puritans say,—from blindly flying to this outward machinery of an Academy, in order to help ourselves. For the very same culture and free inward play of thought which shows how the Corinthian style, or the whimsies about the One Primeval Language, are generated and strengthened in the absence of an Academy, shows us, too, how little any Academy, such as we should be likely to get, would cure them. Every one who knows the characteristics of our national life, and the tendencies so fully discussed in the following pages, knows exactly what an English Academy would be like. One can see the happy family in one's mind's eye as distinctly as if it were already constituted. Lord Stanhope, the Dean of St. Paul's, the Bishop of Oxford, Mr. Gladstone, the Dean of Westminster, Mr. Froude, Mr. Henry Reeve,—everything which is influential, accomplished, and distinguished; and then, some fine morning, a dissatisfaction of the public mind with this brilliant and select coterie, a flight of Corinthian leading articles, and an irruption of Mr. G. A. Sala. Clearly, this is not what will do us good. The very same faults,—the want of sensitiveness of intellectual conscience, the disbelief in right reason, the dislike of authority, —which have hindered our having an Academy and have worked injuriously in our literature, would also hinder us from making our Academy, if we established it, one which would really correct them. And culture, which shows us truly the faults to be corrected, shows us this also just as truly.

It is by a like sort of misunderstanding, again, that Mr. Oscar Browning, one of the assistant-masters at Eton, takes up in the *Quarterly Review* the cudgels for Eton, as if I had attacked Eton, because I have said, in a book about foreign schools, that a man may well prefer to teach his three or four hours a day without keeping a boarding-house; and that there are great dangers in cramming little boys of eight or ten and making them compete for an object of great value to their parents; and, again, that the manufacture and supply of school-books, in England, much needs regulation by some competent authority. Mr. Oscar Browning gives us to understand that at Eton he and others, with perfect satisfaction to themselves and the public, combine the functions of teaching and of keeping a boarding-house; that he knows excellent men (and, indeed, well he may, for a brother of his own, I am told, is one of the best of them), engaged in preparing little boys for competitive examinations, and that the result, as tested at Eton, gives perfect satisfaction. And as to school-books he adds, finally, that Dr. William Smith, the learned and distinguished editor of the *Quarterly Review*, is, as we all know, the compiler of school-books meritorious and many. This is what Mr. Oscar Browning gives us to understand in the *Quarterly Review*, and it is impossible not to read with pleasure what he says. For what can give a finer example of that frankness and manly self-confidence which our great public schools, and none of them so much as Eton, are supposed to inspire, of that buoyant ease in holding up one's head, speaking out what is in one's mind, and flinging off all sheepishness and awkwardness, than to see an Eton assistant-master offering in fact himself as evidence that to combine boarding-house-keeping with teaching is a good thing, and his brother as evidence that to train and race little boys for competitive examinations is a good thing? Nay, and one sees that this frank-hearted Eton self-confidence is contagious; for has not Mr. Oscar Browning managed to fire Dr. William Smith (himself, no doubt, the modestest man alive, and never trained at Eton) with the same spirit, and made him insert in his own *Review* a puff, so to speak, of his own school-books, declaring that they are (as they are) meritorious and many? Nevertheless, Mr. Oscar Browning is wrong in thinking that I wished to run down Eton; and his repetition on behalf of Eton, with this idea in his head, of the strains of his heroic ancestor, Malvina's Oscar, as they are recorded by the family poet, Ossian, is unnecessary. "'The wild boar rushes over their tombs, but he does not disturb their repose. They still love the sport of their youth, and mount the wind with joy." All I meant to say was, that there were unpleasantnesses in uniting the keeping a boarding-house with teaching, and dangers in cramming and racing little boys for competitive examinations, and charlatanism and extravagance in the manufacture and supply of our school-books. But when Mr. Oscar Browning tells us that all these have been happily got rid of in his case, and his brother's case, and Dr. William Smith's case, then I say that this is just what I wish, and I hope other people will follow their good example. All I seek is that such blemishes should not through any negligence, self-love, or want of due self-examination, be suffered to continue.

Natural, as we have said, the sort of misunderstanding just noticed is; yet our usefulness depends upon our being able to clear it away, and to convince those who mechanically serve some stock notion or operation, and thereby go astray, that it is not culture's work or aim to give the victory to some rival fetish, but simply to turn a free and fresh stream of thought upon the whole matter in question. In a thing of more immediate interest, just now, than either of the two we have mentioned, the like misunderstanding prevails; and until it is dissipated, culture can do no good work in the matter. When we criticise the present operation of disestablishing the Irish Church, not by the power of reason and justice, but by the power of the antipathy of the Protestant Nonconformists, English and Scotch, to establishments, we are charged with being dreamers of dreams, which the national will has rudely shattered, for endowing the religious sects all round; or we are called enemies of the Nonconformists, blind partisans of the Anglican Establishment. More than a few words we must give to showing how erroneous are these charges; because if they were true, we should be actually subverting our own design, and playing false to that culture which it is our very purpose to recommend.

Certainly we are no enemies of the Nonconformists; for,

on the contrary, what we aim at is their perfection. Culture, which is the study of perfection, leads us, as we in the following pages have shown, to conceive of true human perfection as a *harmonious* perfection, developing all sides of our humanity; and as a *general* perfection, developing all parts of our society. For if one member suffer, the other members must suffer with it; and the fewer there are that follow the true way of salvation, the harder that way is to find. And while the Nonconformists, the successors and representatives of the Puritans, and like them staunchly walking by the best light they have, make a large part of what is strongest and most serious in this nation, and therefore attract our respect and interest, yet all which, in what follows, is said about Hebraism and Hellenism, has for its main result to show how our Puritans, ancient and modern, have not enough added to their care for walking staunchly by the best light they have, a care that that light be not darkness; how they have developed one side of their humanity at the expense of all others, and have become incomplete and mutilated men in consequence. Thus falling short of harmonious perfection, they fail to follow the true way of salvation. Therefore that way is made the harder for others to find, general perfection is put further off out of our reach, and the confusion and perplexity in which our society now labours is increased by the Nonconformists rather than diminished by them. So while we praise and esteem the zeal of the Nonconformists in walking staunchly by the best light they have, and desire to take no whit from it, we seek to add to this what we call sweetness and light, and to develop their full humanity more perfectly. To seek this is certainly not to be the enemy of the Nonconformists.

But now, with these ideas in our head, we come upon the operation for disestablishing the Irish Church by the power of the Nonconformists' antipathy to religious establishments and endowments. And we see Liberal statesmen, for whose purpose this antipathy happens to be convenient, flattering it all they can; saying that though they have no intention of laying hands on an Establishment which is efficient and popular, like the Anglican Establishment here in England, yet it is in the abstract a fine and good thing that religion should be left to the voluntary support of its promoters, and should thus gain in energy and independence; and Mr. Gladstone has no words strong enough to express his admiration of the refusal of State-aid by the Irish Roman Catholics, who have never yet been seriously asked to accept it, but who would a good deal embarrass him if they demanded it. And we see philosophical politicians, with a turn for swimming with the stream, like Mr. Baxter or Mr. Charles Buxton, and philosophical divines with the same turn, like the Dean of Canterbury, seeking to give a sort of grand stamp of generality and solemnity to this antipathy of the Nonconformists, and to dress it out as a law of human progress in the future. Now, nothing can be pleasanter than swimming with the stream; and we might gladly, if we could, try in our unsystematic way to help Mr. Baxter, and Mr. Charles Buxton, and the Dean of Canterbury, in their labours at once philosophical and popular. But we have got fixed in our minds that a more full and harmonious development of their humanity is what the Nonconformists most want, that narrowness, one-sidedness, and incompleteness is what they most suffer from; in a word, that in what we call *provinciality* they abound, but in what we may call *totality* they fall short.

And they fall short more than the members of Establishments. The great works by which, not only in literature, art, and science generally, but in religion itself, the human spirit has manifested its approaches to totality, and to

a full, harmonious perfection, and by which it stimulates
and helps forward the world's general perfection, come, not
from Nonconformists, but from men who either belong to
Establishments or have been trained in them. A Nonconformist minister, the Rev. Edward White, who has
written a temperate and well-reasoned pamphlet against
Church Establishments, says that "the unendowed and
unestablished communities of England exert full as much
moral and ennobling influence upon the conduct of
statesmen as that Church which is both established and
endowed." That depends upon what one means by moral
and ennobling influence. The believer in machinery may
think that to get a Government to abolish Church-rates or
to legalise marriage with a deceased wife's sister is to exert a
moral and ennobling influence upon Government. But a
lover of perfection, who looks to inward ripeness for the
true springs of conduct, will surely think that as Shakespeare
has done more for the inward ripeness of our statesmen than
Dr. Watts, and has, therefore, done more to moralise and
ennoble them, so an Establishment which has produced
Hooker, Barrow, Butler, has done more to moralise and
ennoble English statesmen and their conduct than communities which have produced the Nonconformist divines.
The fruitful men of English Puritanism and Nonconformity
are men who were trained within the pale of the Establishment,—Milton, Baxter, Wesley. A generation or two
outside the Establishment, and Puritanism produces men
of national mark no more. With the same doctrine and
discipline, men of national mark are produced in Scotland;
but in an Establishment. With the same doctrine and
discipline, men of national and even European mark are
produced in Germany, Switzerland, France; but in
Establishments. Only two religious disciplines seem
exempted, or comparatively exempted, from the operation

of the law which appears to forbid the rearing, outside
of national Churches, of men of the highest spiritual
significance. These two are the Roman Catholic and the
Jewish. And these, both of them, rest on Establishments,
which, though not indeed national, are cosmopolitan; and
perhaps here, what the individual man does not lose by
these conditions of his rearing, the citizen, and the State of
which he is a citizen, loses.

What, now, can be the reason of this undeniable provincialism of the English Puritans and Protestant Nonconformists, a provincialism which has two main types,—a
bitter type and a smug type,—but which in both its types is
vulgarising, and thwarts the full perfection of our humanity? Men of genius and character are born and reared
in this medium as in any other. From the faults of the mass
such men will always be comparatively free, and they will
always excite our interest; yet in this medium they seem to
have a special difficulty in breaking through what bounds
them, and in developing their totality. Surely the reason is,
that the Nonconformist is not in contact with the main
current of national life, like the member of an Establishment. In a matter of such deep and vital concern as
religion, this separation from the main current of the
national life has peculiar importance. In the following essay
we have discussed at length the tendency in us to *Hebraise*,
as we call it; that is, to sacrifice all other sides of our being
to the religious side. This tendency has its cause in the
divine beauty and grandeur of religion, and bears affecting
testimony to them. But we have seen that it has dangers for
us, we have seen that it leads to a narrow and twisted
growth of our religious side itself, and to a failure in perfection. But if we tend to Hebraise even in an Establishment, with the main current of national life flowing round
us, and reminding us in all ways of the variety and fulness

of human existence,—by a Church which is historical as the
State itself is historical, and whose order, ceremonies, and
monuments reach, like those of the State, far beyond any
fancies and devisings of ours; and by institutions such as
the Universities, formed to defend and advance that very
culture and many-sided development which it is the danger
of Hebraising to make us neglect,—how much more must
we tend to Hebraise when we lack these preventives. One
may say that to be reared a member of a national Church is
in itself a lesson of religious moderation, and a help towards
culture and harmonious perfection. Instead of battling for
his own private forms for expressing the inexpressible and
defining the undefinable, a man takes those which have
commended themselves most to the religious life of his
nation; and while he may be sure that within those forms
the religious side of his own nature may find its satisfaction,
he has leisure and composure to satisfy other sides of his
nature as well.

But with the member of a Nonconforming or self-made
religious community how different! The sectary's *eigene
grosse Erfindungen*, as Goethe calls them,—the precious
discoveries of himself and his friends for expressing the
inexpressible and defining the undefinable in peculiar forms
of their own, cannot but, as he has voluntarily chosen them,
and is personally responsible for them, fill his whole
mind. He is zealous to do battle for them and affirm them;
for in affirming them he affirms himself, and that is what we
all like. Other sides of his being are thus neglected, because the religious side, always tending in every serious man
to predominance over our other spiritual sides, is in him
made quite absorbing and tyrannous by the condition of
self-assertion and challenge which he has chosen for himself. And just what is not essential in religion he comes to
mistake for essential, and a thousand times the more

readily because he has chosen it of himself; and religious
activity he fancies to consist in battling for it. All this
leaves him little leisure or inclination for culture; to
which, besides, he has no great institutions not of his own
making, like the Universities connected with the national
Church, to invite him; but only such institutions as, like
the order and discipline of his religion, he may have invented for himself, and invented under the sway of the
narrow and tyrannous notions of religion fostered in him
as we have seen. Thus, while a national establishment of
religion favours totality, *hole-and-corner* forms of religion
(to use an expressive popular word) inevitably favour
provincialism.

But the Nonconformists, and many of our Liberal
friends along with them, have a plausible plan for getting
rid of this provincialism, if, as they can hardly quite deny,
it exists. "Let us all be in the same boat," they cry; "open
the Universities to everybody, and let there be no establishment of religion at all!" Open the Universities by all
means; but, as to the second point about establishment, let
us sift the proposal a little. It does seem at first a little like
that proposal of the fox, who had lost his own tail, to put all
the other foxes in the same case by a general cutting off of
tails; and we know that moralists have decided that the
right course here was, not to adopt this plausible suggestion,
and cut off tails all round, but rather that the other foxes
should keep their tails, and that the fox without a tail
should get one. And so we might be inclined to urge that,
to cure the evil of the Nonconformists' provincialism, the
right way can hardly be to provincialise us all round.

However, perhaps we shall not be provincialised. For
the Rev. Edward White says that probably, "when all good
men alike are placed in a condition of religious equality, and
the whole complicated iniquity of Government Church

patronage is swept away, more of moral and ennobling influence than ever will be brought to bear upon the action of statesmen."

We already have an example of religious equality in our colonies. "In the colonies," says the *Times*, "we see religious communities unfettered by State-control, and the State relieved from one of the most troublesome and irritating responsibilities." But America is the great example alleged by those who are against establishments for religion. Our topic at this moment is the influence of religious establishments on culture; and it is remarkable that Mr. Bright, who has taken lately to representing himself as, above all, a promoter of reason and of the simple natural truth of things, and his policy as a fostering of the growth of intelligence,—just the aims, as is well known, of culture also,—Mr. Bright, in a speech at Birmingham about education, seized on the very point which seems to concern our topic, when he said: "I believe the people of the United States have offered to the world more valuable information during the last forty years than all Europe put together." So America, without religious establishments, seems to get ahead of us all in culture and totality; and these are the cure for provincialism.

On the other hand, another friend of reason and the simple natural truth of things, M. Renan, says of America, in a book he has recently published, what seems to conflict violently with what Mr. Bright says. Mr. Bright avers that not only have the United States thus informed Europe, but they have done it without a great apparatus of higher and scientific instruction, and by dint of all classes in America being "sufficiently educated to be able to read, and to comprehend, and to think; and that, I maintain, is the foundation of all subsequent progress." And then comes

M. Renan, and says: "The sound instruction of the
people is an effect of the high culture of certain classes.
The countries which, like the United States, have created
a considerable popular instruction without any serious
higher instruction, will long have to expiate this fault by
their intellectual mediocrity, their vulgarity of manners,
their superficial spirit, their lack of general intelligence*."

Now, which of these two friends of light are we to
believe? M. Renan seems more to have in view what we
ourselves mean by culture; because Mr. Bright always
has in his eye what he calls "a commendable interest" in
politics and in political agitations. As he said only the other
day at Birmingham: "At this moment,—in fact, I may say
at every moment in the history of a free country,—there is
nothing that is so much worth discussing as politics." And
he keeps repeating, with all the powers of his noble oratory,
the old story, how to the thoughtfulness and intelligence of
the people of great towns we owe all our improvements in the
last thirty years, and how these improvements have hitherto
consisted in Parliamentary reform, and free trade, and
abolition of Church rates, and so on; and how they are now
about to consist in getting rid of minority-members, and in
introducing a free breakfast-table, and in abolishing the
Irish Church by the power of the Nonconformists'
antipathy to establishments, and much more of the same
kind. And though our pauperism and ignorance, and all
the questions which are called social, seem now to be
forcing themselves upon his mind, yet he still goes on with
his glorifying of the great towns, and the Liberals, and their
operations for the last thirty years. It never seems to occur

* "Les pays qui, comme les États-Unis, ont créé un enseignement
populaire considérable sans instruction supérieure sérieuse, expieront
longtemps encore leur faute par leur médiocrité intellectuelle, leur
grossièreté de mœurs, leur esprit superficiel, leur manque d'intelligence générale."

to him that the present troubled state of our social life has anything to do with the thirty years' blind worship of their nostrums by himself and our Liberal friends, or that it throws any doubts upon the sufficiency of this worship. But he thinks what is still amiss is due to the stupidity of the Tories, and will be cured by the thoughtfulness and intelligence of the great towns, and by the Liberals going on gloriously with their political operations as before; or that it will cure itself. So we see what Mr. Bright means by thoughtfulness and intelligence, and in what manner, according to him, we are to grow in them. And, no doubt, in America all classes read their newspaper, and take a commendable interest in politics, more than here or anywhere else in Europe.

But in the following essay we have been led to doubt the sufficiency of all this political operating, pursued mechanically as our race pursues it; and we found that *general intelligence,* as M. Renan calls it, or, as we say, attention to the reason of things, was just what we were without, and that we were without it because we worshipped our machinery so devoutly. Therefore, we conclude that M. Renan, more than Mr. Bright, means by reason and intelligence the same thing as we do; and when he says that America, that chosen home of newspapers and politics, is without general intelligence, we think it likely, from the circumstances of the case, that this is so; and that, in the things of the mind, and in culture and totality, America, instead of surpassing us all, falls short.

And,—to keep to our point of the influence of religious establishments upon culture and a high development of our humanity,—we can surely see reasons why, with all her energy and fine gifts, America does not show more of this development, or more promise of this. In the following essay it will be seen how our society distributes itself into

Barbarians, Philistines, and Populace; and America is just ourselves, with the Barbarians quite left out, and the Populace nearly. This leaves the Philistines for the great bulk of the nation;—a livelier sort of Philistine than ours, and with the pressure and false ideal of our Barbarians taken away, but left all the more to himself and to have his full swing. And as we have found that the strongest and most vital part of English Philistinism was the Puritan and Hebraising middle-class, and that its Hebraising keeps it from culture and totality, so it is notorious that the people of the United States issues from this class, and reproduces its tendencies,—its narrow conception of man's spiritual range and of his one thing needful. From Maine to Florida, and back again, all America Hebraises. Difficult as it is to speak of a people merely from what one reads, yet that, I think, one may without much fear of contradiction say. I mean, when in the United States any spiritual side in man is wakened to activity, it is generally the religious side, and the religious side in a narrow way. Social reformers go to Moses or St. Paul for their doctrines, and have no notion there is anywhere else to go to; earnest young men at schools and universities, instead of conceiving salvation as a harmonious perfection only to be won by unreservedly cultivating many sides in us, conceive of it in the old Puritan fashion, and fling themselves ardently upon it in the old, false ways of this fashion, which we know so well, and such as Mr. Hammond, the American revivalist, has lately at Mr. Spurgeon's Tabernacle been refreshing our memory with.

Now, if America thus Hebraises more than either England or Germany, will any one deny that the absence of religious establishments has much to do with it? We have seen how establishments tend to give us a sense of a historical life of the human spirit, outside and beyond our own fancies and feelings; how they thus tend to suggest new sides and sympathies in us to cultivate; how, further, by saving us from having to invent and fight for our own forms of religion, they give us leisure and calm to steady our view of religion itself,—the most overpowering of objects, as it is the grandest,—and to enlarge our first crude notions of the one thing needful. But, in a serious people, where every one has to choose and strive for his own order and discipline of religion, the contention about these non-essentials occupies his mind. His first crude notions about the one thing needful do not get purged, and they invade the whole spiritual man in him, and then, making a solitude, they call it heavenly peace.

I remember a Nonconformist manufacturer, in a town of the Midland counties, telling me that when he first came there, some years ago, the place had no Dissenters; but he had opened an Independent chapel in it, and now Church and Dissent were pretty equally divided, with sharp contests between them. I said that this seemed a pity. "A pity?" cried he; "not at all! Only think of all the zeal and activity which the collision calls forth!" "Ah, but, my dear friend," I answered, "only think of all the nonsense which you now hold quite firmly, which you would never have held if you had not been contradicting your adversary in it all these years!" The more serious the people, and the more prominent the religious side in it, the greater is the danger of this side, if set to choose out forms for itself and fight for existence, swelling and spreading till it swallows all other spiritual sides up, intercepts and absorbs all nutriment which should have gone to them, and leaves Hebraism rampant in us and Hellenism stamped out.

Culture, and the harmonious perfection of our whole being, and what we call totality, then become quite secondary matters. And even the institutions, which should develop these, take the same narrow and partial view of humanity and its wants as the free religious communities take. Just as the free churches of Mr. Beecher or Brother Noyes, with their provincialism and want of centrality, make mere Hebraisers in religion, and not perfect men, so the university of Mr. Ezra Cornell, a really noble monument of his munificence, yet seems to rest on a misconception of what culture truly is, and to be calculated to produce miners, or engineers, or architects, not sweetness and light.

And, therefore, when the Rev. Edward White asks the same kind of question about America that he has asked about England, and wants to know whether, without religious establishments, as much is not done in America for the higher national life as is done for that life here, we answer in the same way as we did before, that as much is not done. Because to enable and stir up people to read their Bible and the newspapers, and to get a practical knowledge of their business, does not serve to the higher spiritual life of a nation so much as culture, truly conceived, serves; and a true conception of culture is, as M. Renan's words show, just what America fails in.

To the many who think that spirituality, and sweetness, and light, are all moonshine, this will not appear to matter much; but with us, who value them, and who think that we have traced much of our present discomfort to the want of them, it weighs a great deal. So not only do we say that the Nonconformists have got provincialism and lost totality by the want of a religious establishment, but we say that the very example which they bring forward to help their case makes against them; and that when they triumphantly show us America without religious establishments, they only show us a whole nation touched, amidst all its greatness and promise, with that provincialism which it is our aim to extirpate in the English Nonconformists.

But now to evince the disinterestedness which culture teaches us. We have seen the narrowness generated in Puritanism by its hole-and-corner organisation, and we propose to cure it by bringing Puritanism more into contact with the main current of national life. Here we are fully at one with the Dean of Westminster; and, indeed, he and we were trained in the same school to mark the narrowness of Puritanism, and to wish to cure it. But he and others seem disposed simply to give to the present Anglican Establishment a character the most latitudinarian, as it is called, possible; availing themselves for this purpose of the diversity of tendencies and doctrines which does undoubtedly exist already in the Anglican formularies; and then they would say to the Puritans: "Come all of you into this liberally conceived Anglican Establishment." But to say this is hardly, perhaps, to take sufficient account of the course of history, or of the strength of men's feelings in what concerns religion, or of the gravity which may have come to attach to points of religious order and discipline merely. When the Rev. Edward White talks of "sweeping away the whole complicated iniquity of Government Church patronage," he uses language which has been forced upon him by his position, but which is devoid of all real solidity. But when he talks of the religious communities "which have for three hundred years contended for the power of the congregation in the management of their own affairs," then he talks history; and his language has behind it, in my opinion, facts which make the latitudinarianism of our Broad Churchmen quite illusory.

Certainly, culture will never make us think it an essential of religion whether we have in our Church discipline "a popular authority of elders," as Hooker calls it, or whether we have Episcopal jurisdiction. Certainly, Hooker himself did not think it an essential; for in the dedication of his

Ecclesiastical Polity, speaking of these questions of church-discipline which gave occasion to his great work, he says they are, "in truth, for the greatest part, such silly things, that very easiness doth make them hard to be disputed of in serious manner." Hooker's great work against the impugners of the order and discipline of the Church of England was written (and this is too indistinctly seized by many who read it), not because Episcopalianism is essential, but because its impugners maintained that Presbyterianism is essential, and that Episcopalianism is sinful. Neither the one nor the other is either essential or sinful, and much may be said on behalf of both. But what is important to be remarked is, *that both were in the Church of England at the Reformation*, and that Presbyterianism was only extruded gradually. We have mentioned Hooker, and nothing better illustrates what has just been asserted than the following incident in Hooker's own career, which every one has read, for it is related in Isaac Walton's *Life of Hooker*, but of which, probably, the significance has been fully grasped by very few of those who have read it.

Hooker was through the influence of Archbishop Whitgift appointed, in 1585, Master of the Temple; but a great effort had first been made to obtain the place for a Mr. Walter Travers, well known in that day, though now it is Hooker's name which alone preserves his. This Travers was then afternoon-lecturer at the Temple. The Master whose death made the vacancy, Alvey, recommended on his deathbed Travers for his successor. The society was favourable to Travers, and he had the support of the Lord Treasurer Burghley. Although Hooker was appointed to the Mastership, Travers remained afternoon-lecturer, and combated in the afternoons the doctrine which Hooker preached in the mornings. Now, this Travers, originally a Fellow of Trinity College, Cambridge, afterwards afternoon-lecturer at the Temple, recommended for the Mastership by the foregoing Master, whose opinions, it is said, agreed with his, favoured by the Society of the Temple, and supported by the Prime Minister,—this Travers was not an Episcopally ordained clergyman at all. He was a Presbyterian, a partisan of the Geneva church-discipline, as it was then called, and "had taken orders," says Walton, "by the Presbyters in Antwerp." In another place Walton speaks of his orders yet more fully:—"He had disowned," he says, "the English Established Church and Episcopacy, and went to Geneva, and afterwards to Antwerp, to be ordained minister, as he was by Villers and Cartwright and others, the heads of a congregation there; and so came back again more confirmed for the discipline." Villers and Cartwright are in like manner examples of Presbyterianism within the Church of England, which was common enough at that time. But perhaps nothing can better give us a lively sense of its presence there than this history of Travers, which is as if Mr. Binney were now afternoon-reader at Lincoln's Inn or the Temple; were to be a candidate, favoured by the Benchers and by the Prime Minister, for the Mastership; and were only kept out of the post by the accident of the Archbishop of Canterbury's influence with the Queen carrying a rival candidate.

Presbyterianism, with its popular principle of the power of the congregation in the management of their own affairs, was extruded from the Church of England, and men like Travers can no longer appear in her pulpits. Perhaps if a government like that of Elizabeth, with secular statesmen like the Cecils, and ecclesiastical statesmen like Whitgift, could have been prolonged, Presbyterianism might, by a wise mixture of concession and firmness, have been absorbed in the Establishment. Lord Bolingbroke, on a matter of this kind a very clear-judging and impartial witness, says, in a work far too little read, his *Remarks on English History:*—"The measures pursued and the temper observed in Queen Elizabeth's time tended to diminish the religious opposition by a slow, a gentle, and for that very reason an effectual progression. There was even room to hope that when the first fire of the Dissenters' zeal was passed, reasonable terms of union with the Established Church might be accepted by such of them as were not intoxicated with fanaticism. These were friends to order, though they disputed about it. If these friends of Calvin's discipline had been once incorporated with the Established Church, the remaining sectaries would have been of little moment, either for numbers or reputation; and the very means which were proper to gain these friends, were likewise the most effectual to hinder the increase of them, and of the other sectaries in the meantime." The temper and ill judgment of the Stuarts made shipwreck of all policy of this kind. Yet speaking even of the time of the Stuarts, but their early time, Clarendon says that if Bishop Andrewes had succeeded Bancroft at Canterbury, the disaffection of separatists might have been stayed and healed. This, however, was not to be; and Presbyterianism, after exercising for some years the law of the strongest, itself in Charles the Second's reign suffered under this law, and was finally cast out from the Church of England.

Now the points of church discipline at issue between Presbyterianism and Episcopalianism are, as has been said, not essential. They might probably once have been settled in a sense altogether favourable to Episcopalianism. Hooker may have been right in thinking that there were in his time circumstances which made it essential that they should be settled in this sense, though the points in themselves were not essential. But by the very fact of the settlement not having then been effected, of the breach having gone on and widened, of the Nonconformists not having been amicably incorporated with the Establishment, but violently cast out from it, the circumstances are now altogether altered. Isaac Walton, a fervent Churchman, complains that "the principles of the Nonconformists grew at last to such a height and were vented so daringly, that, beside the loss of life and limbs, the Church and State were both forced to use such other severities as will not admit of an excuse, if it had not been to prevent confusion and the perilous consequences of it." But those very severities have of themselves made union on an Episcopalian footing impossible. Besides, Presbyterianism, the popular authority of elders, the power of the congregation in the management of their own affairs, has that warrant given to it by Scripture and by the proceedings of the early Christian Churches, it is so consonant with the spirit of Protestantism which made the Reformation and which has great strength in this country, it is so predominant in the practice of other Reformed Churches, it was so strong in the original Reformed Church of England, that one cannot help doubting whether any settlement which suppressed it could have been really permanent, and whether it would not have kept appearing again and again, and causing dissension.

Well, then, if culture is the disinterested endeavour after man's perfection, will it not make us wish to cure the provincialism of the Nonconformists, not by rendering Churchmen provincial along with them, but by letting their popular church-discipline, formerly present in the National Church, and still present in the affections and practice of a good part of the nation, appear in the national Church once more; and thus to bring Nonconformists into contact again, as their greater fathers were, with the main stream of national life? Why should not a Presbyterian

Church, based on this considerable and important, though not essential principle, of the congregation's power in the church-management, be established,—with equal rank for its chiefs with the chiefs of Episcopacy, and with admissibility of its ministers, under a revised system of patronage and preferment, to benefices,—side by side with the Episcopal Church, as the Calvinist and Lutheran Churches are established side by side in France and Germany? Such a Presbyterian Church would unite the main bodies of Protestants who are now separatists; and separation would cease to be the law of their religious order. And thus,—through this concession on a really considerable point of difference,—that endless splitting into hole-and-corner churches on quite inconsiderable points of difference, which must prevail so long as separatism is the first law of a Nonconformist's religious existence, would be checked. Culture would then find a place among English followers of the popular authority of Elders, as it has long found it among the followers of Episcopal jurisdiction. And this we should gain by merely recognising, regularising, and restoring an element which appeared once in the reformed national Church, and which is considerable and national enough to have a sound claim to appear there still.

So far, then, is culture from making us unjust to the Nonconformists because it forbids us to worship their fetishes, that it even leads us to propose to do more for them than they themselves venture to claim. It leads us, also, to respect what is solid and respectable in their convictions, while their latitudinarian friends make light of it. Not that the forms in which the human spirit tries to express the inexpressible, or the forms by which man tries to worship, have or can have, as has been said, for the follower of perfection, anything necessary or eternal. If the New Testament and the practice of the primitive Christians sanctioned the popular form of church-government a thousand times more expressly than they do, if the Church since Constantine were a thousand times more of a departure from the scheme of primitive Christianity than it can be shown to be, that does not at all make, as is supposed by men in bondage to the letter, the popular form of church-government alone and always sacred and binding, or the work of Constantine a thing to be regretted.

What is alone and always sacred and binding for man is the making progress towards his total perfection; and the machinery by which he does this varies in value according as it helps him to do it. The planters of Christianity had their roots in deep and rich grounds of human life and achievement, both Jewish and also Greek; and had thus a comparatively firm and wide basis amidst all the vehement inspiration of their mighty movement and change. By their strong inspiration they carried men off the old basis of life and culture, whether Jewish or Greek, and generations arose who had their roots in neither world, and were in contact therefore with no full and great stream of human life. If it had not been for some such change as that of the fourth century, Christianity might have lost itself in a multitude of hole-and-corner churches like the churches of English Nonconformity after its founders departed; churches without great men, and without furtherance for the higher life of humanity. At a critical moment came Constantine, and placed Christianity,—or let us rather say, placed the human spirit, whose totality was endangered,— in contact with the main current of human life. And his work was justified by its fruits, in men like Augustine and Dante, and indeed in all the great men of Christianity, Catholics or Protestants, ever since.

And one may go beyond this. M. Albert Réville, whose religious writings are always interesting, says that the conception which cultivated and philosophical Jews now entertain of Christianity and its Founder, is probably destined to become the conception which Christians themselves will entertain. Socinians are fond of saying the same thing about the Socinian conception of Christianity. Now, even if this were true, it would still have been better for a man, during the last eighteen hundred years, to have been a Christian and a member of one of the great Christian communions, than to have been a Jew or a Socinian; because the being in contact with the main stream of human life is of more moment for a man's total spiritual growth, and for his bringing to perfection the gifts committed to him, which is his business on earth, than any speculative opinion which he may hold or think he holds. Luther,—whom we have called a Philistine of genius, and who, because he was a Philistine, had a coarseness and lack of spiritual delicacy which have harmed his disciples, but who, because he was a genius, had splendid flashes of spiritual insight,—Luther says admirably in his Commentary on the Book of Daniel: "A God is simply *that* whereon the human heart rests with trust, faith, hope, and love. If the resting is right, then the God too is right; if the resting is wrong, then the God too is illusory." In other words, the worth of what a man thinks about God and the objects of religion depends on what the man *is*; and what the man *is*, depends upon his having more or less reached the measure of a perfect and total man.

All this is true; and yet culture, as we have seen, has more tenderness for scruples of the Nonconformists than have their Broad Church friends. That is because culture, disinterestedly trying, in its aim at perfection, to see things as they really are, sees how worthy and divine a thing is the religious side in man, though it is not the whole of man. And when Mr. Greg, who differs from us about edification, (and certainly we do not seem likely to agree with him as to what edifies), finding himself moved by some extraneous considerations or other to take a Church's part against its enemies, calls taking a Church's part *returning to base uses*, culture teaches us how out of place is this language, and that to use it shows an inadequate conception of human nature, and that no Church will thank a man for taking its part in this fashion, but will leave him with indifference to the tender mercies of his Benthamite friends. But avoiding Benthamism, or an inadequate conception of the religious side in man, culture makes us also avoid Mialism, or an inadequate conception of man's totality. Therefore to the worth and grandeur of the religious side in man, culture is rejoiced and willing to pay any tribute, except the tribute of man's totality. True, the order and liturgy of the Church of England one may be well contented to live and to die with, and they are such as to inspire an affectionate and revering attachment. True, the reproaches of Nonconformists against this order for "retaining badges of Antichristian recognisance;" and for "corrupting the right form of Church polity with manifold Popish rites and ceremonies;" true, their assertion of the essentialness of their own supposed Scriptural order, and their belief in its eternal fitness, are founded on illusion. True, the whole attitude of horror and holy superiority assumed by Puritanism towards the Church of Rome, is wrong and false, and well merits Sir Henry Wotton's rebuke:—"Take heed of thinking that the farther you go from the Church of Rome, the nearer you are to God." True, one of the best wishes one could form for Mr. Spurgeon or Father Jackson is, that they might be permitted to learn on this side the grave (for if they do not, a considerable surprise is certainly reserved for them on the other) that Whitfield and Wesley were not at all better than St. Francis, and that they themselves are not

at all better than Lacordaire. Yet, in spite of all this, so
noble and divine a thing is religion, so respectable is that
earnestness which desires a prayer-book with one strain of
doctrine, so attaching is the order and discipline by which we
are used to have our religion conveyed, so many claims on
our regard has that popular form of church government for
which Nonconformists contend, so perfectly compatible is
it with all progress towards perfection, that culture would
make us shy even to propose to Nonconformists the acceptance of the Anglican prayer-book and the episcopal order;
and would be forward to wish them a prayer-book of their
own approving, and the church discipline to which they are
attached and accustomed.

Only not at the price of Mialism; that is, of a doctrine
which leaves the Nonconformists in holes and corners, out
of contact with the main current of national life. One can
lay one's finger, indeed, on the line by which this doctrine
has grown up, and see how the essential part of Nonconformity is a popular church-discipline analogous to that of
the other reformed churches, and how its voluntaryism is an
accident. It contended for the establishment of its own
church-discipline as the only true one; and beaten in this
contention, and seeing its rival established, it came down to
the more plausible proposal "to place all good men alike in
a condition of religious equality;" and this plan of proceeding, originally taken as a mere second-best, became, by long
sticking to it and preaching it up, first fair, then righteous,
then the only righteous, then at last necessary to salvation.
This is the plan for remedying the Nonconformists' divorce
from contact with the national life by divorcing churchmen
too from contact with it; that is, as we have familiarly before
put it, the tailless foxes are for cutting off tails all round. But
this the other foxes could not wisely grant, unless it were
proved that tails are of no value. And so, too, unless it is

proved that contact with the main current of national life is of no value (and we have shown that it is of the greatest value), we cannot safely, even to please the Nonconformists in a matter where we would please them as much as possible, admit Mialism.

But now, as we have shown the disinterestedness which culture enjoins, and its obedience not to likings or dislikings, but to the aim of perfection, let us show its flexibility,—its independence of machinery. That other and greater prophet of intelligence, and reason, and the simple natural truth of things,—Mr. Bright,—means by these, as we have seen, a certain set of measures which suit the special ends of Liberal and Nonconformist partisans. For instance, reason and justice towards Ireland mean the abolishment of the iniquitous Protestant ascendency in such a particular way as to suit the Nonconformists' antipathy to establishments. Reason and justice pursued in a different way, by distributing among the three main Churches of Ireland,—the Roman Catholic, the Anglican, and the Presbyterian,—the church property of Ireland, would immediately cease, for Mr. Bright and the Nonconformists, to be reason and justice at all, and would become, as Mr. Spurgeon says, "a setting up of the Roman image." Thus we see that the sort of intelligence reached by culture is more disinterested than the sort of intelligence reached by belonging to the Liberal party in the great towns, and taking a commendable interest in politics. But still more striking is the difference between the two views of intelligence, when we see that culture not only makes a quite disinterested choice of the machinery proper to carry us towards sweetness and light, and to make reason and the will of God prevail, but by even this machinery does not hold stiffly and blindly, and easily passes on beyond it to that for the sake of which it chose it.

For instance: culture leads us to think that the ends of human perfection might be best served by establishing,— that is, by bringing into contact with the main current of the national life,—in Ireland the Roman Catholic and the Presbyterian Churches along with the Anglican Church; and, in England, a Presbyterian or Congregational Church of like rank and *status* with our Episcopalian one. It leads us to think that we should really, in this way, be working to make reason and the will of God prevail; because we should be making Roman Catholics better citizens, and Nonconformists,—nay, and Churchmen along with them,—larger-minded and more complete men. But undoubtedly there are great difficulties in such a plan as this; and the plan is not one which looks very likely to be adopted. It is a plan more for a time of creative statesmen, like the time of Elizabeth, than for a time of instrumental statesmen like the present. The Churchman must rise above his ordinary self in order to favour it; and the Nonconformist has worshipped his fetish of separatism so long that he is likely to wish still to remain, like Ephraim, "a wild ass alone by himself." The centre of power being where it is, our instrumental statesmen have every temptation, as is shown more at large in the following essay, in the first place, to "relieve themselves," as the *Times* says, of troublesome and irritating responsibilities;" in the second place, when they must act, to go along, as they do, with the ordinary self of those on whose favour they depend, to adopt as their own its desires, and to serve them with fidelity, and even, if possible, with impulsiveness. This is the more easy for them, because there are not wanting,— and there never will be wanting,—thinkers like Mr. Baxter, Mr. Charles Buxton, and the Dean of Canterbury, to swim with the stream, but to swim with it philosophically; to call the desires of the ordinary self of any great

section of the community edicts of the national mind and
laws of human progress, and to give them a general, a
philosophic, and an imposing expression. A generous
statesman may honestly, therefore, soon unlearn any disposition to put his tongue in his cheek in advocating these
desires, and may advocate them with fervour and impulsiveness. Therefore a plan such as that which we have indicated does not seem a plan so likely to find favour as a plan
for abolishing the Irish Church by the power of the Nonconformists' antipathy to establishments.

But to tell us that our fond dreams are on that account
shattered is inexact, and is the sort of language which ought
to be addressed to the promoters of intelligence through
public meetings and a commendable interest in politics,
when they fail in their designs, and not to us. For we are
fond stickers to no machinery, not even our own; and we
have no doubt that perfection can be reached without it,—
with free churches as with established churches, and with
instrumental statesmen as with creative statesmen. But it
can never be reached without seeing things as they really
are; and it is to this, therefore, and to no machinery in
the world, that culture sticks fondly. It insists that men
should not mistake, as they are prone to mistake, their
natural taste for the bathos for a relish for the sublime; and
if statesmen, either with their tongue in their cheek or
through a generous impulsiveness, tell them their natural
taste for the bathos is a relish for the sublime, there is the
more need for culture to tell them the contrary.

It is delusion on this point which is fatal, and against
delusion on this point culture works. It is not fatal to our
Liberal friends to labour for free-trade, extension of the
suffrage, and abolition of church-rates, instead of graver
social ends; but it is fatal to them to be told by their
flatterers, and to believe, with our pauperism increasing

more rapidly than our population, that they have performed a great, an heroic work, by occupying themselves exclusively, for the last thirty years, with these Liberal nostrums, and that the right and good course for them now is to go on occupying themselves with the like for the future. It is not fatal to Americans to have no religious establishments and no effective centres of high culture; but it is fatal to them to be told by their flatterers, and to believe, that they are the most intelligent people in the whole world, when of intelligence, in the true and fruitful sense of the word, they even singularly, as we have seen, come short. It is not fatal to the Nonconformists to remain with their separated churches; but it is fatal to them to be told by their flatterers, and to believe, that theirs is the one pure and Christ-ordained way of worshipping God, that provincialism and loss of totality have not come to them from following it, or that provincialism and loss of totality are not evils. It is not fatal to the English nation to abolish the Irish Church by the power of the Nonconformists' antipathy to establishments; but it is fatal to it to be told by its flatterers, and to believe, that it is abolishing it through reason and justice, when it is really abolishing it through this power; or to expect the fruits of reason and justice from anything but the spirit of reason and justice themselves.

Now culture, because of its keen sense of what is really fatal, is all the more disposed to be rather indifferent about what is not fatal. And because machinery is the one concern of our actual politics, and an inward working, and not machinery, is what we most want, we keep advising our ardent young Liberal friends to think less of machinery, to stand more aloof from the arena of politics at present, and rather to try and promote, with us, an inward working. They do not listen to us, and they rush into the arena of politics, where their merits, indeed, seem to be little appreciated as yet; and then they complain of the reformed constituencies, and call the new Parliament a Philistine Parliament. As if a nation, nourished and reared as ours has been, could give us, just yet, anything but a Philistine Parliament!—and would a Barbarian Parliament be even so good, or a Populace Parliament? For our part, we rejoice to see our dear old friends, the Hebraising Philistines, gathered in force in the Valley of Jehoshaphat previous to their final conversion, which will certainly come. But to attain this conversion, we must not try to oust them from their places, and to contend for machinery with them, but we must work on them inwardly and cure their spirit. Ousted they will not be, but transformed. Ousted they do not deserve to be, and will not be.

For *the days of Israel are innumerable*; and in its blame of Hebraising too, and in its praise of Hellenising, culture must not fail to keep its flexibility, and to give to its judgments that passing and provisional character which we have seen it impose on its preferences and rejections of machinery. Now, and for us, it is a time to Hellenise, and to praise knowing; for we have Hebraised too much, and have over-valued doing. But the habits and discipline received from Hebraism remain for our race an eternal possession; and, as humanity is constituted, one must never assign to them the second rank to-day, without being prepared to restore them to the first rank to-morrow. Let us conclude by marking this distinctly.

To walk staunchly by the best light one has, to be strict and sincere with oneself, not to be of the number of those who say and do not, to be in earnest,—this is the discipline by which alone man is enabled to rescue his life from thraldom to the passing moment and to his bodily senses, to ennoble it, and to make it eternal. And this discipline has

been nowhere so effectively taught as in the school of
Hebraism. Sophocles and Plato knew as well as the author
of the Epistle to the Hebrews that "without holiness no
man shall see God," and their notion of what goes to make
up holiness was larger than his. But the intense and convinced energy with which the Hebrew, both of the Old and
of the New Testament, threw himself upon his ideal of
righteousness, and which inspired the incomparable definition of the great Christian virtue, faith,—*the substance of
things hoped for, the evidence of things not seen,*—this energy
of devotion to its ideal has belonged to Hebraism alone.
As our idea of holiness enlarges, and our scope of
perfection widens beyond the narrow limits to which the
over-rigour of Hebraising has tended to confine it, we
shall yet come again to Hebraism for that devout energy
in embracing our ideal, which alone can give to man
the happiness of doing what he knows. "If ye know
these things, happy are ye if ye do them!"—the last
word for infirm humanity will always be that. For
this word, reiterated with a power now sublime, now
affecting, but always admirable, our race will, as long as the
world lasts, return to Hebraism; and the Bible, which
preaches this word, will forever remain, as Goethe called
it, not only a national book, but the Book of the Nations.
Again and again, after what seemed breaches and separa-
tions, the prophetic promise to Jerusalem will still be true:—
*Lo, thy sons come, whom thou sentest away; they come
gathered from the west unto the east by the word of the Holy
One, rejoicing in the remembrance of God.*

INTRODUCTION

In one of his speeches a short time ago, that fine speaker and famous Liberal, Mr. Bright, took occasion to have a fling at the friends and preachers of culture. "People who talk about what they call *culture!*" said he contemptuously; "by which they mean a smattering of the two dead languages of Greek and Latin." And he went on to remark, in a strain with which modern speakers and writers have made us very familiar, how poor a thing this culture is, how little good it can do to the world, and how absurd it is for its possessors to set much store by it. And the other day a younger Liberal than Mr. Bright, one of a school whose mission it is to bring into order and system that body of truth with which the earlier Liberals merely fumbled, a member of the University of Oxford, and a very clever writer, Mr. Frederic Harrison, developed, in the systematic and stringent manner of his school, the thesis which Mr. Bright had propounded in only general terms. "Perhaps the very silliest cant of the day," said Mr. Frederic Harrison, "is the cant about culture. Culture is a desirable quality in a critic of new books, and sits well on a professor of *belles lettres;* but as applied to politics, it means simply a turn for small fault-finding, love of selfish ease, and indecision in action. The man of culture is in politics one of the poorest mortals alive. For simple pedantry and want of good sense no man is his equal. No assumption is too unreal, no end is too unpractical for him. But the active exercise of politics requires common sense, sympathy, trust, resolution and enthusiasm, qualities which your man of culture has carefully rooted up, lest they damage the delicacy of his critical olfactories. Perhaps they are the only class of responsible beings in the community who cannot with safety be entrusted with power."

Now for my part I do not wish to see men of culture asking to be entrusted with power; and, indeed, I have freely said, that in my opinion the speech most proper, at present, for a man of culture to make to a body of his fellow-countrymen who get him into a committee-room, is Socrates's: *Know thyself!* and this is not a speech to be made by men wanting to be entrusted with power. For this very indifference to direct political action I have been taken to task by the *Daily Telegraph*, coupled, by a strange perversity of fate, with just that very one of the Hebrew prophets whose style I admire the least, and called "an elegant Jeremiah." It is because I say (to use the words which the *Daily Telegraph* puts in my mouth):—"You mustn't make a fuss because you have no vote,—that is vulgarity; you mustn't hold big meetings to agitate for reform bills and to repeal corn laws,—that is the very height of vulgarity,"— it is for this reason that I am called, sometimes an elegant Jeremiah, sometimes a spurious Jeremiah, a Jeremiah about the reality of whose mission the writer in the *Daily Telegraph* has his doubts. It is evident, therefore, that I have so taken my line as not to be exposed to the whole brunt of Mr. Frederic Harrison's censure. Still, I have often spoken in praise of culture, I have striven to make all my works and ways serve the interests of culture. I take culture to be something a great deal more than what Mr. Frederic Harrison and others call it: "a desirable quality in a critic of new books." Nay, even though to a certain extent I am disposed to agree with Mr. Frederic Harrison, that men of culture are just the class of responsible beings in this community of ours who cannot properly, at present, be entrusted with power, I am not sure that I do not think this the fault of our community rather than of the men of culture. In short, although, like Mr. Bright and Mr. Frederic Harrison, and the editor of the *Daily Telegraph*, and a large body of valued friends of mine, I am a Liberal, yet I am a Liberal tempered by experience, reflection, and renouncement, and I am, above all, a believer in culture. Therefore I propose now to try and enquire, in the simple unsystematic way which best suits both my taste and my powers, what culture really is, what good it can do, what is our own special need of it; and I shall seek to find some plain grounds on which a faith in culture—both my own faith in it and the faith of others—may rest securely.

CHAPTER I

SWEETNESS AND LIGHT

THE disparagers of culture make its motive curiosity; sometimes, indeed, they make its motive mere exclusiveness and vanity. The culture which is supposed to plume itself on a smattering of Greek and Latin is a culture which is begotten by nothing so intellectual as curiosity; it is valued either out of sheer vanity and ignorance, or else as an engine of social and class distinction, separating its holder, like a badge or title, from other people who have not got it. No serious man would call this *culture*, or attach any value to it, as culture, at all. To find the real ground for the very differing estimate which serious people will set upon culture, we must find some motive for culture in the terms of which may lie a real ambiguity; and such a motive the word *curiosity* gives us.

I have before now pointed out that we English do not, like the foreigners, use this word in a good sense as well as in a bad sense. With us the word is always used in a somewhat disapproving sense A liberal and intelligent eagerness about the things of the mind may be meant by a foreigner when he speaks of curiosity, but with us the word always conveys a certain notion of frivolous and unedifying activity. In the *Quarterly Review*, some little time ago, was an estimate of the celebrated French critic, M. Sainte-Beuve, and a very inadequate estimate it in my judgment was. And its inadequacy consisted chiefly in this: that in our English way it left out of sight the double sense really involved in the word *curiosity*, thinking enough was said to stamp M. Sainte-Beuve with blame if it was said that he was impelled in his operations as a critic by curiosity, and omitting either to perceive that M. Sainte-Beuve himself, and many other people with him, would consider that this was praiseworthy and not blameworthy, or to point out why it ought really to be accounted worthy of blame and not of praise. For as there is a curiosity about intellectual matters which is futile, and merely a disease, so there is certainly a curiosity, —a desire after the things of the mind simply for their own sakes and for the pleasure of seeing them as they are,— which is, in an intelligent being, natural and laudable. Nay, and the very desire to see things as they are, implies a balance and regulation of mind which is not often attained without fruitful effort, and which is the very opposite of the blind and diseased impulse of mind which is what we mean to blame when we blame curiosity. Montesquieu says:— "The first motive which ought to impel us to study is the desire to augment the excellence of our nature, and to render an intelligent being yet more intelligent." This is the true ground to assign for the genuine scientific passion, however manifested, and for culture, viewed simply as a fruit of this passion; and it is a worthy ground, even though we let the term *curiosity* stand to describe it.

But there is of culture another view, in which not solely the scientific passion, the sheer desire to see things as they are, natural and proper in an intelligent being, appears as the ground of it. There is a view in which all the love of our neighbour, the impulses towards action, help, and beneficence, the desire for removing human error, clearing human confusion, and diminishing human misery, the noble aspiration to leave the world better and happier than we found it,—motives eminently such as are called social,— come in as part of the grounds of culture, and the main and pre-eminent part. Culture is then properly described not as having its origin in curiosity, but as having its origin in the love of perfection; it is *a study of perfection.* It moves by the force, not merely or primarily of the scientific passion for pure knowledge, but also of the moral and social passion for doing good. As, in the first view of it, we took for its worthy motto Montesquieu's words: "To render an intelligent being yet more intelligent!" so, in the second view of it, there is no better motto which it can have than these words of Bishop Wilson: "To make reason and the will of God prevail!"

Only, whereas the passion for doing good is apt to be overhasty in determining what reason and the will of God say, because its turn is for acting rather than thinking, and it wants to be beginning to act; and whereas it is apt to take its own conceptions, which proceed from its own state of development and share in all the imperfections and immaturities of this, for a basis of action; what distinguishes culture is, that it is possessed by the scientific passion as well as by the passion of doing good; that it demands worthy notions of reason and the will of God, and does not readily suffer its own crude conceptions to substitute themselves for them. And knowing that no action or institution can be salutary and stable which is not based on reason and the will of God, it is not so bent on acting and instituting, even with the great aim of diminishing human error and misery ever before its thoughts, but that it can remember that acting and instituting are of little use, unless we know how and what we ought to act and to institute.

This culture is more interesting and more far-reaching than that other, which is founded solely on the scientific passion for knowing. But it needs times of faith and ardour, times when the intellectual horizon is opening and widening all round us, to flourish in. And is not the close and bounded intellectual horizon within which we have long lived and moved now lifting up, and are not new lights finding free passage to shine in upon us? For a long time there was no passage for them to make their way in upon us, and then it was of no use to think of adapting the world's action to them. Where was the hope of making reason and the will of God prevail among people who had a routine which they had christened reason and the will of God, in which they were inextricably bound, and beyond which they had no power of looking? But now the iron force of adhesion to the old routine,—social, political, religious,—has wonderfully yielded; the iron force of exclusion of all which is new has wonderfully yielded. The danger now is, not that people should obstinately refuse to allow anything but their old routine to pass for reason and the will of God, but either that they should allow some novelty or other to pass for these too easily, or else that they should underrate the importance of them altogether, and think it enough to follow action for its own sake, without troubling themselves to make reason and the will of God prevail therein. Now, then, is the moment for culture to be of service, culture which believes in making reason and the will of God prevail, believes in perfection, is the study and pursuit of perfection, and is no longer debarred, by a rigid invincible exclusion of whatever is new, from getting acceptance for its ideas, simply because they are new.

The moment this view of culture is seized, the moment it is regarded not solely as the endeavour to see things as they are, to draw towards a knowledge of the universal order which seems to be intended and aimed at in the world, and which it is a man's happiness to go along with or his misery to go counter to,—to learn, in short, the will of God, —the moment, I say, culture is considered not merely as the endeavour to *see* and *learn* this, but as the endeavour, also, to make it *prevail*, the moral, social, and beneficent character of culture becomes manifest. The mere endeavour to see and learn the truth for our own personal satisfaction is indeed a commencement for making it prevail, a preparing the way for this, which always serves this, and is wrongly, therefore, stamped with blame absolutely in itself and not only in its caricature and degeneration. But perhaps it has got stamped with blame, and disparaged with the dubious title of curiosity, because in comparison with this wider endeavour of such great and plain utility it looks selfish, petty, and unprofitable.

And religion, the greatest and most important of the efforts by which the human race has manifested its impulse to perfect itself,—religion, that voice of the deepest human experience,—does not only enjoin and sanction the aim which is the great aim of culture, the aim of setting ourselves to ascertain what perfection is and to make it prevail; but also, in determining generally in what human perfection consists, religion comes to a conclusion identical with that which culture,—culture seeking the determination of this question through *all* the voices of human experience which have been heard upon it, of art, science, poetry, philosophy, history, as well as of religion, in order to give a greater fulness and certainty to its solution,—likewise reaches. Religion says: *The kingdom of God is within you;* and culture, in like manner, places human perfection in an *internal* condition, in the growth and predominance of our humanity proper, as distinguished from our animality. It places it in the ever-increasing efficacy and in the general harmonious expansion of those gifts of thought and feeling which make the peculiar dignity, wealth, and happiness of human nature. As I have said on a former occasion: "It is in making endless additions to itself, in the endless expansion of its powers, in endless growth in wisdom and beauty, that the spirit of the human race finds its ideal. To reach this ideal, culture is an indispensable aid, and that is the true value of culture."

Not a having and a resting, but a growing and a becoming, is the character of perfection as culture conceives it; and here, too, it coincides with religion.

And because men are all members of one great whole, and the sympathy which is in human nature will not allow one member to be indifferent to the rest or to have a perfect welfare independent of the rest, the expansion of our humanity, to suit the idea of perfection which culture forms, must be a *general* expansion. Perfection, as culture conceives it, is not possible while the individual remains isolated. The individual is required, under pain of being stunted and enfeebled in his own development if he disobeys, to carry others along with him in his march towards perfection, to be continually doing all he can to enlarge and increase the volume of the human stream sweeping thitherward. And here, once more, culture lays on us the same obligation as religion, which says, as Bishop Wilson has admirably put it, that "to promote the kingdom of God is to increase and hasten one's own happiness."

But, finally, perfection,—as culture, from a thorough disinterested study of human nature and human experience learns to conceive it,—is a harmonious expansion of *all* the powers which make the beauty and worth of human nature, and is not consistent with the over-development of any one power at the expense of the rest. Here culture goes beyond religion, as religion is generally conceived by us.

If culture, then, is a study of perfection, and of harmonious perfection, general perfection, and perfection which consists in becoming something rather than in having something, in an inward condition of the mind and spirit, not in an outward set of circumstances,—it is clear that culture, instead of being the frivolous and useless thing which Mr. Bright, and Mr. Frederic Harrison, and many other Liberals are apt to call it, has a very important function to fulfil for mankind. And this function is particularly important in our modern world, of which the whole civilisation is, to a much greater degree than the civilisation of Greece and Rome, mechanical and external, and tends constantly to become more so. But above all in our own country has culture a weighty part to perform, because here that mechanical character, which civilisation tends to take everywhere, is shown in the most eminent degree. Indeed nearly all the characters of perfection, as culture teaches us to fix them, meet in this country with some powerful tendency which thwarts them and sets them at defiance. The idea of perfection as an *inward* condition of the mind and spirit is at variance with the mechanical and material civilisation in esteem with us, and nowhere, as I have said, so much in esteem as with us. The idea of perfection as a *general* expansion of the human family is at variance with our strong individualism, our hatred of all limits to the unrestrained swing of the individual's personality, our maxim of "every man for himself." Above all the idea of perfection as a *harmonious* expansion of human nature is at variance with our want of flexibility, with our inaptitude for seeing more than one side of a thing, with our intense energetic absorption in the particular pursuit we happen to be following. So culture has a rough task to achieve in this country. Its preachers have, and are likely long to have, a hard time of it, and they will much oftener be regarded, for a great while to come, as elegant or spurious Jeremiahs, than as friends and benefactors. That, however, will not prevent their doing in the end good service if they persevere. And meanwhile, the mode of action they have to pursue, and the sort of habits they must fight against, ought to be made quite clear for every one to see who may be willing to look at the matter attentively and dispassionately.

Faith in machinery is, I said, our besetting danger; often

in machinery most absurdly disproportioned to the end
which this machinery, if it is to do any good at all, is to
serve; but always in machinery, as if it had a value in and for
itself. What is freedom but machinery? what is population
but machinery? what is coal but machinery? what are railroads but machinery? what is wealth but machinery? what
are, even, religious organisations but machinery? Now almost every voice in England is accustomed to speak of these
things as if they were precious ends in themselves, and therefore had some of the characters of perfection indisputably
joined to them. I have before now noticed Mr. Roebuck's
stock argument for proving the greatness and happiness of
England as she is, and for quite stopping the mouths of all
gainsayers. Mr. Roebuck is never weary of reiterating this
argument of his, so I do not know why I should be weary of
noticing it. "May not every man in England say what he
likes?"—Mr. Roebuck perpetually asks; and that, he
thinks, is quite sufficient, and when every man may say
what he likes, our aspirations ought to be satisfied. But the
aspirations of culture, which is the study of perfection, are
not satisfied, unless what men say, when they may say what
they like, is worth saying,—has good in it, and more good
than bad. In the same way the *Times*, replying to some
foreign strictures on the dress, looks, and behaviour of the
English abroad, urges that the English ideal is that every
one should be free to do and to look just as he likes. But
culture indefatigably tries, not to make what each raw person may like, the rule by which he fashions himself; but to
draw ever nearer to a sense of what is indeed beautiful,
graceful, and becoming, and to get the raw person to like
that.

And in the same way with respect to railroads and coal.
Every one must have observed the strange language current during the late discussions as to the possible failure of

our supplies of coal. Our coal, thousands of people were saying, is the real basis of our national greatness; if our coal runs short, there is an end of the greatness of England. But what *is* greatness?—culture makes us ask. Greatness is a spiritual condition worthy to excite love, interest, and admiration; and the outward proof of possessing greatness is that we excite love, interest, and admiration. If England were swallowed up by the sea to-morrow, which of the two, a hundred years hence, would most excite the love, interest, and admiration of mankind,—would most, therefore, show the evidences of having possessed greatness, —the England of the last twenty years, or the England of Elizabeth, of a time of splendid spiritual effort, but when our coal, and our industrial operations depending on coal, were very little developed? Well, then, what an unsound habit of mind it must be which makes us talk of things like coal or iron as constituting the greatness of England, and how salutary a friend is culture, bent on seeing things as they are, and thus dissipating delusions of this kind and fixing standards of perfection that are real!

Wealth, again, that end to which our prodigious works for material advantage are directed,—the commonest of commonplaces tells us how men are always apt to regard wealth as a precious end in itself; and certainly they have never been so apt thus to regard it as they are in England at the present time. Never did people believe anything more firmly, than nine Englishmen out of ten at the present day believe that our greatness and welfare are proved by our being so very rich. Now, the use of culture is that it helps us, by means of its spiritual standard of perfection, to regard wealth as but machinery, and not only to say as a matter of words that we regard wealth as but machinery, but really to perceive and feel that it is so. If it were not for this purging effect wrought upon our minds by culture, the whole world, the future as well as the present, would inevitably belong to the Philistines. The people who believe most that our greatness and welfare are proved by our being very rich, and who most give their lives and thoughts to becoming rich, are just the very people whom we call Philistines. Culture says: "Consider these people, then, their way of life, their habits, their manners, the very tones of their voice; look at them attentively; observe the literature they read, the things which give them pleasure, the words which come forth out of their mouths, the thoughts which make the furniture of their minds; would any amount of wealth be worth having with the condition that one was to become just like these people by having it?" And thus culture begets a dissatisfaction which is of the highest possible value in stemming the common tide of men's thoughts in a wealthy and industrial community, and which saves the future, as one may hope, from being vulgarised, even if it cannot save the present.

Population, again, and bodily health and vigour, are things which are nowhere treated in such an unintelligent, misleading, exaggerated way as in England. Both are really machinery; yet how many people all around us do we see rest in them and fail to look beyond them! Why, one has heard people, fresh from reading certain articles of the *Times* on the Registrar-General's returns of marriages and births in this country, who would talk of our large English families in quite a solemn strain, as if they had something in itself beautiful, elevating, and meritorious in them; as if the British Philistine would have only to present himself before the Great Judge with his twelve children, in order to be received among the sheep as a matter of right!

But bodily health and vigour, it may be said, are not to be classed with wealth and population as mere machinery; they have a more real and essential value. True; but only as they are more intimately connected with a perfect spiritual condition than wealth or population are. The moment we disjoin them from the idea of a perfect spiritual condition, and pursue them, as we do pursue them, for their own sake and as ends in themselves, our worship of them becomes as mere worship of machinery, as our worship of wealth or population, and as unintelligent and vulgarising a worship as that is. Every one with anything like an adequate idea of human perfection has distinctly marked this subordination to higher and spiritual ends of the cultivation of bodily vigour and activity. "Bodily exercise profiteth little; but godliness is profitable unto all things," says the author of the Epistle to Timothy. And the utilitarian Franklin says just as explicitly:—"Eat and drink such an exact quantity as suits the constitution of thy body, *in reference to the services of the mind*." But the point of view of culture, keeping the mark of human perfection simply and broadly in view, and not assigning to this perfection, as religion or utilitarianism assign to it, a special and limited character,—this point of view, I say, of culture is best given by these words of Epictetus:—"It is a sign of ἀφυΐα," says he,—that is, of a nature not finely tempered,—"to give yourselves up to things which relate to the body; to make, for instance, a great fuss about exercise, a great fuss about eating, a great fuss about drinking, a great fuss about walking, a great fuss about riding. All these things ought to be done merely by the way: the formation of the spirit and character must be our real concern." This is admirable; and, indeed, the Greek word εὐφυΐα, a finely tempered nature, gives exactly the notion of perfection as culture brings us to conceive it: a harmonious perfection, a perfection in which the characters of beauty and intelligence are both present, which unites "the two noblest of things,"—as Swift, who of one of the two, at any rate, had himself all too little, most happily calls them in his *Battle of the Books*,—"the two noblest of things, *sweetness and light*." The εὐφυής is the man who tends towards sweetness and light; the ἀφυής, on the other hand, is our Philistine. The immense spiritual significance of the Greeks is due to their having been inspired with this central and happy idea of the essential character of human perfection; and Mr. Bright's misconception of culture, as a smattering of Greek and Latin, comes itself, after all, from this wonderful significance of the Greeks having affected the very machinery of our education, and is in itself a kind of homage to it.

In thus making sweetness and light to be characters of perfection, culture is of like spirit with poetry, follows one law with poetry. Far more than on our freedom, our population, and our industrialism, many amongst us rely upon our religious organisations to save us. I have called religion a yet more important manifestation of human nature than poetry, because it has worked on a broader scale for perfection, and with greater masses of men. But the idea of beauty and of a human nature perfect on all its sides, which is the dominant idea of poetry, is a true and invaluable idea, though it has not yet had the success that the idea of conquering the obvious faults of our animality, and of a human nature perfect on the moral side,—which is the dominant idea of religion,—has been enabled to have; and it is destined, adding to itself the religious idea of a devout energy, to transform and govern the other.

The best art and poetry of the Greeks, in which religion and poetry are one, in which the idea of beauty and of a human nature perfect on all sides adds to itself a religious and devout energy, and works in the strength of that, is on this account of such surpassing interest and instructiveness for us, though it was,—as, having regard to the human race in general, and, indeed, having regard to the Greeks themselves, we must own,—a premature attempt, an attempt which for success needed the moral and religious fibre in humanity to be more braced and developed than it had yet been. But Greece did not err in having the idea of beauty, harmony, and complete human perfection, so present and paramount. It is impossible to have this idea too present and paramount; only, the moral fibre must be braced too. And we, because we have braced the moral fibre, are not on that account in the right way, if at the same time the idea of beauty, harmony, and complete human perfection, is wanting or misapprehended amongst us; and evidently it *is* wanting or misapprehended at present. And when we rely as we do on our religious organisations, which in themselves do not and cannot give us this idea, and think we have done enough if we make them spread and prevail, then, I say, we fall into our common fault of over-valuing machinery.

Nothing is more common than for people to confound the inward peace and satisfaction which follows the subduing of the obvious faults of our animality with what I may call absolute inward peace and satisfaction,—the peace and satisfaction which are reached as we draw near to complete spiritual perfection, and not merely to moral perfection, or rather to relative moral perfection. No people in the world have done more and struggled more to attain this relative moral perfection than our English race has. For no people in the world has the command to *resist the devil*, to *overcome the wicked one*, in the nearest and most obvious sense of those words, had such a pressing force and reality. And we have had our reward, not only in the great worldly prosperity which our obedience to this command has brought us, but also, and far more, in great inward peace and satisfaction. But to me few things are more pathetic than to see people, on the strength of the inward peace and satisfaction which their rudimentary efforts towards perfection have brought them, employ, concerning their incomplete perfection and the religious organisations within which they have found it, language which properly applies only to complete perfection, and is a far-off echo of the human soul's prophecy of it. Religion itself, I need hardly say, supplies them in abundance with this grand language. And very freely do they use it; yet it is really the severest criticism of such an incomplete perfection as alone we have yet reached through our religious organisations.

The impulse of the English race towards moral development and self-conquest has nowhere so powerfully manifested itself as in Puritanism. Nowhere has Puritanism found so adequate an expression as in the religious organisation of the Independents. The modern Independents have a newspaper, the *Nonconformist*, written with great sincerity and ability. The motto, the standard, the profession of faith which this organ of theirs carries aloft, is: "The Dissidence of Dissent and the Protestantism of the Protestant religion." There is sweetness and light, and an ideal of complete harmonious human perfection! One need not go to culture and poetry to find language to judge it. Religion, with its instinct for perfection, supplies language to judge it, language too which is in our mouths every day. "Finally, be of one mind, united in feeling," says St. Peter. There is an ideal which judges the Puritan ideal: "The Dissidence of Dissent and the Protestantism of the Protestant religion!" And religious organisations like this are what people believe in, rest in, would give their lives for! Such, I say, is the wonderful virtue of even the beginnings of perfection, of having conquered even the plain faults of our animality, that the religious organisation which has helped us to do it can seem to us something precious, salutary, and to be propagated, even when it wears such a brand of imperfection on its forehead as this. And men have got such a habit of giving to the language of religion a special application, of making it a mere jargon, that for the condemnation which religion itself passes on the shortcomings of their religious organisations they have no ear; they are sure to cheat themselves and to explain this condemnation away. They can only be reached by the criticism which culture, like poetry, speaking a language not to be sophisticated, and resolutely testing these organisations by the ideal of a human perfection complete on all sides, applies to them.

But men of culture and poetry, it will be said, are again and again failing, and failing conspicuously, in the necessary first stage to a harmonious perfection, in the subduing of the great obvious faults of our animality, which it is the glory of these religious organisations to have helped us to subdue. True, they do often so fail. They have often been without the virtues as well as the faults of the Puritan; it has been one of their dangers that they so felt the Puritan's faults that they too much neglected the practice of his virtues. I will not, however, exculpate them at the Puritan's expense. They have often failed in morality, and morality is indispensable And they have been punished for their failure, as the Puritan has been rewarded for his performance. They have been punished wherein they erred; but their ideal of beauty, of sweetness and light, and a human nature complete on all its sides, remains the true ideal of perfection still; just as the Puritan's ideal of perfection remains narrow and inadequate, although for what he did well he has been richly rewarded. Notwithstanding the mighty results of the Pilgrim Fathers' voyage, they and their standard of perfection are rightly judged when we figure to ourselves Shakespeare or Virgil,—souls in whom sweetness

4   W A

and light, and all that in human nature is most humane, were eminent,—accompanying them on their voyage, and think what intolerable company Shakespeare and Virgil would have found them! In the same way let us judge the religious organisations which we see all around us. Do not let us deny the good and the happiness which they have accomplished; but do not let us fail to see clearly that their idea of human perfection is narrow and inadequate, and that the Dissidence of Dissent and the Protestantism of the Protestant religion will never bring humanity to its true goal. As I said with regard to wealth: Let us look at the life of those who live in and for it,—so I say with regard to the religious organisations. Look at the life imaged in such a newspaper as the *Nonconformist*,—a life of jealousy of the Establishment, disputes, tea-meetings, openings of chapels, sermons; and then think of it as an ideal of a human life completing itself on all sides, and aspiring with all its organs after sweetness, light, and perfection!

Another newspaper, representing, like the *Nonconformist*, one of the religious organisations of this country, was a short time ago giving an account of the crowd at Epsom on the Derby day, and of all the vice and hideousness which was to be seen in that crowd; and then the writer turned suddenly round upon Professor Huxley, and asked him how he proposed to cure all this vice and hideousness without religion. I confess I felt disposed to ask the asker this question: and how do you propose to cure it with such a religion as yours? How is the ideal of a life so unlovely, so unattractive, so incomplete, so narrow, so far removed from a true and satisfying ideal of human perfection, as is the life of your religious organisation as you yourself reflect it, to conquer and transform all this vice and hideousness? Indeed, the strongest plea for the study of perfection as pursued by culture, the clearest proof of the actual inadequacy

of the idea of perfection held by the religious organisations,
—expressing, as I have said, the most wide-spread effort
which the human race has yet made after perfection,—is to
be found in the state of our life and society with these in
possession of it, and having been in possession of it I know
not how many hundred years. We are all of us included
in some religious organisation or other; we all call ourselves, in the sublime and aspiring language of religion
which I have before noticed, *children of God.* Children of
God;—it is an immense pretension!—and how are we to
justify it? By the works which we do, and the words
which we speak. And the work which we collective
children of God do, our grand centre of life, our *city* which
we have builded for us to dwell in, is London! London,
with its unutterable external hideousness, and with its internal canker of *publicè egestas, privatim opulentia,*—to use
the words which Sallust puts into Cato's mouth about
Rome,—unequalled in the world! The word, again, which
we children of God speak, the voice which most hits our
collective thought, the newspaper with the largest circulation in England, nay, with the largest circulation in the
whole world, is the *Daily Telegraph!* I say that when our
religious organisations,—which I admit to express the most
considerable effort after perfection that our race has yet
made,—land us in no better result than this, it is high time
to examine carefully their idea of perfection, to see whether
it does not leave out of account sides and forces of human
nature which we might turn to great use; whether it
would not be more operative if it were more complete.
And I say that the English reliance on our religious
organisations and on their ideas of human perfection just
as they stand, is like our reliance on freedom, on muscular
Christianity, on population, on coal, on wealth,—mere
belief in machinery, and unfruitful; and that it is whole-

somely counteracted by culture, bent on seeing things as they are, and on drawing the human race onwards to a more complete, a harmonious perfection.

Culture, however, shows its single-minded love of perfection, its desire simply to make reason and the will of God prevail, its freedom from fanaticism, by its attitude towards all this machinery, even while it insists that it *is* machinery. Fanatics, seeing the mischief men do themselves by their blind belief in some machinery or other,—whether it is wealth and industrialism, or whether it is the cultivation of bodily strength and activity, or whether it is a political organisation,—or whether it is a religious organisation,—oppose with might and main the tendency to this or that political and religious organisation, or to games and athletic exercises, or to wealth and industrialism, and try violently to stop it. But the flexibility which sweetness and light give, and which is one of the rewards of culture pursued in good faith, enables a man to see that a tendency may be necessary, and even, as a preparation for something in the future, salutary, and yet that the generations or individuals who obey this tendency are sacrificed to it, that they fall short of the hope of perfection by following it; and that its mischiefs are to be criticised, lest it should take too firm a hold and last after it has served its purpose.

Mr. Gladstone well pointed out, in a speech at Paris,—and others have pointed out the same thing,—how necessary is the present great movement towards wealth and industrialism, in order to lay broad foundations of material well-being for the society of the future. The worst of these justifications is, that they are generally addressed to the very people engaged, body and soul, in the movement in question; at all events, that they are always seized with the greatest avidity by these people, and taken by them as quite justifying their life; and that thus they tend to harden them in their sins. Now, culture admits the necessity of the movement towards fortune-making and exaggerated industrialism, readily allows that the future may derive benefit from it; but insists, at the same time, that the passing generations of industrialists,—forming, for the most part, the stout main body of Philistinism,—are sacrificed to it. In the same way, the result of all the games and sports which occupy the passing generation of boys and young men may be the establishment of a better and sounder physical type for the future to work with. Culture does not set itself against the games and sports; it congratulates the future, and hopes it will make a good use of its improved physical basis; but it points out that our passing generation of boys and young men is, meantime, sacrificed. Puritanism was perhaps necessary to develop the moral fibre of the English race, Nonconformity to break the yoke of ecclesiastical domination over men's minds and to prepare the way for freedom of thought in the distant future; still, culture points out that the harmonious perfection of generations of Puritans and Nonconformists has been, in consequence, sacrificed. Freedom of speech may be necessary for the society of the future, but the young lions of the *Daily Telegraph* in the meanwhile are sacrificed. A voice for every man in his country's government may be necessary for the society of the future, but meanwhile Mr. Beales and Mr. Bradlaugh are sacrificed.

Oxford, the Oxford of the past, has many faults; and she has heavily paid for them in defeat, in isolation, in want of hold upon the modern world. Yet we in Oxford, brought up amidst the beauty and sweetness of that beautiful place, have not failed to seize one truth:—the truth that beauty and sweetness are essential characters of a complete human perfection. When I insist on this, I am all in the faith and tradition of Oxford. I say boldly that this our sentiment for beauty and sweetness, our sentiment against hideousness and rawness, has been at the bottom of our attachment to so many beaten causes, of our opposition to so many triumphant movements. And the sentiment is true, and has never been wholly defeated, and has shown its power even in its defeat. We have not won our political battles, we have not carried our main points, we have not stopped our adversaries' advance, we have not marched victoriously with the modern world; but we have told silently upon the mind of the country, we have prepared currents of feeling which sap our adversaries' position when it seems gained, we have kept up our own communications with the future. Look at the course of the great movement which shook Oxford to its centre some thirty years ago! It was directed, as any one who reads Dr. Newman's *Apology* may see, against what in one word may be called "Liberalism." Liberalism prevailed; it was the appointed force to do the work of the hour; it was necessary, it was inevitable that it should prevail. The Oxford movement was broken, it failed; our wrecks are scattered on every shore:—

Quæ regio in terris nostri non plena laboris?

But what was it, this Liberalism, as Dr. Newman saw it, and as it really broke the Oxford movement? It was the great middle-class Liberalism, which had for the cardinal points of its belief the Reform Bill of 1832, and local self-government, in politics; in the social sphere, free-trade, unrestricted competition, and the making of large industrial fortunes; in the religious sphere, the Dissidence of Dissent and the Protestantism of the Protestant religion. I do not say that other and more intelligent forces than this were not opposed to the Oxford movement: but this was the force which really beat it; this was the force which Dr. Newman felt himself fighting with; this was the force which till only the other day seemed to be the paramount force in this country, and to be in possession of the future; this was the force whose achievements fill Mr. Lowe with such inexpressible admiration, and whose rule he was so horror-struck to see threatened. And where is this great force of Philistinism now? It is thrust into the second rank, it is become a power of yesterday, it has lost the future. A new power has suddenly appeared, a power which it is impossible yet to judge fully, but which is certainly a wholly different force from middle-class Liberalism; different in its cardinal points of belief, different in its tendencies in every sphere. It loves and admires neither the legislation of middle-class Parliaments, nor the local self-government of middle-class vestries, nor the unrestricted competition of middle-class industrialists, nor the dissidence of middle-class Dissent and the Protestantism of middle-class Protestant religion. I am not now praising this new force, or saying that its own ideals are better; all I say is, that they are wholly different. And who will estimate how much the currents of feeling created by Dr. Newman's movement, the keen desire for beauty and sweetness which it nourished, the deep aversion it manifested to the hardness and vulgarity of middle-class Liberalism, the strong light it turned on the hideous and grotesque illusions of middle-class Protestantism,—who will estimate how much all these contributed to swell the tide of secret dissatisfaction which has mined the ground under the self-confident Liberalism of the last thirty years, and has prepared the way for its sudden collapse and supersession? It is in this manner that the sentiment of Oxford for beauty and sweetness conquers, and in this manner long may it continue to conquer!

In this manner it works to the same end as culture, and there is plenty of work for it yet to do. I have said that the new and more democratic force which is now superseding our old middle-class Liberalism cannot yet be rightly judged. It has its main tendencies still to form. We hear promises of its giving us administrative reform, law reform, reform of education, and I know not what; but those promises come rather from its advocates, wishing to make a good plea for it and to justify it for superseding middle-class Liberalism, than from clear tendencies which it has itself yet developed. But meanwhile it has plenty of well-intentioned friends against whom culture may with advantage continue to uphold steadily its ideal of human perfection; that this is *an inward spiritual activity, having for its characters increased sweetness, increased light, increased life, increased sympathy.* Mr. Bright, who has a foot in both worlds, the world of middle-class Liberalism and the world of democracy, but who brings most of his ideas from the world of middle-class Liberalism in which he was bred, always inclines to inculcate that faith in machinery to which, as we have seen, Englishmen are so prone, and which has been the bane of middle-class Liberalism. He complains with a sorrowful indignation of people who "appear to have no proper estimate of the value of the franchise;" he leads his disciples to believe,—what the Englishman is always too ready to believe,—that the having a vote, like the having a large family, or a large business, or large muscles, has in itself some edifying and perfecting effect upon human nature. Or else he cries out to the democracy,—"the men," as he calls them, "upon whose shoulders the greatness of England rests,"—he cries out to them: "See what you have done! I look over this country and see the cities you have built, the railroads you have made, the manufactures you have produced, the cargoes which freight the ships of the greatest mercantile navy the world has ever seen! I see that you have converted by your labours what was once a wilderness, these islands, into a fruitful garden; I know that you have created this wealth, and are a nation whose name is a word of power throughout all the world." Why, this is just the very style of laudation with which Mr. Roebuck or Mr. Lowe debauch the minds of the middle classes, and make such Philistines of them. It is the same fashion of teaching a man to value himself not on what he *is*, not on his progress in sweetness and light, but on the number of the railroads he has constructed, or the bigness of the tabernacle he has built. Only the middle classes are told they have done it all with their energy, self-reliance, and capital, and the democracy are told they have done it all with their hands and sinews. But teaching the democracy to put its trust in achievements of this kind is merely training them to be Philistines to take the place of the Philistines whom they are superseding; and they too, like the middle class, will be encouraged to sit down at the banquet of the future without having on a wedding garment, and nothing excellent can then come from them. Those who know their besetting faults, those who have watched them and listened to them, or those who will read the instructive account recently given of them by one of themselves, the *Journeyman Engineer*, will agree that the idea which culture sets before us of perfection,—an increased spiritual activity, having for its characters increased sweetness, increased light, increased life, increased sympathy,—is an idea which the new democracy needs far more than the idea of the blessedness of the franchise, or the wonderfulness of its own industrial performances.

Other well-meaning friends of this new power are for leading it, not in the old ruts of middle-class Philistinism, but in ways which are naturally alluring to the feet of democracy, though in this country they are novel and untried ways. I may call them the ways of Jacobinism. Violent indignation with the past, abstract systems of renovation applied wholesale, a new doctrine drawn up in black and white for elaborating down to the very smallest details a rational society for the future,—these are the ways of Jacobinism. Mr. Frederic Harrison and other disciples of Comte,—one of them, Mr. Congreve, is an old friend of mine, and I am glad to have an opportunity of pub-licly expressing my respect for his talents and character, —are among the friends of democracy who are for leading it in paths of this kind. Mr. Frederic Harrison is very hostile to culture, and from a natural enough motive; for culture is the eternal opponent of the two things which are the signal marks of Jacobinism,—its fierceness, and its addiction to an abstract system. Culture is always assigning to system-makers and systems a smaller share in the bent of human destiny than their friends like. A current in people's minds sets towards new ideas; people are dissatisfied with their old narrow stock of Philistine ideas, Anglo-Saxon ideas, or any other; and some man, some Bentham or Comte, who has the real merit of having early and strongly felt and helped the new current, but who brings plenty of narrowness and mistakes of his own into his feeling and help of it, is credited with being the author of the whole current, the fit person to be entrusted with its regulation and to guide the human race.

The excellent German historian of the mythology of Rome, Preller, relating the introduction at Rome under the Tarquins of the worship of Apollo, the god of light, healing, and reconciliation, will have us observe that it was not so much the Tarquins who brought to Rome the new worship of Apollo, as a current in the mind of the Roman people which set powerfully at that time towards a new worship of this kind, and away from the old run of Latin and Sabine religious ideas. In a similar way, culture directs our attention to the natural current there is in human affairs, and to its continual working, and will not let us rivet our faith upon any one man and his doings. It makes us see, not only his good side, but also how much in him was of necessity limited and transient; nay, it even feels a pleasure, a sense of an increased freedom and of an ampler future, in so doing.

I remember, when I was under the influence of a mind to which I feel the greatest obligations, the mind of a man who was the very incarnation of sanity and clear sense, a man the most considerable, it seems to me, whom America has yet produced,—Benjamin Franklin,—I remember the relief with which, after long feeling the sway of Franklin's imperturbable common-sense, I came upon a project of his for a new version of the Book of Job, to replace the old version, the style of which, says Franklin, has become obsolete, and thence less agreeable. "I give," he continues, "a few verses, which may serve as a sample of the kind of version I would recommend." We all recollect the famous verse in our translation: "Then Satan answered the Lord and said: 'Doth Job fear God for nought?'" Franklin makes this: "Does Your Majesty imagine that Job's good conduct is the effect of mere personal attachment and affection?" I well remember how when first I read that, I drew a deep breath of relief, and said to myself: "After all, there is a stretch of humanity beyond Franklin's victorious good sense!" So, after hearing Bentham cried loudly up as the renovator of modern society, and Bentham's mind and ideas proposed as the rulers of our future, I open the *Deontology*. There I read: "While Xenophon was writing his history and Euclid teaching geometry, Socrates and Plato were talking nonsense under pretence of talking wisdom and morality. This morality of theirs consisted in words, this wisdom of theirs was the denial of matters known to every man's experience." From the moment of reading that, I am delivered from the bondage of Bentham! the fanaticism of his adherents can touch me no longer; I feel the inadequacy of his mind and ideas for supplying the rule of human society, for perfection.

Culture tends always thus to deal with the men of a system, of disciples, of a school; with men like Comte or, the late Mr. Buckle, or Mr. Mill. However much it may find to admire in these personages, or in some of them, it nevertheless remembers the text: "Be not ye called Rabbi!" and it soon passes on from any Rabbi. But Jacobinism loves a Rabbi; it does not want to pass on from its Rabbi in pursuit of a future and still unreached perfection; it wants its Rabbi and his ideas to stand for perfection, that they may with the more authority recast the world; and for Jacobinism, therefore, culture,—eternally passing onwards and seeking,—is an impertinence and an offence. But culture, just because it resists this tendency of Jacobinism to impose on us a man with limitations and errors of his own along with the true ideas of which he is the organ, really does the world and Jacobinism itself a service.

So, too, Jacobinism, in its fierce hatred of the past and of those whom it makes liable for the sins of the past, cannot away with the inexhaustible indulgence proper to culture, the consideration of circumstances, the severe judgment of actions joined to the merciful judgment of persons. "The man of culture is in politics," cries Mr. Frederic Harrison, "one of the poorest mortals alive!" Mr. Frederic Harrison wants to be doing business, and he complains that the man of culture stops him with a "turn for small fault-finding, love of selfish ease, and indecision in action." Of what use is culture, he asks, except for "a critic of new books or a professor of *belles lettres?*" Why, it is of use because, in presence of the fierce exasperation which breathes, or rather, I may say, hisses, through the whole production in which Mr. Frederic Harrison asks that question, it reminds us that the perfection of human nature is sweetness and light. It is of use because, like religion,—that other effort after perfection,—it testifies that, where bitter envying and strife are, there is confusion and every evil work.

The pursuit of perfection, then, is the pursuit of sweetness and light. He who works for sweetness works in the end for light also; he who works for light works in the end for sweetness also. But he who works for sweetness and light united, works to make reason and the will of God prevail. He who works for machinery, he who works for hatred, works only for confusion. Culture looks beyond machinery, culture hates hatred; culture has one great passion, the passion for sweetness and light. It has one even yet greater!—the passion for making them *prevail*. It is not satisfied till we *all* come to a perfect man; it knows that the sweetness and light of the few must be imperfect until the raw and unkindled masses of humanity are touched with sweetness and light. If I have not shrunk from saying that we must work for sweetness and light, so neither have I shrunk from saying that we must have a broad basis, must have sweetness and light for as many as possible. Again and again I have insisted how those are the happy moments of humanity, how those are the marking epochs of a people's life, how those are the flowering times for literature and art and all the creative power of genius, when there is a *national* glow of life and thought, when the whole of society is in the fullest measure permeated by thought, sensible to beauty, intelligent and alive. Only it must be *real* thought and *real* beauty; *real* sweetness and *real* light. Plenty of people will try to give the masses, as they call them, an intellectual food prepared and adapted in the way they think proper for the actual condition of the masses.

The ordinary popular literature is an example of this way of working on the masses. Plenty of people will try to indoctrinate the masses with the set of ideas and judgments constituting the creed of their own profession or party. Our religious and political organisations give an example of this way of working on the masses. I condemn neither way; but culture works differently. It does not try to teach down to the level of inferior classes; it does not try to win them for this or that sect of its own, with ready-made judgments and watchwords. It seeks to do away with classes; to make the best that has been thought and known in the world current everywhere; to make all men live in an atmosphere of sweetness and light, where they may use ideas, as it uses them itself, freely,—nourished and not bound by them.

This is the *social idea*; and the men of culture are the true apostles of equality. The great men of culture are those who have had a passion for diffusing, for making prevail, for carrying from one end of society to the other, the best knowledge, the best ideas of their time; who have laboured to divest knowledge of all that was harsh, uncouth, difficult, abstract, professional, exclusive; to humanise it, to make it efficient outside the clique of the cultivated and learned, yet still remaining the *best* knowledge and thought of the time, and a true source, therefore, of sweetness and light. Such a man was Abelard in the Middle Ages, in spite of all his imperfections; and thence the boundless emotion and enthusiasm which Abelard excited. Such were Lessing and Herder in Germany, at the end of the last century; and their services to Germany were in this way inestimably precious. Generations will pass, and literary monuments will accumulate, and works far more perfect than the works of Lessing and Herder will be produced in Germany; and yet the names of these two men will fill a German with a

reverence and enthusiasm such as the names of the most
gifted masters will hardly awaken. And why? Because
they *humanised* knowledge; because they broadened the
basis of life and intelligence; because they worked powerfully to diffuse sweetness and light, to make reason and
the will of God prevail. With Saint Augustine they said:
"Let us not leave Thee alone to make in the secret of
thy knowledge, as thou didst before the creation of the
firmament, the division of light from darkness; let the
children of thy spirit, placed in their firmament, make
their light shine upon the earth, mark the division of
night and day, and announce the revolution of the times;
for the old order is passed, and the new arises; the night is
spent, the day is come forth; and thou shalt crown
the year with thy blessing, when thou shalt send forth
labourers into thy harvest sown by other hands than theirs;
when thou shalt send forth new labourers to new seed-times,
whereof the harvest shall be not yet."

CHAPTER II

DOING AS ONE LIKES

I HAVE been trying to show that culture is, or ought to be, the study and pursuit of perfection; and that of perfection, as pursued by culture, beauty and intelligence, or, in other words, sweetness and light, are the main characters. But hitherto I have been insisting chiefly on beauty, or sweetness, as a character of perfection. To complete rightly my design, it evidently remains to speak also of intelligence, or light, as a character of perfection.

First, however, I ought perhaps to notice that, both here and on the other side of the Atlantic, all sorts of objections are raised against the "religion of culture," as the objectors mockingly call it, which I am supposed to be promulgating. It is said to be a religion proposing parmaceti, or some scented salve or other, as a cure for human miseries; a religion breathing a spirit of cultivated inaction, making its believer refuse to lend a hand at uprooting the definite evils on all sides of us, and filling him with antipathy against the reforms and reformers which try to extirpate them. In general, it is summed up as being not practical, or,—as some critics familiarly put it,—all moonshine. That Alcibiades, the editor of the *Morning Star*, taunts me, as its promulgator, with living out of the world and knowing nothing of life and men. That great austere toiler, the editor of the *Daily Telegraph*, upbraids me,—but kindly, and more in sorrow than in anger,—for trifling with æsthetics and poetical fancies, while he himself, in that arsenal of his in Fleet Street, is bearing the burden and heat of the day. An intelligent American newspaper, the *Nation*, says that it is very easy to sit in one's study and find fault with the course of modern society, but the thing is to propose practical improvements for it. While, finally, Mr. Frederic Harrison, in a very good-tempered and witty satire, which makes me quite understand his having apparently achieved such a conquest of my young Prussian friend, Arminius, at last gets moved to an almost stern moral impatience, to behold, as he says, "Death, sin, cruelty stalk among us, filling their maws with innocence and youth," and me, in the midst of the general tribulation, handing out my pouncet-box.

It is impossible that all these remonstrances and reproofs should not affect me, and I shall try my very best, in completing my design and in speaking of light as one of the characters of perfection, and of culture as giving us light, to profit by the objections I have heard and read, and to drive at practice as much as I can, by showing the communications and passages into practical life from the doctrine which I am inculcating.

It is said that a man with my theories of sweetness and light is full of antipathy against the rougher or coarser movements going on around him, that he will not lend a hand to the humble operation of uprooting evil by their means, and that therefore the believers in action grow impatient with them. But what if rough and coarse action, ill-calculated action, action with insufficient light, is, and has for a long time been, our bane? What if our urgent want now is, not to act at any price, but rather to lay in a stock of light for our difficulties? In that case, to refuse to lend a hand to the rougher and coarser movements going on round us, to make the primary need, both for oneself and others, to consist in enlightening ourselves and qualifying ourselves to act less at random, is surely the best and in real truth the most practical line our endeavours can take. So that if I can show what my opponents call rough or coarse action, but what I would rather call random and ill-regulated action,—action with insufficient light, action pursued because we like to be doing something and doing it as we please, and do not like the trouble of thinking and the severe constraint of any kind of rule,—if I can show this to be, at the present moment, a practical mischief and dangerous to us, then I have found a practical use for light in correcting this state of things, and have only to exemplify how, in cases which fall under everybody's observation, it may deal with it.

When I began to speak of culture, I insisted on our bondage to machinery, on our proneness to value machinery as an end in itself, without looking beyond it to the end for which alone, in truth, it is valuable. Freedom, I said, was one of those things which we thus worshipped in itself, without enough regarding the ends for which freedom is to be desired. In our common notions and talk about freedom, we eminently show our idolatry of machinery. Our prevalent notion is,—and I quoted a number of instances to prove it,—that it is a most happy and important thing for a man merely to be able to do as he likes. On what he is to do when he is thus free to do as he likes, we do not lay so much stress. Our familiar praise of the British Constitution under which we live, is that it is a system of checks,—a system which stops and paralyses any power in interfering with the free action of individuals. To this effect Mr. Bright, who loves to walk in the old ways of the Constitution, said forcibly in one of his great speeches, what many other people are every day saying less forcibly, that the central idea of English life and politics is *the assertion of personal liberty*. Evidently this is so; but evidently, also, as feudalism, which with its ideas and habits of subordination was for many centuries silently behind the British

Constitution, dies out, and we are left with nothing but our system of checks, and our notion of its being the great right and happiness of an Englishman to do as far as possible what he likes, we are in danger of drifting towards anarchy. We have not the notion, so familiar on the Continent and to antiquity, of *the State*—the nation in its collective and corporate character, entrusted with stringent powers for the general advantage, and controlling individual wills in the name of an interest wider than that of individuals. We say, what is very true, that this notion is often made instrumental to tyranny; we say that a State is in reality made up of the individuals who compose it, and that every individual is the best judge of his own interests. Our leading class is an aristocracy, and no aristocracy likes the notion of a State-authority greater than itself, with a stringent administrative machinery superseding the decorative inutilities of lord-lieutenancy, deputy-lieutenancy, and the *posse comitatûs*, which are all in its own hands. Our middle class, the great representative of trade and Dissent, with its maxims of every man for himself in business, every man for himself in religion, dreads a powerful administration which might somehow interfere with it; and besides, it has its own decorative inutilities of vestrymanship and guardianship, which are to this class what lord-lieutenancy and the county magistracy are to the aristocratic class, and a stringent administration might either take these functions out of its hands, or prevent its exercising them in its own comfortable, independent manner, as at present.

Then as to our working class. This class, pressed constantly by the hard daily compulsion of material wants, is naturally the very centre and stronghold of our national idea, that it is man's ideal right and felicity to do as he likes. I think I have somewhere related how M. Michelet said to me of the people of France, that it was "a nation

of barbarians civilised by the conscription." He meant
that through their military service the idea of public
duty and of discipline was brought to the mind of these
masses, in other respects so raw and uncultivated. Our
masses are quite as raw and uncultivated as the French;
and so far from their having the idea of public duty and of
discipline, superior to the individual's self-will, brought to
their mind by a universal obligation of military service,
such as that of the conscription,—so far from their having
this, the very idea of a conscription is so at variance with
our English notion of the prime right and blessedness of
doing as one likes, that I remember the manager of the
Clay Cross works in Derbyshire told me during the
Crimean war, when our want of soldiers was much felt
and some people were talking of a conscription, that
sooner than submit to a conscription the population of that
district would flee to the mines, and lead a sort of Robin
Hood life under ground.

For a long time, as I have said, the strong feudal habits
of subordination and deference continued to tell upon the
working class. The modern spirit has now almost entirely
dissolved those habits, and the anarchical tendency of our
worship of freedom in and for itself, of our superstitious
faith, as I say, in machinery, is becoming very manifest.
More and more, because of this our blind faith in machinery, because of our want of light to enable us to look
beyond machinery to the end for which machinery is
valuable, this and that man, and this and that body of men,
all over the country, are beginning to assert and put in
practice an Englishman's right to do what he likes; his
right to march where he likes, meet where he likes, enter
where he likes, hoot as he likes, threaten as he likes,
smash as he likes. All this, I say, tends to anarchy; and
though a number of excellent people, and particularly my

see Intro p XXVI

friends of the Liberal or progressive party, as they call themselves, are kind enough to reassure us by saying that these are trifles, that a few transient outbreaks of rowdyism signify nothing, that our system of liberty is one which itself cures all the evils which it works, that the educated and intelligent classes stand in overwhelming strength and majestic repose, ready, like our military force in riots, to act at a moment's notice,—yet one finds that one's Liberal friends generally say this because they have such faith in themselves and their nostrums, when they shall return, as the public welfare requires, to place and power. But this faith of theirs one cannot exactly share, when one has so long had them and their nostrums at work, and sees that they have not prevented our coming to our present embarrassed condition. And one finds, also, that the outbreaks of rowdyism tend to become less and less of trifles, to become more frequent rather than less frequent; and that meanwhile our educated and intelligent classes remain in their majestic repose, and somehow or other, whatever happens, their overwhelming strength, like our military force in riots, never does act.

How, indeed, *should* their overwhelming strength act, when the man who gives an inflammatory lecture, or breaks down the park railings, or invades a Secretary of State's office, is only following an Englishman's impulse to do as he likes; and our own conscience tells us that we ourselves have always regarded this impulse as something primary and sacred? Mr. Murphy lectures at Birmingham, and showers on the Catholic population of that town "words," says the Home Secretary, Mr. Hardy, "only fit to be addressed to thieves or murderers." What then? Mr. Murphy has his own reasons of several kinds. He suspects the Roman Catholic Church of designs upon Mrs. Murphy; and he says, if mayors and magistrates do not care for their wives and daughters, he does. But, above all, he is doing as he likes; or, in worthier language, asserting his personal liberty. "I will carry out my lectures if they walk over my body as a dead corpse; and I say to the Mayor of Birmingham that he is my servant while I am in Birmingham, and as my servant he must do his duty and protect me." Touching and beautiful words, which find a sympathetic chord in every British bosom! The moment it is plainly put before us that a man is asserting his personal liberty, we are half disarmed; because we are believers in freedom, and not in some dream of a right reason to which the assertion of our freedom is to be subordinated. Accordingly, the Secretary of State had to say that although the lecturer's language was "only fit to be addressed to thieves or murderers," yet, "I do not think he is to be deprived, I do not think that anything I have said could justify the inference that he is to be deprived, of the right of protection in a place built by him for the purpose of these lectures; because the language was not language which afforded grounds for a criminal prosecution." No, nor to be silenced by Mayor, or Home Secretary, or any administrative authority on earth, simply on their notion of what is discreet and reasonable! This is in perfect consonance with our public opinion, and with our national love for the assertion of personal liberty.

In quite another department of affairs, an experienced and distinguished Chancery Judge relates an incident which is just to the same effect as this of Mr. Murphy. A testator bequeathed 300*l.* a year, to be for ever applied as a pension to some person who had been unsuccessful in literature, and whose duty should be to support and diffuse, by his writings, the testator's own views, as enforced in the testator's publications. The views were not worth a straw and the bequest was appealed against in the Court of Chancery on the ground of its absurdity; but, being only absurd, it was upheld, and the so-called charity was established. Having, I say, at the bottom of our English hearts a very strong belief in freedom, and a very weak belief in right reason, we are soon silenced when a man pleads the prime right to do as he likes, because this is the prime right for ourselves too; and even if we attempt now and then to mumble something about reason, yet we have ourselves thought so little about this and so much about liberty, that we are in conscience forced, when our brother Philistine with whom we are meddling turns boldly round upon us and asks: *Have you any light?*—to shake our heads ruefully, and to let him go his own way after all.

There are many things to be said on behalf of this exclusive attention of ours to liberty, and of the relaxed habits of government which it has engendered. It is very easy to mistake or to exaggerate the sort of anarchy from which we are in danger through them. We are not in danger from Fenianism, fierce and turbulent as it may show itself; for against this our conscience is free enough to let us act resolutely and put forth our overwhelming strength the moment there is any real need for it. In the first place, it never was any part of our creed that the great right and blessedness of an Irishman, or, indeed, of anybody on earth except an Englishman, is to do as he likes; and we can have no scruple at all about abridging, if necessary, a non-Englishman's assertion of personal liberty. The British Constitution, its checks, and its prime virtues, are for Englishmen. We may extend them to others out of love and kindness; but we find no real divine law written on our hearts constraining us so to extend them. And then the difference between an Irish Fenian and an English rough is so immense, and the case, in dealing with the Fenian, so much more clear! He is so evidently desperate and dangerous, a man of a conquered race, a Papist, with centuries

of ill-usage to inflame him against us, with an alien
religion established in his country by us at his expense, with
no admiration of our institutions, no love of our virtues, no
talents for our business, no turn for our comfort! Show
him our symbolical Truss Manufactory on the finest site in
Europe, and tell him that British industrialism and individualism can bring a man to that, and he remains cold!
Evidently, if we deal tenderly with a sentimentalist like this,
it is out of pure philanthropy.

But with the Hyde Park rioter how different! He is our
own flesh and blood; he is a Protestant; he is framed by
nature to do as we do, hate what we hate, love what we
love; he is capable of feeling the symbolical force of the
Truss Manufactory; the question of questions, for him, is
a wages question. That beautiful sentence Sir Daniel
Gooch quoted to the Swindon workmen, and which I
treasure as Mrs. Gooch's Golden Rule, or the Divine In-
junction "Be ye Perfect" done into British,—the sentence
Sir Daniel Gooch's mother repeated to him every morning
when he was a boy going to work: "*Ever remember, my
dear Dan, that you should look forward to being some day
manager of that concern!*"—this fruitful maxim is perfectly
fitted to shine forth in the heart of the Hyde Park rough
also, and to be his guiding-star through life. He has no
visionary schemes of revolution and transformation, though
of course he would like his class to rule, as the aristocratic
class like their class to rule, and the middle class theirs.
But meanwhile our social machine is a little out of order;
there are a good many people in our paradisiacal centres of
industrialism and individualism taking the bread out of one
another's mouths. The rough has not yet quite found his
groove and settled down to his work, and so he is just
asserting his personal liberty a little, going where he likes,
assembling where he likes, bawling as he likes, hustling as

he likes. Just as the rest of us,—as the country squires in the aristocratic class, as the political dissenters in the middle class,—he has no idea of a *State*, of the nation in its collective and corporate character controlling, as government, the free swing of this or that one of its members in the name of the higher reason of all of them, his own as well as that of others. He sees the rich, the aristocratic class, in occupation of the executive government, and so if he is stopped from making Hyde Park a bear-garden or the streets impassable, he says he is being butchered by the aristocracy.

His apparition is somewhat embarrassing, because too many cooks spoil the broth; because, while the aristocratic and middle classes have long been doing as they like with great vigour, he has been too undeveloped and submissive hitherto to join in the game; and now, when he does come, he comes in immense numbers, and is rather raw and rough. But he does not break many laws, or not many at one time; and, as our laws were made for very different circumstances from our present (but always with an eye to Englishmen doing as they like), and as the clear letter of the law must be against our Englishman who does as he likes and not only the spirit of the law and public policy, and as Government must neither have any discretionary power nor act resolutely on its own interpretation of the law if any one disputes it, it is evident our laws give our playful giant, in doing as he likes, considerable advantage. Besides, even if he can be clearly proved to commit an illegality in doing as he likes, there is always the resource of not putting the law in force, or of abolishing it. So he has his way, and if he has his way he is soon satisfied for the time. However, he falls into the habit of taking it oftener and oftener, and at last begins to create by his operations a confusion of which mischievous people can take advantage, and which at any rate, by troubling the common course of business throughout the country, tends to cause distress, and so to increase the sort of anarchy and social disintegration which had previously commenced. And thus that profound sense of settled order and security, without which a society like ours cannot live and grow at all, sometimes seems to be beginning to threaten us with taking its departure.

Now, if culture, which simply means trying to perfect oneself, and one's mind as part of oneself, brings us light, and if light shows us that there is nothing so very blessed in merely doing as one likes, that the worship of the mere freedom to do as one likes is worship of machinery, that the really blessed thing is to like what right reason ordains, and to follow her authority, then we have got a practical benefit out of culture. We have got a much wanted principle, a principle of authority, to counteract the tendency to anarchy which seems to be threatening us.

But how to organise this authority, or to what hands to entrust the wielding of it? How to get your *State*, summing up the right reason of the community, and giving effect to it, as circumstances may require, with vigour? And here I think I see my enemies waiting for me with a hungry joy in their eyes. But I shall elude them.

The *State*, the power most representing the right reason of the nation, and most worthy, therefore, of ruling,—of exercising, when circumstances require it, authority over us all,—is for Mr. Carlyle the aristocracy. For Mr. Lowe, it is the middle class with its incomparable Parliament. For the Reform League, it is the working class, the class with "the brightest powers of sympathy and readiest powers of action." Now, culture, with its disinterested pursuit of perfection, culture, simply trying to see things as they are, in order to seize on the best and to make it prevail, is surely well fitted to help us to judge rightly, by all the aids of observing, reading, and thinking, the qualifications and titles to our confidence of these three candidates for authority, and can thus render us a practical service of no mean value.

So when Mr. Carlyle, a man of genius to whom we have all at one time or other been indebted for refreshment and stimulus, says we should give rule to the aristocracy, mainly because of its dignity and politeness, surely culture is useful in reminding us, that in our idea of perfection the characters of beauty and intelligence are both of them present, and sweetness and light, the two noblest of things, are united. Allowing, therefore, with Mr. Carlyle, the aristocratic class to possess sweetness, culture insists on the necessity of light also, and shows us that aristocracies, being by the very nature of things inaccessible to ideas, unapt to see how the world is going, must be somewhat wanting in light, and must therefore be, at a moment when light is our great requisite, inadequate to our needs. Aristocracies, those children of the established fact, are for epochs of concentration. In epochs of expansion, epochs such as that in which we now live, epochs when always the warning voice is again heard: *Now is the judgment of this world*—in such epochs aristocracies with their natural clinging to the established fact, their want of sense for the flux of things, for the inevitable transitoriness of all human institutions, are bewildered and helpless. Their serenity, their high spirit, their power of haughty resistance,—the great qualities of an aristocracy, and the secret of its distinguished manners and dignity,—these very qualities, in an epoch of expansion, turn against their possessors. Again and again I have said how the refinement of an aristocracy may be precious and educative to a raw nation as a kind of shadow of true refinement; how its serenity and dignified freedom from petty cares may serve as a useful foil to set off the vulgarity and hideousness of that type of life which a hard

middle class tends to establish, and to help people to see this
vulgarity and hideousness in their true colours. From such
an ignoble spectacle as that of poor Mrs. Lincoln,—a
spectacle to vulgarise a whole nation,—aristocracies undoubtedly preserve us. But the true grace and serenity is
that of which Greece and Greek art suggest the admirable
ideals of perfection,—a serenity which comes from having
made order among ideas and harmonised them; whereas
the serenity of aristocracies, at least the peculiar serenity of
aristocracies of Teutonic origin, appears to come from
their never having had any ideas to trouble them. And
so, in a time of expansion like the present, a time for
ideas, one gets, perhaps, in regarding an aristocracy, even
more than the idea of serenity, the idea of futility and
sterility.

One has often wondered whether upon the whole earth
there is anything so unintelligent, so unapt to perceive how
the world is really going, as an ordinary young Englishman
of our upper class. Ideas he has not, and neither has he
that seriousness of our middle class which is, as I have often
said, the great strength of this class, and may become its
salvation. Why, a man may hear a young Dives of the
aristocratic class, when the whim takes him to sing the
praises of wealth and material comfort, sing them with a
cynicism from which the conscience of the veriest Philistine of our industrial middle class would recoil in affright.
And when, with the natural sympathy of aristocracies for
firm dealing with the multitude, and his uneasiness at our
feeble dealing with it at home, an unvarnished young
Englishman of our aristocratic class applauds the absolute
rulers on the Continent, he in general manages completely
to miss the grounds of reason and intelligence which alone
can give any colour of justification, any possibility of
existence, to those rulers, and applauds them on grounds

which it would make their own hair stand on end to listen to.

And all this time we are in an epoch of expansion; and the essence of an epoch of expansion is a movement of ideas, and the one salvation of an epoch of expansion is a harmony of ideas. The very principle of the authority which we are seeking as a defence against anarchy is right reason, ideas, light. The more, therefore, an aristocracy calls to its aid its innate forces,—its impenetrability, its high spirit, its power of haughty resistance,—to deal with an epoch of expansion, the graver is the danger, the greater the certainty of explosion, the surer the aristocracy's defeat; for it is trying to do violence to nature instead of working along with it. The best powers shown by the best men of an aristocracy at such an epoch are, it will be observed, non-aristocratical powers, powers of industry, powers of intelligence; and these powers, thus exhibited, tend really not to strengthen the aristocracy, but to take their owners out of it, to expose them to the dissolving agencies of thought and change, to make them men of the modern spirit and of the future. If, as sometimes happens, they add to their non-aristocratical qualities of labour and thought, a strong dose of aristocratical qualities also,—of pride, defiance, turn for resistance—this truly aristocratical side of them, so far from adding any strength to them, really neutralises their force and makes them impracticable and ineffective.

Knowing myself to be indeed sadly to seek, as one of my many critics says, in "a philosophy with coherent, inter-dependent, subordinate and derivative principles," I continually have recourse to a plain man's expedient of trying to make what few simple notions I have, clearer and more intelligible to myself, by means of example and illustration. And having been brought up at Oxford in the bad old times, when we were stuffed with Greek and Aristotle, and thought nothing of preparing ourselves by the study of modern languages,—as after Mr. Lowe's great speech at Edinburgh we shall do,—to fight the battle of life with the waiters in foreign hotels, my head is still full of a lumber of phrases we learnt at Oxford from Aristotle, about virtue being in a mean, and about excess and defect, and so on. Once when I had had the advantage of listening to the Reform debates in the House of Commons, having heard a number of interesting speakers, and among them Lord Elcho and Sir Thomas Bateson, I remember it struck me, applying Aristotle's machinery of the mean to my ideas about our aristocracy, that Lord Elcho was exactly the perfection, or happy mean, or virtue, of aristocracy, and Sir Thomas Bateson the excess; and I fancied that by observing these two we might see both the inadequacy of aristocracy to supply the principle of authority needful for our present wants, and the danger of its trying to supply it when it was not really competent for the business. On the one hand, in Lord Elcho, showing plenty of high spirit, but remarkable, far above and beyond his gift of high spirit, for the fine tempering of his high spirit, for ease, serenity, politeness,—the great virtues, as Mr. Carlyle says, of aristocracy,—in this beautiful and virtuous mean, there seemed evidently some insufficiency of light; while, on the other hand, Sir Thomas Bateson, in whom the high spirit of aristocracy, its impenetrability, defiant courage, and pride of resistance, were developed even in excess, was manifestly capable, if he had his way given him, of causing us great danger, and, indeed, of throwing the whole commonwealth into confusion. Then I reverted to that old fundamental notion of mine about the grand merit of our race being really our honesty. And the very helplessness of our aristocratic or governing class in dealing with our perturbed social condition gave me a sort of pride and satisfaction; because I saw they were, as a whole, too honest to try and manage a business for which they did not feel themselves capable.

Surely, now, it is no inconsiderable boon which culture confers upon us, if in embarrassed times like the present it enables us to look at the ins and the outs of things in this way, without hatred and without partiality, and with a disposition to see the good in everybody all round. And I try to follow just the same course with our middle class as with our aristocracy. Mr. Lowe talks to us of this strong middle part of the nation, of the unrivalled deeds of our Liberal middle-class Parliament, of the noble, the heroic work it has performed in the last thirty years; and I begin to ask myself if we shall not, then, find in our middle class the principle of authority we want, and if we had not better take administration as well as legislation away from the weak extreme which now administers for us, and commit both to the strong middle part. I observe, too, that the heroes of middle-class Liberalism, such as we have hitherto known it, speak with a kind of prophetic anticipation of the great destiny which awaits them, and as if the future was clearly theirs. The advanced party, the progressive party, the party in alliance with the future, are the names they like to give themselves. "The principles which will obtain recognition in the future," says Mr. Miall, a personage of deserved eminence among the political Dissenters, as they are called, who have been the backbone of middle-class Liberalism—"the principles which will obtain recognition in the future are the principles for which I have long and zealously laboured. I qualified myself for joining in the work of harvest by doing to the best of my ability the duties of seed time." These duties, if one is to gather them from the works of the great Liberal party in the last thirty years, are, as I have elsewhere summed them up, the advocacy of free-trade, of parliamentary reform, of abolition of church-rates, of voluntaryism in religion and education, of non-interference of the State between employers and employed, and of marriage with one's deceased wife's sister.

Now I know, when I object that all this is machinery, the great Liberal middle class has by this time grown cunning enough to answer that it always meant more by these things than meets the eye; that it has had that within which passes show, and that we are soon going to see, in a Free Church and all manner of good things, what it was. But I have learned from Bishop Wilson (if Mr. Frederic Harrison will forgive my again quoting that poor old hierophant of a decayed superstition): "If we would really know our heart let us impartially view our actions;" and I cannot help thinking that if our Liberals had had so much sweetness and light in their inner minds as they allege, more of it must have come out in their sayings and doings.

An American friend of the English Liberals says, indeed, that their Dissidence of Dissent has been a mere instrument of the political Dissenters for making reason and the will of God prevail (and no doubt he would say the same of marriage with one's deceased wife's sister); and that the abolition of a State Church is merely the Dissenter's means to this end, just as culture is mine. Another American defender of theirs says just the same of their industrialism and free-trade; indeed, this gentleman, taking the bull by the horns, proposes that we should for the future call industrialism culture, and the industrialists the men of culture, and then of course there can be no longer any misapprehension about their true character; and besides the pleasure of being wealthy and comfortable, they will have authentic recognition as vessels of sweetness and light.

All this is undoubtedly specious; but I must remark that the culture of which I talked was an endeavour to come at reason and the will of God by means of reading, observing, and thinking; and that whoever calls anything else culture, may, indeed, call it so if he likes, but then he talks of something quite different from what I talked of. And, again, as culture's way of working for reason and the will of God is by directly trying to know more about them, while the Dissidence of Dissent is evidently in itself no effort of this kind, nor is its Free Church, in fact, a church with worthier conceptions of God and the ordering of the world than the State Church professes, but with mainly the same conceptions of these as the State Church has, only that every man is to comport himself as he likes in professing them,—this being so, I cannot at once accept the Nonconformity any more than the industrialism and the other great works of our Liberal middle class as proof positive that this class is in possession of light, and that here is the true seat of authority for which we are in search; but I must try a little further, and seek for other indications which may enable me to make up my mind.

Why should we not do with the middle class as we have done with the aristocratic class,—find in it some representative men who may stand for the virtuous mean of this class, for the perfection of its present qualities and mode of being, and also for the excess of them. Such men must clearly not be men of genius like Mr. Bright; for, as I have formerly said, so far as a man has genius he tends to take himself out of the category of class altogether, and to become simply a man. Mr. Bright's brother, Mr. Jacob Bright, would, perhaps, be more to the purpose; he seems to sum up very well in himself, without disturbing influences, the general liberal force of the middle class, the force by which it has done its great works of free-trade, parliamentary reform, voluntaryism, and so on, and the spirit in which it has done them. Now it is clear, from what has been already said, that there has been at least an apparent want of light in the force and spirit through which these great works have been done, and that the works have worn in consequence too much a look of machinery. But this will be clearer still if we take, as the happy mean of the middle class, not Mr. Jacob Bright, but his colleague in the representation of Manchester, Mr. Bazley. Mr. Bazley sums up for us, in general, the middle class, its spirit and its works, at least as well as Mr. Jacob Bright; and he has given us, moreover, a famous sentence, which bears directly on the resolution of our present question,—whether there is light enough in our middle class to make it the proper seat of the authority we wish to establish. When there was a talk some little while ago about the state of middle-class education, Mr. Bazley, as the representative of that class, spoke some memorable words:—"There had been a cry that middle class education ought to receive more attention. He confessed himself very much surprised by the clamour that was raised. He did not think that class need excite the sympathy either of the legislature or the public." Now this satisfaction of Mr. Bazley with the mental state of the middle class was truly representative, and makes good his claim to stand as the beautiful and virtuous mean of that class. But it is obviously at variance with our definition of culture, or the pursuit of light and perfection, which made light and perfection consist, not in resting and being, but in growing and becoming, in a perpetual advance in beauty and wisdom. So the middle class is by its essence, as one may say, by its incomparable self-satisfaction decisively expressed through its beautiful and virtuous mean, self-excluded from wielding an authority of which light is to be the very soul.

Clear as this is, it will be made clearer still if we take some representative man as the excess of the middle class, and remember that the middle class, in general, is to be conceived as a body swaying between the qualities of its mean and of its excess, and on the whole, of course, as human nature is constituted, inclining rather towards the excess than the mean. Of its excess no better representative can possibly be imagined than the Rev. W. Cattle, a Dissenting minister from Walsall, who came before the public in connection with the proceedings at Birmingham of Mr. Murphy, already mentioned. Speaking in the midst of an irritated population of Catholics, the Rev. W. Cattle exclaimed:—"I say, then, away with the Mass! It is from the bottomless pit; and in the bottomless pit shall all liars have their part, in the lake that burneth with fire and brimstone." And again: "When all the praties were black in Ireland, why didn't the priests say the hocus-pocus over them, and make them all good again?" He shared, too, Mr. Murphy's fears of some invasion of his domestic happiness: "What I wish to say to you as Protestant husbands is, *Take care of your wives!*" And, finally, in the true vein of an Englishman doing as he likes, a vein of which I have at some length pointed out the present dangers, he recommended for imitation the example of some churchwardens at Dublin, among whom, said he, "there was a Luther and also a Melancthon," who had made very short work with some ritualist or other, hauled him down from his pulpit, and kicked him out of church. Now it is manifest, as I said in the case of Sir Thomas Bateson, that if we let this excess of the sturdy English middle class, this conscientious Protestant Dissenter, so strong, so self-reliant, so fully persuaded in his own mind, have his way, he would be capable, with his want of light—or, to use the language of the religious world, with his zeal without knowledge—of

stirring up strife which neither he nor any one else could
easily compose.

And then comes in, as it did also with the aristocracy,
the honesty of our race, and by the voice of another
middle-class man, Alderman Wilson, Alderman of the City
of London and Colonel of the City of London Militia,
proclaims that it has twinges of conscience, and that it will
not attempt to cope with our social disorders, and to deal
with a business which it feels to be too high for it. Every
one remembers how this virtuous Alderman-Colonel, or
Colonel-Alderman, led his militia through the London
streets; how the bystanders gathered to see him pass; how
the London roughs, asserting an Englishman's best and
most blissful right of doing what he likes, robbed and beat
the bystanders; and how the blameless warrior-magistrate
refused to let his troops interfere. "The crowd," he
touchingly said afterwards, "was mostly composed of fine
healthy strong men, bent on mischief; if he had allowed his
soldiers to interfere they might have been overpowered,
their rifles taken from them and used against them by the
mob; a riot, in fact, might have ensued, and been attended
with bloodshed, compared with which the assaults and loss
of property that actually occurred would have been as
nothing." Honest and affecting testimony of the English
middle class to its own inadequacy for the authoritative
part one's admiration would sometimes incline one to
assign to it! "Who are we," they say by the voice of their
Alderman-Colonel, "that we should not be overpowered
if we attempt to cope with social anarchy, our rifles taken
from us and used against us by the mob, and we, perhaps,
robbed and beaten ourselves? Or what light have we,
beyond a free-born Englishman's impulse to do as he
likes, which could justify us in preventing, at the cost
of bloodshed, other free-born Englishmen from doing as

they like, and robbing and beating us as much as they please?"

This distrust of themselves as an adequate centre of authority does not mark the working class, as was shown by their readiness the other day in Hyde Park to take upon themselves all the functions of government. But this comes from the working class being, as I have often said, still an embryo, of which no one can yet quite foresee the final development; and from its not having the same experience and self-knowledge as the aristocratic and middle classes. Honesty it no doubt has, just like the other classes of Englishmen, but honesty in an inchoate and untrained state; and meanwhile its powers of action, which are, as Mr. Frederic Harrison says, exceedingly ready, easily run away with it. That it cannot at present have a sufficiency of light which comes by culture,—that is, by reading, observing, and thinking,—is clear from the very nature of its condition; and, indeed, we saw that Mr. Frederic Harrison, in seeking to make a free stage for its bright powers of sympathy and ready powers of action, had to begin by throwing overboard culture, and flouting it as only fit for a professor of *belles lettres*. Still, to make it perfectly manifest that no more in the working class than in the aristocratic and middle classes can one find an adequate centre of authority,—that is, as culture teaches us to conceive our required authority, of light,—let us again follow, with this class, the method we have followed with the aristocratic and middle classes, and try to bring before our minds representative men, who may figure to us its virtue and its excess.

We must not take, of course, men like the chiefs of the Hyde Park demonstration, Colonel Dickson or Mr. Beales; because Colonel Dickson, by his martial profession and dashing exterior, seems to belong properly, like Julius Cæsar

and Mirabeau and other great popular leaders, to the aristocratic class, and to be carried into the popular ranks only
by his ambition or his genius; while Mr. Beales belongs
to our solid middle class, and, perhaps, if he had not been
a great popular leader, would have been a Philistine. But
Mr. Odger, whose speeches we have all read, and of
whom his friends relate, besides, much that is favourable,
may very well stand for the beautiful and virtuous mean
of our present working class; and I think everybody will
admit that in Mr. Odger, as in Lord Elcho, there is manifestly, with all his good points, some insufficiency of light.
The excess of the working class, in its present state of
development, is perhaps best shown in Mr. Bradlaugh, the
iconoclast, who seems to be almost for baptizing us all in
blood and fire into his new social dispensation, and to whose
reflections, now that I have once been set going on Bishop
Wilson's track, I cannot forbear commending this maxim
of the good old man: "Intemperance in talk makes a dread-
ful havoc in the heart." Mr. Bradlaugh, like Sir Thomas
Bateson and the Rev. W. Cattle, is evidently capable, if he
had his head given him, of running us all into great dangers
and confusion. I conclude, therefore—what, indeed, few
of those who do me the honour to read this disquisition are
likely to dispute,—that we can as little find in the working
class as in the aristocratic or in the middle class our much-
wanted source of authority, as culture suggests it to us.

Well, then, what if we tried to rise above the idea of
class to the idea of the whole community, *the State*, and to
find our centre of light and authority there? Every one of
us has the idea of country, as a sentiment; hardly any one of
us has the idea of *the State*, as a working power. And why?
Because we habitually live in our ordinary selves, which do
not carry us beyond the ideas and wishes of the class to
which we happen to belong. And we are all afraid of giving

to the State too much power, because we only conceive of
the State as something equivalent to the class in occupation
of the executive government, and are afraid of that class
abusing power to its own purposes. If we strengthen the
State with the aristocratic class in occupation of the
executive government, we imagine we are delivering ourselves up captive to the ideas and wishes of our fierce
aristocratical baronet Sir Thomas Bateson; if with the
middle class in occupation of the executive government,
to those of our truculent middle-class Dissenting minister,
the Rev. W. Cattle; if with the working class, to those
of its notorious tribune, Mr. Bradlaugh. And with
much justice; owing to the exaggerated notion which we
English, as I have said, entertain of the right and blessedness of the mere doing as one likes, of the affirming oneself, and oneself just as it is. People of the aristocratic class
want to affirm their ordinary selves, their likings and dislikings; people of the middle class the same, people of the
working class the same. By our every-day selves, however,
we are separate, personal, at war; we are only safe from one
another's tyranny when no one has any power; and this
safety, in its turn, cannot save us from anarchy. And when,
therefore, anarchy presents itself as a danger to us, we
know not where to turn.

But by our *best self* we are united, impersonal, at harmony. We are in no peril from giving authority to this,
because it is the truest friend we all of us can have; and
when anarchy is a danger to us, to this authority we may
turn with sure trust. Well, and this is the very self which
culture, or the study of perfection, seeks to develop in us;
at the expense of our old untransformed self, taking pleasure only in doing what it likes or is used to do, and ex-
posing us to the risk of clashing with every one else who is
doing the same! So that our poor culture, which is flouted

as so unpractical, leads us to the very ideas capable of meeting the great want of our present embarrassed times! We want an authority, and we find nothing but jealous classes, checks, and a deadlock; culture suggests the idea of *the State*. We find no basis for a firm State-power in our ordinary selves; culture suggests one to us in our *best self*.

It cannot but acutely try a tender conscience to be accused, in a practical country like ours, of keeping aloof from the work and hope of a multitude of earnest-hearted men, and of merely toying with poetry and æsthetics. So it is with no little sense of relief that I find myself thus in the position of one who makes a contribution in aid of the practical necessities of our times. The great thing, it will be observed, is to find our *best* self, and to seek to affirm nothing but that; not,—as we English with our over-value for merely being free and busy have been so accustomed to do,—resting satisfied with a self which comes uppermost long before our best self, and affirming that with blind energy. In short,—to go back yet once more to Bishop Wilson,—of these two excellent rules of Bishop Wilson's for a man's guidance: "Firstly, never go against the best light you have; secondly, take care that your light be not darkness," we English have followed with praiseworthy zeal the first rule, but we have not given so much heed to the second. We have gone manfully, the Rev. W. Cattle and the rest of us, according to the best light we have; but we have not taken enough care that this should be really the best light possible for us, that it should not be darkness. And, our honesty being very great, conscience has whispered to us that the light we were following, our ordinary self, was, indeed, perhaps, only an inferior self, only darkness; and that it would not do to impose this seriously on all the world.

But our best self inspires faith, and is capable of affording a serious principle of authority. For example. We are on our way to what the late Duke of Wellington, with his strong sagacity, foresaw and admirably described as "a revolution by due course of law." This is undoubtedly,—if we are still to live and grow, and this famous nation is not to stagnate and dwindle away on the one hand, or, on the other, to perish miserably in mere anarchy and confusion,—what we are on the way to. Great changes there must be, for a revolution cannot accomplish itself without great changes; yet order there must be, for without order a revolution cannot accomplish itself by due course of law. So whatever brings risk of tumult and disorder, multitudinous processions in the streets of our crowded towns, multitudinous meetings in their public places and parks,—demonstrations perfectly unnecessary in the present course of our affairs,—our best self, or right reason, plainly enjoins us to set our faces against. It enjoins us to encourage and uphold the occupants of the executive power, whoever they may be, in firmly prohibiting them. But it does this clearly and resolutely, and is thus a real principle of authority, because it does it with a free conscience; because in thus provisionally strengthening the executive power, it knows that it is not doing this merely to enable Sir Thomas Bateson to affirm himself as against Mr. Bradlaugh, or the Rev. W. Cattle to affirm himself as against both. It knows that it is stablishing *the State*, or organ of our collective best self, of our national right reason; and it has the testimony of conscience that it is stablishing the State on behalf of whatever great changes are needed, just as much as on behalf of order; stablishing it to deal just as stringently, when the time comes, with Sir Thomas Bateson's Protestant ascendency, or with the Rev. W. Cattle's sorry education of his children, as it deals with Mr. Bradlaugh's street-processions.

CHAPTER III

BARBARIANS, PHILISTINES,
POPULACE

FROM a man without a philosophy no one can expect
philosophical completeness. Therefore I may observe without shame, that in trying to get a distinct notion of our
aristocratic, our middle, and our working class, with a view
of testing the claims of each of these classes to become a
centre of authority, I have omitted, I find, to complete the
old-fashioned analysis which I had the fancy of applying,
and have not shown in these classes, as well as the virtuous
mean and the excess, the defect also. I do not know that
the omission very much matters. Still, as clearness is the one
merit which a plain, unsystematic writer, without a philosophy, can hope to have, and as our notion of the three
great English classes may perhaps be made clearer if we see
their distinctive qualities in the defect, as well as in the
excess and in the mean, let us try, before proceeding further,
to remedy this omission.

It is manifest, if the perfect and virtuous mean of that
fine spirit which is the distinctive quality of aristocracies, is
to be found in Lord Elcho's chivalrous style, and its excess
in Sir Thomas Bateson's turn for resistance, that its defect
must lie in a spirit not bold and high enough, and in an
excessive and pusillanimous unaptness for resistance. If,
again, the perfect and virtuous mean of that force by which
our middle class has done its great works, and of that self-
reliance with which it contemplates itself and them, is to
be seen in the performances and speeches of Mr. Bazley,

and the excess of that force and of that self-reliance in the performances and speeches of the Rev. W. Cattle, then it is manifest that their defect must lie in a helpless inaptitude for the great works of the middle class, and in a poor and despicable lack of its self-satisfaction.

To be chosen to exemplify the happy mean of a good quality, or set of good qualities, is evidently a praise to a man; nay, to be chosen to exemplify even their excess, is a kind of praise. Therefore I could have no hesitation in taking Lord Elcho and Mr. Bazley, the Rev. W. Cattle and Sir Thomas Bateson, to exemplify, respectively, the mean and the excess of aristocratic and middle-class qualities. But perhaps there might be a want of urbanity in singling out this or that personage as the representative of defect. Therefore I shall leave the defect of aristocracy unillustrated by any representative man. But with oneself one may always, without impropriety, deal quite freely; and, indeed, this sort of plain-dealing with oneself has in it, as all the moralists tell us, something very wholesome. So I will venture to humbly offer myself as an illustration of defect in those forces and qualities which make our middle class what it is. The too well-founded reproaches of my opponents declare how little I have lent a hand to the great works of the middle class; for it is evidently these works, and my slackness at them, which are meant, when I am said to "refuse to lend a hand to the humble operation of uprooting certain definite evils" (such as church-rates and others), and that therefore "the believers in action grow impatient" with me. The line, again, of a still unsatisfied seeker which I have followed, the idea of self-transformation, of growing towards some measure of sweetness and light not yet reached, is evidently at clean variance with the perfect self-satisfaction current in my class, the middle class, and may serve to indicate in me, therefore, the extreme defect of this feeling. But these confessions, though salutary, are bitter and unpleasant.

To pass, then, to the working class. The defect of this class would be the falling short in what Mr. Frederic Harrison calls those "bright powers of sympathy and ready powers of action," of which we saw in Mr. Odger the virtuous mean, and in Mr. Bradlaugh the excess. The working class is so fast growing and rising at the present time, that instances of this defect cannot well be now very common. Perhaps Canning's "Needy Knife-Grinder" (who is dead, and therefore cannot be pained at my taking him for an illustration) may serve to give us the notion of defect in the essential quality of a working class; or I might even cite (since, though he is alive in the flesh, he is dead to all heed of criticism) my poor old poaching friend, Zephaniah Diggs, who, between his hare-snaring and his gin-drinking, has got his powers of sympathy quite dulled and his powers of action in any great movement of his class hopelessly impaired. But examples of this defect belong, as I have said, to a bygone age rather than to the present.

The same desire for clearness, which has led me thus to extend a little my first analysis of the three great classes of English society, prompts me also to improve my nomenclature for them a little, with a view to making it thereby more manageable. It is awkward and tiresome to be always saying the aristocratic class, the middle class, the working class. For the middle class, for that great body which, as we know, "has done all the great things that have been done in all departments," and which is to be conceived as moving between its two cardinal points of Mr. Bazley, our commercial member of Parliament, and the Rev. W. Cattle, our fanatical Protestant Dissenter,—for this class we have a designation which now has become pretty well known, and which we may as well still keep for them,

the designation of Philistines. What this term means I have
so often explained that I need not repeat it here. For the
aristocratic class, conceived mainly as a body moving
between the two cardinal points of our chivalrous Lord
Elcho and our defiant baronet, Sir Thomas Bateson,
we have as yet got no special designation. Almost all
my attention has naturally been concentrated on my own
class, the middle class, with which I am in closest sympathy,
and which has been, besides, the great power of our day,
and has had its praises sung by all speakers and newspapers.

Still the aristocratic class is so important in itself, and
the weighty functions which Mr. Carlyle proposes at the
present critical time to commit to it must add so much to
its importance, that it seems neglectful, and a strong instance of that want of coherent philosophic method for
which Mr. Frederic Harrison blames me, to leave the
aristocratic class so much without notice and denomina-
tion. It may be thought that the characteristic which I
have occasionally mentioned as proper to aristocracies,—
their natural inaccessibility, as children of the established
fact, to ideas,—points to our extending to this class also
the designation of Philistines; the Philistine being, as is
well known, the enemy of the children of light or servants
of the idea. Nevertheless, there seems to be an inconvenience in thus giving one and the same designation to two
very different classes; and besides, if we look into the thing
closely, we shall find that the term Philistine conveys a
sense which makes it more peculiarly appropriate to our
middle class than to our aristocratic. For *Philistine* gives
the notion of something particularly stiff-necked and perverse in the resistance to light and its children; and therein
it specially suits our middle class, who not only do not
pursue sweetness and light, but who even prefer to them that
sort of machinery of business, chapels, tea-meetings, and

addresses from Mr. Murphy and the Rev. W. Cattle, which makes up the dismal and illiberal life on which I have so often touched. But the aristocratic class has actually, as we have seen, in its well-known politeness, a kind of image or shadow of sweetness; and as for light, if it does not pursue light, it is not that it perversely cherishes some dismal and illiberal existence in preference to light, but it is lured off from following light by those mighty and eternal seducers of our race which weave for this class their most irresistible charms,—by worldly splendour, security, power and pleasure. These seducers are exterior goods, but in a way they are goods; and he who is hindered by them from caring for light and ideas, is not so much doing what is perverse as what is too natural.

Keeping this in view, I have in my own mind often indulged myself with the fancy of employing, in order to designate our aristocratic class, the name of *The Barbarians*. The Barbarians, to whom we all owe so much, and who reinvigorated and renewed our worn-out Europe, had, as is well known, eminent merits; and in this country, where we are for the most part sprung from the Barbarians, we have never had the prejudice against them which prevails among the races of Latin origin. The Barbarians brought with them that staunch individualism, as the modern phrase is, and that passion for doing as one likes, for the assertion of personal liberty, which appears to Mr. Bright the central idea of English life, and of which we have, at any rate, a very rich supply. The stronghold and natural seat of this passion was in the nobles of whom our aristocratic class are the inheritors; and this class, accordingly, have signally manifested it, and have done much by their example to recommend it to the body of the nation, who already, indeed, had it in their blood. The Barbarians, again, had the passion for field-sports; and they have handed it on to our aristocratic class, who of this passion too, as of the passion for asserting one's personal liberty, are the great natural stronghold. The care of the Barbarians for the body, and for all manly exercises; the vigour, good looks, and fine complexion which they acquired and perpetuated in their families by these means,—all this may be observed still in our aristocratic class. The chivalry of the Barbarians, with its characteristics of high spirit, choice manners, and distinguished bearing,—what is this but the attractive commencement of the politeness of our aristocratic class? In some Barbarian noble, no doubt, one would have admired, if one could have been then alive to see it, the rudiments of Lord Elcho. Only, all this culture (to call it by that name) of the Barbarians was an exterior culture mainly. It consisted principally in outward gifts and graces, in looks, manners, accomplishments, prowess. The chief inward gifts which had part in it were the most exterior, so to speak, of inward gifts, those which come nearest to outward ones; they were courage, a high spirit, self-confidence. Far within, and unawakened, lay a whole range of powers of thought and feeling, to which these interesting productions of nature had, from the circumstances of their life, no access. Making allowances for the difference of the times, surely we can observe precisely the same thing now in our aristocratic class. In general its culture is exterior chiefly; all the exterior graces and accomplishments, and the more external of the inward virtues, seem to be principally its portion. It now, of course, cannot but be often in contact with those studies by which, from the world of thought and feeling, true culture teaches us to fetch sweetness and light; but its hold upon these very studies appears remarkably external, and unable to exert any deep power upon its spirit. Therefore the one insufficiency which we noted in the perfect mean of this class, Lord Elcho, was an insufficiency of light. And owing to the same causes, does not a subtle criticism lead us to make, even on the good looks and politeness of our aristocratic class, and of even the most fascinating half of that class, the feminine half, the one qualifying remark, that in these charming gifts there should perhaps be, for ideal perfection, a shade more *soul?*

I often, therefore, when I want to distinguish clearly the aristocratic class from the Philistines proper, or middle class, name the former, in my own mind, *the Barbarians.* And when I go through the country, and see this and that beautiful and imposing seat of theirs crowning the landscape, "There," I say to myself, "is a great fortified post of the Barbarians."

It is obvious that that part of the working class which, working diligently by the light of Mrs. Gooch's Golden Rule, looks forward to the happy day when it will sit on thrones with Mr. Bazley and other middle-class potentates, to survey, as Mr. Bright beautifully says, "the cities it has built, the railroads it has made, the manufactures it has produced, the cargoes which freight the ships of the greatest mercantile navy the world has ever seen,"—it is obvious, I say, that this part of the working class is, or is in a fair way to be, one in spirit with the industrial middle class. It is notorious that our middle-class Liberals have long looked forward to this consummation, when the working class shall join forces with them, aid them heartily to carry forward their great works, go in a body to their tea-meetings, and, in short, enable them to bring about their millennium. That part of the working class, therefore, which does really seem to lend itself to these great aims, may, with propriety, be numbered by us among the Philistines. That part of it, again, which so much occupies the attention of philanthropists at present,—the part which gives all its energies to organising itself, through trades' unions and other means, so as to constitute, first, a great working-class power, independent of the middle and aristocratic classes, and then, by dint of numbers, give the law to them, and itself reign absolutely,—this lively and interesting part must also, according to our definition, go with the Philistines; because it is its class and its class-instinct which it seeks to affirm, its ordinary self, not its best self; and it is a machinery, an industrial machinery, and power and pre-eminence and other external goods, which fill its thoughts, and not an inward perfection. It is wholly occupied, according to Plato's subtle expression, with the things of itself and not its real self, with the things of the State and not the real State. But that vast portion, lastly, of the working class which, raw and half-developed, has long lain half-hidden amidst its poverty and squalor, and is now issuing from its hiding-place to assert an Englishman's heaven-born privilege of doing as he likes, and is beginning to perplex us by marching where it likes, meeting where it likes, bawling what it likes, breaking what it likes,—to this vast residuum we may with great propriety give the name of *Populace*.

Thus we have got three distinct terms, *Barbarians, Philistines, Populace*, to denote roughly the three great classes into which our society is divided; and though this humble attempt at a scientific nomenclature falls, no doubt, very far short in precision of what might be required from a writer equipped with a complete and coherent philosophy, yet, from a notoriously unsystematic and unpretending writer, it will, I trust, be accepted as sufficient.

But in using this new, and, I hope, convenient division of English society, two things are to be borne in mind. The first is, that since, under all our class divisions, there is a common basis of human nature, therefore, in every one of us, whether we be properly Barbarians, Philistines, or Populace, there exists, sometimes only in germ and potentially, sometimes more or less developed, the same tendencies and passions which have made our fellow-citizens of other classes what they are. This consideration is very important, because it has great influence in begetting that spirit of indulgence which is a necessary part of sweetness, and which, indeed, when our culture is complete, is, as I have said, inexhaustible. Thus, an English Barbarian who examines himself will, in general, find himself to be not so entirely a Barbarian but that he has in him, also, something of the Philistine, and even something of the Populace as well. And the same with Englishmen of the two other classes.

This is an experience which we may all verify every day. For instance, I myself (I again take myself as a sort of *corpus vile* to serve for illustration in a matter where serving for illustration may not by every one be thought agreeable), I myself am properly a Philistine,—Mr. Swinburne would add, the son of a Philistine. And although, through circumstances which will perhaps one day be known if ever the affecting history of my conversion comes to be written, I have, for the most part, broken with the ideas and the tea-meetings of my own class, yet I have not, on that account, been brought much the nearer to the ideas and works of the Barbarians or of the Populace. Nevertheless, I never take a gun or a fishing-rod in my hands without feeling that I have in the ground of my nature the self-same seeds which, fostered by circumstances, do so much to make the Barbarian; and that, with the Barbarian's advantages, I might have rivalled him. Place me in one of his great fortified posts, with these seeds of a love for field-sports sown in my nature, with all the means of developing them, with all pleasures at my command, with most whom I met deferring to me, every one I met smiling on me, and with every appearance of permanence and security before me and behind me,—then I too might have grown, I feel, into a very passable child of the established fact, of commendable spirit and politeness, and, at the same time, a little inaccessible to ideas and light; not, of course, with either the eminent fine spirit of Lord Elcho, or the eminent power of resistance of Sir Thomas Bateson, but, according to the measure of the common run of mankind, something between the two. And as to the Populace, who, whether he be Barbarian or Philistine, can look at them without sympathy, when he remembers how often,—every time that we snatch up a vehement opinion in ignorance and passion, every time that we long to crush an adversary by sheer violence, every time that we are envious, every time that we are brutal, every time that we adore mere power or success, every time that we add our voice to swell a blind clamour against some unpopular personage, every time that we trample savagely on the fallen,—he has found in his own bosom the eternal spirit of the Populace, and that there needs only a little help from circumstances to make it triumph in him untameably?

The second thing to be borne in mind I have indicated several times already. It is this. All of us, so far as we are Barbarians, Philistines, or Populace, imagine happiness to consist in doing what one's ordinary self likes. What one's ordinary self likes differs according to the class to which one belongs, and has its severer and its lighter side; always, however, remaining machinery, and nothing more. The graver self of the Barbarian likes honours and consideration; his more relaxed self, field-sports and pleasure. The graver self of one kind of Philistine likes fanaticism, business, and money-making; his more relaxed self, comfort and tea-meetings. Of another kind of Philistine, the graver self likes rattening; the relaxed self, deputations, or hearing Mr. Odger speak. The sterner self of the Populace likes bawling, hustling, and smashing; the lighter self, beer. But in each class there are born a certain number of natures with a curiosity about their best self, with a bent for seeing things as they are, for disentangling themselves from machinery, for simply concerning themselves with reason and the will of God, and doing their best to make these prevail;—for the pursuit, in a word, of perfection. To certain manifestations of this love for perfection mankind have accustomed themselves to give the name of genius; implying, by this name, something original and heaven-bestowed in the passion. But the passion is to be found far beyond those manifestations of it to which the world usually gives the name of genius, and in which there is, for the most part, a *talent* of some kind or other, a special and striking faculty of execution, informed by the heaven-bestowed ardour, or genius. It is to be found in many manifestations besides these, and may best be called, as we have called it, the love and pursuit of perfection; culture being the true nurse of the pursuing love, and sweetness and light the true character of the pursued perfection. Natures with this bent emerge in all classes,—among the Barbarians, among the Philistines, among the Populace. And this bent always tends to take them out of their class, and to make their distinguishing characteristic not their Barbarianism or their Philistinism, but their *humanity*. They have, in general, a rough time of it in their lives; but they are sown more abundantly than one might think, they appear where and when one least expects it, they set up a fire which enfilades, so to speak, the class with which they are ranked; and, in general, by the extrication of their best self as the self to develop, and by the simplicity of the ends fixed by them as paramount, they hinder the unchecked predominance of that class-life which is the affirmation of our ordinary self, and seasonably disconcert mankind in their worship of machinery.

Therefore, when we speak of ourselves as divided into Barbarians, Philistines, and Populace, we must be understood always to imply that within each of these classes there are a certain number of *aliens*, if we may so call them,— persons who are mainly led, not by their class spirit, but by a general *humane* spirit, by the love of human perfection; and that this number is capable of being diminished or augmented. I mean, the number of those who will succeed in developing this happy instinct will be greater or smaller, in proportion both to the force of the original instinct within them, and to the hindrance or encouragement which it meets with from without. In almost all who have it, it is mixed with some infusion of the spirit of an ordinary self, some quantity of class-instinct, and even, as has been shown, of more than one class-instinct at the same time; so that, in general, the extrication of the best self, the predominance of the *humane* instinct, will very much depend upon its meeting, or not, with what is fitted to help and elicit it. At a moment, therefore, when it is agreed that we want a source of authority, and when it seems probable that the right source is our best self, it becomes of vast importance to see whether or not the things around us are, in general, such as to help and elicit our best self, and if they are not, to see why they are not, and the most promising way of mending them.

Now, it is clear that the very absence of any powerful authority amongst us, and the prevalent doctrine of the duty and happiness of doing as one likes, and asserting our personal liberty, must tend to prevent the erection of any very strict standard of excellence, the belief in any very paramount authority of right reason, the recognition of our best self as anything very recondite and hard to come at. It may be, as I have said, a proof of our honesty that we do not attempt to give to our ordinary self, as we have it in action, predominant authority, and to impose its rule upon other people. But it is evident, also, that it is not easy, with our style of proceeding, to get beyond the notion of an ordinary self at all, or to get the paramount authority of a commanding best self, or right reason, recognised. The learned Martinus Scriblerus well says:—"The taste of the bathos is implanted by nature itself in the soul of man; till, perverted by custom or example, he is taught, or rather compelled, to relish the sublime." But with us everything seems directed to prevent any such perversion of us by custom or example as might compel us to relish the sublime; by all means we are encouraged to keep our natural taste for the bathos unimpaired.

// I have formerly pointed out how in literature the absence of any authoritative centre, like an Academy, tends to do this. Each section of the public has its own literary organ, and the mass of the public is without any suspicion that the value of these organs is relative to their being nearer a certain ideal centre of correct information, taste, and intelligence, or farther away from it. I have said that within certain limits, which any one who is likely to read this will have no difficulty in drawing for himself, my old adversary, the *Saturday Review*, may, on matters of literature and taste, be fairly enough regarded, relatively to the mass of newspapers which treat these matters, as a kind of organ of reason. But I remember once conversing with a company of Nonconformist admirers of some lecturer who had let off a great firework, which the *Saturday Review* said was all noise and false lights, and feeling my way as tenderly as I could about the effect of this unfavourable judgment upon those with whom I was conversing. "Oh," said one who was their spokesman, with the most tranquil air of conviction, "it is true the *Saturday Review* abuses the lecture, but the *British Banner*" (I am not quite sure it was the *British Banner*, but it was some newspaper of that stamp) "says that the *Saturday Review* is quite wrong." The speaker had evidently no notion that there was a scale of value for judgments on these topics, and that the judgments of the *Saturday Review* ranked high on this scale, and those of the *British Banner* low; the taste of the bathos implanted by nature in the literary judgments of man had never, in my friend's case, encountered any let or hindrance.

Just the same in religion as in literature. We have most of us little idea of a high standard to choose our guides by, of a great and profound spirit, which is an authority, while inferior spirits are none. It is enough to give importance to things that this or that person says them decisively, and has a large following of some strong kind when he says them. This habit of ours is very well shown in that able and interesting work of Mr. Hepworth Dixon's, which we were all reading lately, *The Mormons, by One of Themselves.* Here, again, I am not quite sure that my memory serves me as to the exact title, but I mean the well-known book in which Mr. Hepworth Dixon described the Mormons, and other similar religious bodies in America, with so much detail and such warm sympathy. In this work it seems enough for Mr. Dixon that this or that doctrine has its Rabbi, who talks big to him, has a staunch body of disciples, and, above all, has plenty of rifles. That there are any further stricter tests to be applied to a doctrine, before it is pronounced important, never seems to occur to him. "It is easy to say," he writes of the Mormons, "that these saints are dupes and fanatics, to laugh at Joe Smith and his church, but what then? *The great facts remain.* Young and his people are at Utah; a church of 200,000 souls; an army of 20,000 rifles." But if the followers of a doctrine are really dupes, or worse, and its promulgators are really fanatics, or worse, it gives the doctrine no seriousness or authority the more that there should be found 200,000 souls,—200,000 of the innumerable multitude with a natural taste for the bathos,—to hold it, and 20,000 rifles to defend it. And again, of another religious organisation in America: "A fair and open field is not to be refused when hosts so mighty throw down wager of battle on behalf of what they hold to be true, however strange their faith may seem." A fair and open field is not to be refused to any speaker; but this solemn way of heralding him is quite out of place, unless he has, for the best reason and spirit of man, some significance. "Well, but," says Mr. Hepworth Dixon, "a theory which has been accepted by men like Judge Edmonds, Dr. Hare, Elder Frederick, and Professor Bush!" And again: "Such are, in brief, the bases of what Newman Weeks, Sarah Horton, Deborah Butler, and the associated brethren, proclaimed in Rolt's Hall as the new covenant!" If he was summing up an account of the doctrine of Plato or of St. Paul, and of its followers, Mr. Hepworth Dixon could not be more earnestly reverential. But the question is, Have personages like Judge Edmonds, and Newman Weeks, and Elderess Polly, and Elderess Antoinette, and the rest of Mr. Hepworth Dixon's heroes and heroines, anything of the weight and significance for the best reason and spirit of man that Plato and St. Paul have? Evidently they, at present, have not; and a very small taste of them and their doctrines ought to have convinced Mr. Hepworth Dixon that they never could have. "But," says he, "the magnetic power which Shakerism is exercising on American thought would of itself compel us,"—and so on. Now as far as real thought

is concerned,—thought which affects the best reason and
spirit of man, the scientific or the imaginative thought of
the world, the only thought which deserves speaking of in
this solemn way,—America has up to the present time been
hardly more than a province of England, and even now
would not herself claim to be more than abreast of England;
and of this only real human thought, English thought itself
is not just now, as we must all admit, the most significant
factor. Neither, then, can American thought be; and the
magnetic power which Shakerism exercises on American
thought is about as important, for the best reason and spirit
of man, as the magnetic power which Mr. Murphy exercises on Birmingham Protestantism. And as we shall
never get rid of our natural taste for the bathos in religion,
—never get access to a best self and right reason which
may stand as a serious authority,—by treating Mr. Murphy
as his own disciples treat him, seriously, and as if he was
as much an authority as any one else: so we shall never
get rid of it while our able and popular writers treat their
Joe Smiths and Deborah Butlers, with their so many
thousand souls and so many thousand rifles, in the like
exaggerated and misleading manner, and so do their best
to confirm us in a bad mental habit to which we are
already too prone.

If our habits make it hard for us to come at the idea of
a high best self, of a paramount authority, in literature or
religion, how much more do they make this hard in the
sphere of politics! In other countries the governors, not
depending so immediately on the favour of the governed,
have everything to urge them, if they know anything of
right reason (and it is at least supposed that governors
should know more of this than the mass of the governed),
to set it authoritatively before the community. But our
whole scheme of government being representative, every

one of our governors has all possible temptation, instead of
setting up before the governed who elect him, and on
whose favour he depends, a high standard of right reason,
to accommodate himself as much as possible to their natural
taste for the bathos; and even if he tries to go counter to it,
to proceed in this with so much flattering and coaxing, that
they shall not suspect their ignorance and prejudices to be
anything very unlike right reason, or their natural taste for
the bathos to differ much from a relish for the sublime.
Every one is thus in every possible way encouraged to trust
in his own heart; but "he that trusteth in his own heart,"
says the Wise Man, "is a fool;" and at any rate this, which
Bishop Wilson says, is undeniably true: "The number of
those who need to be awakened is far greater than that of
those who need comfort."

But in our political system everybody is comforted. Our
guides and governors who have to be elected by the influence of the Barbarians, and who depend on their favour,
sing the praises of the Barbarians, and say all the smooth
things that can be said of them. With Mr. Tennyson, they
celebrate "the great broad-shouldered genial Englishman,"
with his "sense of duty," his "reverence for the laws," and
his "patient force," who saves us from the "revolts, re-
publics, revolutions, most no graver than a schoolboy's
barring out," which upset other and less broad-shouldered
nations. Our guides who are chosen by the Philistines and
who have to look to their favour, tell the Philistines how
"all the world knows that the great middle class of this
country supplies the mind, the will, and the power requisite
for all the great and good things that have to be done," and
congratulate them on their "earnest good sense, which
penetrates through sophisms, ignores commonplaces, and
gives to conventional illusions their true value." Our
guides who look to the favour of the Populace, tell them

that "theirs are the brightest powers of sympathy, and the readiest powers of action."

Harsh things are said too, no doubt, against all the great classes of the community; but these things so evidently come from a hostile class, and are so manifestly dictated by the passions and prepossessions of a hostile class, and not by right reason, that they make no serious impression on those at whom they are launched, but slide easily off their minds. For instance, when the Reform League orators inveigh against our cruel and bloated aristocracy, these invectives so evidently show the passions and point of view of the Populace, that they do not sink into the minds of those at whom they are addressed, or awaken any thought or self-examination in them. Again, when Sir Thomas Bateson describes the Philistines and the Populace as influenced with a kind of hideous mania for emasculating the aristocracy, that reproach so clearly comes from the wrath and excited imagination of the Barbarians, that it does not much set the Philistines and the Populace thinking. Or when Mr. Lowe calls the Populace drunken and venal, he so evidently calls them this in an agony of apprehension for his Philistine or middle-class Parliament, which has done so many great and heroic works, and is now threatened with mixture and debasement, that the Populace do not lay his words seriously to heart.

So the voice which makes a permanent impression on each of our classes is the voice of its friends, and this is from the nature of things, as I have said, a comforting voice. The Barbarians remain in the belief that the great broad-shouldered genial Englishman may be well satisfied with himself; the Philistines remain in the belief that the great middle class of this country, with its earnest common-sense penetrating through sophisms and ignoring commonplaces, may be well satisfied with itself; the Populace, that the working man with his bright powers of sympathy and ready powers of action, may be well satisfied with himself. What hope, at this rate, of extinguishing the taste of the bathos implanted by nature itself in the soul of man, or of inculcating the belief that excellence dwells among high and steep rocks, and can only be reached by those who sweat blood to reach her?

But it will be said, perhaps, that candidates for political influence and leadership, who thus caress the self-love of those whose suffrages they desire, know quite well that they are not saying the sheer truth as reason sees it, but that they are using a sort of conventional language, or what we call clap-trap, which is essential to the working of representative institutions. And therefore, I suppose, we ought rather to say with Figaro: *Qui est-ce qu'on trompe ici?* Now, I admit that often, but not always, when our governors say smooth things to the self-love of the class whose political support they want, they know very well that they are overstepping, by a long stride, the bounds of truth and soberness; and while they talk, they in a manner, no doubt, put their tongue in their cheek. Not always; because, when a Barbarian appeals to his own class to make him their representative and give him political power, he, when he pleases their self-love by extolling broad-shouldered genial Englishmen with their sense of duty, reverence for the laws, and patient force, pleases his own self-love and extols himself, and is, therefore, himself ensnared by his own smooth words. And so, too, when a Philistine wants to be sent to Parliament by his brother Philistines, and extols the earnest good sense which characterises Manchester and supplies the mind, the will, and the power, as the *Daily News* eloquently says, requisite for all the great and good things that have to be done, he intoxicates and deludes himself as well as his brother Philistines who hear him.

But it is true that a Barbarian often wants the political support of the Philistines; and he unquestionably, when he flatters the self-love of Philistinism, and extols, in the approved fashion, its energy, enterprise, and self-reliance, knows that he is talking clap-trap, and so to say, puts his tongue in his cheek. On all matters where Nonconformity and its catchwords are concerned, this insincerity of Barbarians needing Nonconformist support, and, therefore, flattering the self-love of Nonconformity and repeating its catchwords without the least real belief in them, is very noticeable. When the Nonconformists, in a transport of blind zeal, threw out Sir James Graham's useful Education Clauses in 1843, one-half of their parliamentary advocates, no doubt, who cried aloud against "trampling on the religious liberty of the Dissenters by taking the money of Dissenters to teach the tenets of the Church of England," put their tongue in their cheek while they so cried out. And perhaps there is even a sort of motion of Mr. Frederic Harrison's tongue towards his cheek when he talks of "the shriek of superstition," and tells the working class that "theirs are the brightest powers of sympathy and the readiest powers of action." But the point on which I would insist is, that this involuntary tribute to truth and soberness on the part of certain of our governors and guides never reaches at all the mass of us governed, to serve as a lesson to us, to abate our self-love, and to awaken in us a suspicion that our favourite prejudices may be, to a higher reason, all nonsense. Whatever by-play goes on among the more intelligent of our leaders, we do not see it; and we are left to believe that, not only in our own eyes, but in the eyes of our representative and ruling men, there is nothing more admirable than our ordinary self, whatever our ordinary self happens to be, Barbarian, Philistine, or Populace.

Thus everything in our political life tends to hide from

us that there is anything wiser than our ordinary selves, and to prevent our getting the notion of a paramount right reason. Royalty itself, in its idea the expression of the collective nation, and a sort of constituted witness to its best mind, we try to turn into a kind of grand advertising van, meant to give publicity and credit to the inventions, sound or unsound, of the ordinary self of individuals.

I remember, when I was in North Germany, having this very strongly brought to my mind in the matter of schools and their institution. In Prussia, the best schools are Crown patronage schools, as they are called; schools which have been established and endowed (and new ones are to this day being established and endowed) by the Sovereign himself out of his own revenues, to be under the direct control and management of him or of those representing him, and to serve as types of what schools should be. The Sovereign, as his position raises him above many prejudices and littlenesses, and as he can always have at his disposal the best advice, has evident advantages over private founders in well planning and directing a school; while at the same time his great means and his great influence secure, to a well-planned school of his, credit and authority. This is what, in North Germany, the governors do in the matter of education for the governed; and one may say that they thus give the governed a lesson, and draw out in them the idea of a right reason higher than the suggestions of an ordinary man's ordinary self.

But in England how different is the part which in this matter our governors are accustomed to play! The Licensed Victuallers or the Commercial Travellers propose to make a school for their children; and I suppose, in the matter of schools, one may call the Licensed Victuallers or the Commercial Travellers ordinary men, with their natural taste for the bathos still strong; and a Sovereign with the

advice of men like Wilhelm von Humboldt or Schleiermacher may, in this matter, be a better judge, and nearer to
right reason.   And it will be allowed, probably, that right
reason would suggest that, to have a sheer school of Licensed Victuallers' children, or a sheer school of Commercial
Travellers' children, and to bring them all up, not only at
home but at school too, in a kind of odour of licensed
victualism or of bagmanism, is not a wise training to give
to these children.   And in Germany, I have said, the action
of the national guides or governors is to suggest and provide
a better.   But, in England, the action of the national guides
or governors is, for a Royal Prince or a great Minister to go
down to the opening of the Licensed Victuallers' or of the
Commercial Travellers' school, to take the chair, to extol
the energy and self-reliance of the Licensed Victuallers or
the Commercial Travellers, to be all of their way of thinking, to predict full success to their schools, and never so
much as to hint to them that they are probably doing a very
foolish thing, and that the right way to go to work with their
children's education is quite different.   And it is the same in
almost every department of affairs.   While, on the Continent, the idea prevails that it is the business of the heads and
representatives of the nation, by virtue of their superior
means, power, and information, to set an example and to
provide suggestions of right reason, among us the idea is that
the business of the heads and representatives of the nation is
to do nothing of the kind, but to applaud the natural taste
for the bathos showing itself vigorously in any part of the
community, and to encourage its works.

Now I do not say that the political system of foreign
countries has not inconveniences which may outweigh the
inconveniences of our own political system; nor am I the
least proposing to get rid of our own political system and
to adopt theirs.   But a sound centre of authority being

what, in this disquisition, we have been led to seek, and right reason, or our best self, appearing alone to offer such a sound centre of authority, it is necessary to take note of the chief impediments which hinder, in this country, the extrication or recognition of this right reason as a paramount authority, with a view to afterwards trying in what way they can best be removed.

This being borne in mind, I proceed to remark how not only do we get no suggestions of right reason, and no rebukes of our ordinary self, from our governors, but a kind of philosophical theory is widely spread among us to the effect that there is no such thing at all as a best self and a right reason having claim to paramount authority, or, at any rate, no such thing ascertainable and capable of being made use of; and that there is nothing but an infinite number of ideas and works of our ordinary selves, and suggestions of our natural taste for the bathos, pretty nearly equal in value, which are doomed either to an irreconcilable conflict, or else to a perpetual give and take; and that wisdom consists in choosing the give and take rather than the conflict, and in sticking to our choice with patience and good humour.

And, on the other hand, we have another philosophical theory rife among us, to the effect that without the labour of perverting ourselves by custom or example to relish right reason, but by continuing all of us to follow freely our natural taste for the bathos, we shall, by the mercy of Providence, and by a kind of natural tendency of things, come in due time to relish and follow right reason.

The great promoters of these philosophical theories are our newspapers, which, no less than our parliamentary representatives, may be said to act the part of guides and governors to us; and these favourite doctrines of theirs I call, —or should call, if the doctrines were not preached by authorities I so much respect,—the first, a peculiarly British form of Atheism, the second, a peculiarly British form of Quietism. The first-named melancholy doctrine is preached in the *Times* with great clearness and force of style; indeed, it is well known, from the example of the poet Lucretius and others, what great masters of style the atheistic doctrine has always counted among its promulgators. "It is of no use," says the *Times*, "for us to attempt to force upon our neighbours our several likings and dislikings. We must take things as they are. Everybody has his own little vision of religious or civil perfection. Under the evident impossibility of satisfying everybody, we agree to take our stand on equal laws and on a system as open and liberal as is possible. The result is that everybody has more liberty of action and of speaking here than anywhere else in the Old World." We come again here upon Mr. Roebuck's celebrated definition of happiness, on which I have so often commented: "I look around me and ask what is the state of England? Is not every man able to say what he likes? I ask you whether the world over, or in past history, there is anything like it? Nothing. I pray that our unrivalled happiness may last." This is the old story of our system of checks and every Englishman doing as he likes, which we have already seen to have been convenient enough so long as there were only the Barbarians and the Philistines to do what they liked, but to be getting inconvenient, and productive of anarchy, now that the Populace wants to do what it likes too.

But for all that, I will not at once dismiss this famous doctrine, but will first quote another passage from the *Times*, applying the doctrine to a matter of which we have just been speaking,—education. "The difficulty here" (in providing a national system of education), says the *Times*, "does not reside in any removable arrangements. It is

6   W A

inherent and native in the actual and inveterate state of things in this country. All these powers and personages, all these conflicting influences and varieties of character, exist, and have long existed among us; they are fighting it out, and will long continue to fight it out, without coming to that happy consummation when some one element of the British character is to destroy or to absorb all the rest." There it is; the various promptings of the natural taste for the bathos in this man and that amongst us are fighting it out; and the day will never come (and, indeed, why should we wish it to come?) when one man's particular sort of taste for the bathos shall tyrannise over another man's; nor when right reason (if that may be called an element of the British character) shall absorb and rule them all. "The whole system of this country, like the constitution we boast to inherit, and are glad to uphold, is made up of established facts, prescriptive authorities, existing usages, powers that be, persons in possession, and communities or classes that have won dominion for themselves, and will hold it against all comers." Every force in the world, evidently, except the one reconciling force, right reason! Sir Thomas Bateson here, the Rev. W. Cattle on this side, Mr. Bradlaugh on that!—pull devil, pull baker! Really, presented with the mastery of style of our leading journal, the sad picture, as one gazes upon it, assumes the iron and inexorable solemnity of tragic Destiny.

After this, the milder doctrine of our other philosophical teacher, the *Daily News*, has, at first, something very attractive and assuaging. The *Daily News* begins, indeed, in appearance, to weave the iron web of necessity round us like the *Times*. "The alternative is between a man's doing what he likes and his doing what some one else, probably not one whit wiser than himself, likes." This points to the tacit compact, mentioned in my last paper, between the Bar-

barians and the Philistines, and into which it is hoped that
the Populace will one day enter; the compact, so creditable
to English honesty, that since each class has only the
ideas and aims of its ordinary self to give effect to, none of
them shall, if it exercise power, treat its ordinary self
too seriously, or attempt to impose it on others; but shall
let these others,—the Rev. W. Cattle, for instance, in
his Papist-baiting, and Mr. Bradlaugh in his Hyde Park
anarchy-mongering,—have their fling. But then the
Daily News suddenly lights up the gloom of necessitarianism with bright beams of hope. "No doubt," it
says, "the common reason of society ought to check the
aberrations of individual eccentricity." This common reason
of society looks very like our best self or right reason,
to which we want to give authority, by making the action
of the *State*, or nation in its collective character, the expression of it. But of this project of ours, the *Daily News*,
with its subtle dialectics, makes havoc. "Make the State
the organ of the common reason?"—it says. "You may
make it the organ of something or other, but how can you
be certain that reason will be the quality which will be
embodied in it?" You cannot be certain of it, undoubtedly,
if you never try to bring the thing about; but the question
is, the action of the State being the action of the collective
nation and the action of the collective nation carrying
naturally great publicity, weight, and force of example with
it, whether we should not try to put into the action of the
State as much as possible of right reason, or our best self,
which may, in this manner, come back to us with new
force and authority; may have visibility, form, and influence; and help to confirm us, in the many moments
when we are tempted to be our ordinary selves merely, in
resisting our natural taste of the bathos rather than in giving
way to it?

But no! says our teacher: "It is better there should be an infinite variety of experiments in human action, because, as the explorers multiply, the true track is more likely to be discovered. The common reason of society can check the aberrations of individual eccentricity only by acting on the individual reason; and it will do so in the main sufficiently, if left to this natural operation." This is what I call the specially British form of Quietism, or a devout, but excessive reliance on an over-ruling Providence. Providence, as the moralists are careful to tell us, generally works in human affairs by human means; so when we want to make right reason act on individual inclination, our best self on our ordinary self, we seek to give it more power of doing so by giving it public recognition and authority, and embodying it, so far as we can, in the State. It seems too much to ask of Providence, that while we, on our part, leave our congenital taste for the bathos to its natural operation and its infinite variety of experiments, Providence should mysteriously guide it into the true track, and compel it to relish the sublime. At any rate, great men and great institutions have hitherto seemed necessary for producing any considerable effect of this kind. No doubt we have an infinite variety of experiments, and an ever-multiplying multitude of explorers. Even in these few chapters I have enumerated many: the *British Banner*, Judge Edmonds, Newman Weeks, Deborah Butler, Elderess Polly, Brother Noyes, the Rev. W. Cattle, the Licensed Victuallers, the Commercial Travellers, and I know not how many more; and the members of the noble army are swelling every day. But what a depth of Quietism, or rather, what an over-bold call on the direct interposition of Providence, to believe that these interesting explorers will discover the true track, or at any rate, "will do so in the main well enough" (whatever that may mean) if left to their natural operation; that is, by going on as they

are! Philosophers say, indeed, that we learn virtue by performing acts of virtue; but to say that we shall learn virtue
by performing any acts to which our natural taste for the
bathos carries us, that the Rev. W. Cattle comes at his best
self by Papist-baiting, or Newman Weeks and Deborah
Butler at right reason by following their noses, this certainly
does appear over-sanguine.

It is true, what we want is to make right reason act on
individual reason, the reason of individuals; all our search
for authority has that for its end and aim. The *Daily News*
says, I observe, that all my argument for authority "has a
non-intellectual root;" and from what I know of my own
mind and its poverty I think this so probable, that I should
be inclined easily to admit it, if it were not that, in the first
place, nothing of this kind, perhaps, should be admitted
without examination; and, in the second, a way of account-
ing for the charge being made, in this particular instance,
without good grounds, appears to present itself. What seems
to me to account here, perhaps, for the charge, is the want
of flexibility of our race, on which I have so often remarked.
I mean, it being admitted that the conformity of the individual reason of the Rev. W. Cattle or Mr. Bradlaugh with
right reason is our true object, and not the mere restraining
them, by the strong arm of the State, from Papist-baiting or
railing-breaking,—admitting this, we English have so little
flexibility that we cannot readily perceive that the State's
restraining them from these indulgences may yet fix clearly
in their minds that, to the collective nation, these indulgences appear irrational and unallowable, may make them
pause and reflect, and may contribute to bringing, with
time, their individual reason into harmony with right reason. But in no country, owing to the want of intellectual
flexibility above mentioned, is the leaning which is our
natural one, and, therefore, needs no recommending to us,

so sedulously recommended, and the leaning which is not our natural one, and, therefore, does not need dispraising to us, so sedulously dispraised, as in ours. To rely on the individual being, with us, the natural leaning, we will hear of nothing but the good of relying on the individual; to act through the collective nation on the individual being not our natural leaning, we will hear nothing in recommendation of it. But the wise know that we often need to hear most of that to which we are least inclined, and even to learn to employ, in certain circumstances, that which is capable, if employed amiss, of being a danger to us.

Elsewhere this is certainly better understood than here. In a recent number of the *Westminster Review*, an able writer, but with precisely our national want of flexibility of which I have been speaking, has unearthed, I see, for our present needs, an English translation, published some years ago, of Wilhelm von Humboldt's book, *The Sphere and Duties of Government*. Humboldt's object in this book is to show that the operation of government ought to be severely limited to what directly and immediately relates to the security of person and property. Wilhelm von Humboldt, one of the most beautiful souls that have ever existed, used to say that one's business in life was first to perfect oneself by all the means in one's power, and secondly to try and create in the world around one an aristocracy, the most numerous that one possibly could, of talents and characters. He saw, of course, that, in the end, everything comes to this,—that the individual must act for himself, and must be perfect in himself; and he lived in a country, Germany, where people were disposed to act too little for themselves, and to rely too much on the Government. But even thus, such was his flexibility, so little was he in bondage to a mere abstract maxim, that he saw very well that for his purpose itself, of enabling the individual to stand perfect on his own foundations and to do without the State, the action of the State would for long, long years be necessary. And soon after he wrote his book on *The Sphere and Duties of Government*, Wilhelm von Humboldt became Minister of Education in Prussia; and from his ministry all the great reforms which give the control of Prussian education to the State,—the transference of the management of public schools from their old boards of trustees to the State, the obligatory State-examination for schools, the obligatory State-examination for schoolmasters, and the foundation of the great State-University of Berlin,—take their origin. This his English reviewer says not a word of. But, writing for a people whose dangers lie, as we have seen, on the side of their unchecked and unguided individual action, whose dangers none of them lie on the side of an over-reliance on the State, he quotes just so much of Wilhelm von Humboldt's example as can flatter them in their propensities, and do them no good; and just what might make them think, and be of use to them, he leaves on one side. This precisely recalls the manner, it will be observed, in which we have seen that our royal and noble personages proceed with the Licensed Victuallers.

In France the action of the State on individuals is yet more preponderant than in Germany; and the need which friends of human perfection feel for what may enable the individual to stand perfect on his own foundations is all the stronger. But what says one of the staunchest of these friends, M. Renan, on State action; and even State action in that very sphere where in France it is most excessive, the sphere of education? Here are his words:—" A Liberal believes in liberty, and liberty signifies the non-intervention of the State. *But such an ideal is still a long way off from us, and the very means to remove it to an indefinite distance would be precisely the State's withdrawing its action too soon.*" And this, he adds, is even truer of education than of any other department of public affairs.

We see, then, how indispensable to that human perfection which we seek is, in the opinion of good judges, some public recognition and establishment of our best self, or right reason. We see how our habits and practice oppose themselves to such a recognition, and the many inconveniences which we therefore suffer. But now let us try to go a little deeper, and to find, beneath our actual habits and practice, the very ground and cause out of which they spring.

CHAPTER IV

HEBRAISM AND HELLENISM

THIS fundamental ground is our preference of doing to thinking. Now this preference is a main element in our nature, and as we study it we find ourselves opening up a number of large questions on every side.

Let me go back for a moment to Bishop Wilson, who says:—"First, never go against the best light you have; secondly, take care that your light be not darkness." We show, as a nation, laudable energy and persistence in walking according to the best light we have, but are not quite careful enough, perhaps, to see that our light be not darkness. This is only another version of the old story that energy is our strong point and favourable characteristic rather than intelligence. But we may give to this idea a more general form still, in which it will have a yet larger range of application. We may regard this energy driving at practice, this paramount sense of the obligation of duty, self-control, and work, this earnestness in going manfully with the best light we have, as one force. And we may regard the intelligence driving at those ideas which are, after all, the basis of right practice, the ardent sense for all the new and changing combinations of them which man's development brings with it, the indomitable impulse to know and adjust them perfectly, as another force. And these two forces we may regard as in some sense rivals,—rivals not by the necessity of their own nature, but as exhibited in man and his history,—and rivals dividing the empire of the world between them. And to give these forces names from the two races of men who have supplied the most signal and splendid manifestations of them, we may call them respectively the forces of Hebraism and Hellenism. Hebraism and Hellenism,—between these two points of influence moves our world. At one time it feels more powerfully the attraction of one of them, at another time of the other; and it ought to be, though it never is, evenly and happily balanced between them.

The final aim of both Hellenism and Hebraism, as of all great spiritual disciplines, is no doubt the same: man's perfection or salvation. The very language which they both of them use in schooling us to reach this aim is often identical. Even when their language indicates by variation,—sometimes a broad variation, often a but slight and subtle variation,—the different courses of thought which are uppermost in each discipline, even then the unity of the final end and aim is still apparent. To employ the actual words of that discipline with which we ourselves are all of us most familiar, and the words of which, therefore, come most home to us, that final end and aim is "that we might be partakers of the divine nature." These are the words of a Hebrew apostle, but of Hellenism and Hebraism alike this is, I say, the aim. When the two are confronted, as they very often are confronted, it is nearly always with what I may call a rhetorical purpose; the speaker's whole design is to exalt and enthrone one of the two, and he uses the other only as a foil and to enable him the better to give effect to his purpose. Obviously, with us, it is usually Hellenism which is thus reduced to minister to the triumph of Hebraism. There is a sermon on Greece and the Greek spirit by a man never to be mentioned without interest and respect, Frederick Robertson, in which this rhetorical use of Greece and the Greek spirit, and the inadequate exhibition of them necessarily consequent upon this, is almost ludicrous, and would be censurable if it were not to be explained by the exigencies of a sermon. On the other hand, Heinrich Heine, and other writers of his sort, give us the spectacle of the tables completely turned, and of Hebraism brought in just as a foil and contrast to Hellenism, and to make the superiority of Hellenism more manifest. In both these cases there is injustice and misrepresentation. The aim and end of both Hebraism and Hellenism is, as I have said, one and the same, and this aim and end is august and admirable.

Still, they pursue this aim by very different courses. The uppermost idea with Hellenism is to see things as they really are; the uppermost idea with Hebraism is conduct and obedience. Nothing can do away with this ineffaceable difference. The Greek quarrel with the body and its desires is, that they hinder right thinking, the Hebrew quarrel with them is, that they hinder right acting. "He that keepeth the law, happy is he;" "Blessed is the man that feareth the Eternal, that delighteth greatly in his commandments,"—that is the Hebrew notion of felicity; and, pursued with passion and tenacity, this notion would not let the Hebrew rest till, as is well known, he had at last got out of the law a network of prescriptions to enwrap his whole life, to govern every moment of it, every impulse, every action. The Greek notion of felicity, on the other hand, is perfectly conveyed in these words of a great French moralist: "*C'est le bonheur des hommes*"—when? when they abhor that which is evil?—no; when they exercise themselves in the law of the Lord day and night?—no; when they die daily? —no; when they walk about the New Jerusalem with palms in their hands?—no; but when they think aright, when their thought hits: "*quand ils pensent juste*." At the bottom of both the Greek and the Hebrew notion is the desire, native in man, for reason and the will of God, the feeling after the universal order,—in a word, the love of God. But, while Hebraism seizes upon certain plain, capital intimations of the universal order, and rivets itself, one may say, with unequalled grandeur of earnestness and intensity on the study and observance of them, the bent of Hellenism is to follow, with flexible activity, the whole play of the universal order, to be apprehensive of missing any part of it, of sacrificing one part to another, to slip away from resting in this or that intimation of it, however capital. An unclouded clearness of mind, an unimpeded play of thought, is what this bent drives at. The governing idea of Hellenism is *spontaneity of consciousness;* that of Hebraism, *strictness of conscience.*

Christianity changed nothing in this essential bent of Hebraism to set doing above knowing. Self-conquest, self-devotion, the following not our own individual will, but the will of God, *obedience*, is the fundamental idea of this form, also, of the discipline to which we have attached the general name of Hebraism. Only, as the old law and the network of prescriptions with which it enveloped human life were evidently a motive-power not driving and searching enough to produce the result aimed at,—patient continuance in well doing, self-conquest,—Christianity substituted for them boundless devotion to that inspiring and affecting pattern of self-conquest offered by Jesus Christ; and by the new motive-power, of which the essence was this, though the love and admiration of Christian churches have for centuries been employed in varying, amplifying, and adorning the plain description of it, Christianity, as St. Paul truly says, "establishes the law," and in the strength of the ampler power which she has thus supplied to fulfil it, has accomplished the miracles, which we all see, of her history.

So long as we do not forget that both Hellenism and Hebraism are profound and admirable manifestations of man's life, tendencies, and powers, and that both of them aim at a like final result, we can hardly insist too strongly

on the divergence of line and of operation with which they
proceed. It is a divergence so great that it most truly, as
the prophet Zechariah says, "has raised up thy sons, O
Zion, against thy sons, O Greece!" The difference whether
it is by doing or by knowing that we set most store, and
the practical consequences which follow from this difference, leave their mark on all the history of our race and of
its development. Language may be abundantly quoted
from both Hellenism and Hebraism to make it seem that
one follows the same current as the other towards the same
goal. They are, truly, borne towards the same goal; but
the currents which bear them are infinitely different. It
is true, Solomon will praise knowing: "Understanding is
a well-spring of life unto him that hath it." And in the
New Testament, again, Jesus Christ is a "light," and
"truth makes us free." It is true, Aristotle will undervalue knowing: "In what concerns virtue," says he, "three
things are necessary—knowledge, deliberate will, and per-
severance; but, whereas the two last are all-important, the
first is a matter of little importance." It is true that with
the same impatience with which St. James enjoins a man
to be not a forgetful hearer, but a *doer of the work*, Epictetus
exhorts us to *do* what we have demonstrated to ourselves
we ought to do; or he taunts us with futility, for being
armed at all points to prove that lying is wrong, yet all the
time continuing to lie. It is true, Plato, in words which are
almost the words of the New Testament or the Imitation,
calls life a learning to die. But underneath the superficial
agreement the fundamental divergence still subsists. The
understanding of Solomon is "the walking in the way of the
commandments;" this is "the way of peace," and it is of
this that blessedness comes. In the New Testament, the
truth which gives us the peace of God and makes us free, is
the love of Christ constraining us to crucify, as he did, and

with a like purpose of moral regeneration, the flesh with its
affections and lusts, and thus establishing, as we have seen,
the law. To St. Paul it appears possible to "hold the truth
in unrighteousness," which is just what Socrates judged
impossible. The moral virtues, on the other hand, are with
Aristotle but the porch and access to the intellectual, and
with these last is blessedness. That partaking of the divine
life, which both Hellenism and Hebraism, as we have said,
fix as their crowning aim, Plato expressly denies to the man
of practical virtue merely, of self-conquest with any other
motive than that of perfect intellectual vision. He reserves
it for the lover of pure knowledge, of seeing things as they
really are,—the φιλομαθής.

Both Hellenism and Hebraism arise out of the wants of
human nature, and address themselves to satisfying those
wants. But their methods are so different, they lay stress on
such different points, and call into being by their respective
disciplines such different activities, that the face which
human nature presents when it passes from the hands of one
of them to those of the other, is no longer the same. To get
rid of one's ignorance, to see things as they are, and by seeing
them as they are to see them in their beauty, is the simple
and attractive ideal which Hellenism holds out before
human nature; and from the simplicity and charm of this
ideal, Hellenism, and human life in the hands of Hellenism,
is invested with a kind of aërial ease, clearness, and
radiancy; they are full of what we call sweetness and light.
Difficulties are kept out of view, and the beauty and
rationalness of the ideal have all our thoughts. "The best
man is he who most tries to perfect himself, and the happiest
man is he who most feels that he *is* perfecting himself,"—
this account of the matter by Socrates, the true Socrates of
the *Memorabilia*, has something so simple, spontaneous, and
unsophisticated about it, that it seems to fill us with clear-

ness and hope when we hear it. But there is a saying which I have heard attributed to Mr. Carlyle about Socrates,—a very happy saying, whether it is really Mr. Carlyle's or not, —which excellently marks the essential point in which Hebraism differs from Hellenism. "Socrates," this saying goes, "is terribly *at ease in Zion*." Hebraism,—and here is the source of its wonderful strength,—has always been severely pre-occupied with an awful sense of the impossibility of being at ease in Zion; of the difficulties which oppose themselves to man's pursuit or attainment of that perfection of which Socrates talks so hopefully, and, as from this point of view one might almost say, so glibly. It is all very well to talk of getting rid of one's ignorance, of seeing things in their reality, seeing them in their beauty; but how is this to be done when there is something which thwarts and spoils all our efforts?

This something is *sin*; and the space which sin fills in Hebraism, as compared with Hellenism, is indeed prodigious. This obstacle to perfection fills the whole scene, and perfection appears remote and rising away from earth, in the background. Under the name of sin, the difficulties of knowing oneself and conquering oneself which impede man's passage to perfection, become, for Hebraism, a positive, active entity hostile to man, a mysterious power which I heard Dr. Pusey the other day, in one of his impressive sermons, compare to a hideous hunchback seated on our shoulders, and which it is the main business of our lives to hate and oppose. The discipline of the Old Testament may be summed up as a discipline teaching us to abhor and flee from sin; the discipline of the New Testament, as a discipline teaching us to die to it. As Hellenism speaks of thinking clearly, seeing things in their essence and beauty, as a grand and precious feat for man to achieve, so Hebraism speaks of becoming conscious of sin, of awakening to a sense of sin, as a feat of this kind. It is obvious to what wide divergence these differing tendencies, actively followed, must lead. As one passes and repasses from Hellenism to Hebraism, from Plato to St. Paul, one feels inclined to rub one's eyes and ask oneself whether man is indeed a gentle and simple being, showing the traces of a noble and divine nature; or an unhappy chained captive, labouring with groanings that cannot be uttered to free himself from the body of this death.

Apparently it was the Hellenic conception of human nature which was unsound, for the world could not live by it. Absolutely to call it unsound, however, is to fall into the common error of its Hebraising enemies; but it was unsound at that particular moment of man's development, it was premature. The indispensable basis of conduct and self-control, the platform upon which alone the perfection aimed at by Greece can come into bloom, was not to be reached by our race so easily; centuries of probation and discipline were needed to bring us to it. Therefore the bright promise of Hellenism faded, and Hebraism ruled the world. Then was seen that astonishing spectacle, so well marked by the often-quoted words of the prophet Zechariah, when men of all languages and nations took hold of the skirt of him that was a Jew, saying:—"*We will go with you, for we have heard that God is with you.*" And the Hebraism which thus received and ruled a world all gone out of the way and altogether become unprofitable, was, and could not but be, the later, the more spiritual, the more attractive development of Hebraism. It was Christianity; that is to say, Hebraism aiming at self-conquest and rescue from the thrall of vile affections, not by obedience to the letter of a law, but by conformity to the image of a self-sacrificing example. To a world stricken with moral enervation Christianity offered its spectacle of

an inspired self-sacrifice; to men who refused themselves
nothing, it showed one who refused himself everything;—
"*my Saviour banished joy!*" says George Herbert. When
the *alma Venus*, the life-giving and joy-giving power of
nature, so fondly cherished by the pagan world, could not
save her followers from self-dissatisfaction and ennui, the
severe words of the apostle came bracingly and refreshingly:
"Let no man deceive you with vain words, for because of
these things cometh the wrath of God upon the children of
disobedience." Through age after age and generation after
generation, our race, or all that part of our race which
was most living and progressive, was *baptized into a death;*
and endeavoured, by suffering in the flesh, to cease from sin.
Of this endeavour, the animating labours and afflictions of
early Christianity, the touching asceticism of mediæval
Christianity, are the great historical manifestations. Literary monuments of it, each in its own way incomparable,
remain in the Epistles of St. Paul, in St. Augustine's Confessions, and in the two original and simplest books of the
Imitation*.

Of two disciplines laying their main stress, the one, on
clear intelligence, the other, on firm obedience; the one,
on comprehensively knowing the grounds of one's duty,
the other, on diligently practising it; the one, on taking all
possible care (to use Bishop Wilson's words again) that the
light we have be not darkness, the other, that according to
the best light we have we diligently walk,—the priority
naturally belongs to that discipline which braces all man's
moral powers, and founds for him an indispensable basis
of character. And, therefore, it is justly said of the Jewish
people, who were charged with setting powerfully forth
that side of the divine order to which the words *conscience*
and *self-conquest* point, that they were "entrusted with the

* The two first books.

oracles of God;" as it is justly said of Christianity, which
followed Judaism and which set forth this side with a much
deeper effectiveness and a much wider influence, that the
wisdom of the old Pagan world was foolishness compared
to it. No words of devotion and admiration can be too
strong to render thanks to these beneficent forces which
have so borne forward humanity in its appointed work of
coming to the knowledge and possession of itself; above all,
in those great moments when their action was the whole-
somest and the most necessary.

But the evolution of these forces, separately and in
themselves, is not the whole evolution of humanity,—their
single history is not the whole history of man; whereas
their admirers are always apt to make it stand for the whole
history. Hebraism and Hellenism are, neither of them, the
law of human development, as their admirers are prone to
make them; they are, each of them, *contributions* to human
development,—august contributions, invaluable contributions; and each showing itself to us more august, more invaluable, more preponderant over the other, according to
the moment in which we take them, and the relation in
which we stand to them. The nations of our modern world,
children of that immense and salutary movement which
broke up the Pagan world, inevitably stand to Hellenism in
a relation which dwarfs it, and to Hebraism in a relation
which magnifies it. They are inevitably prone to take
Hebraism as the law of human development, and not as
simply a contribution to it, however precious. And yet the
lesson must perforce be learned, that the human spirit is
wider than the most priceless of the forces which bear it
onward, and that to the whole development of man Hebraism itself is, like Hellenism, but a contribution.

Perhaps we may help ourselves to see this clearer by an
illustration drawn from the treatment of a single great idea

which has profoundly engaged the human spirit, and has given it eminent opportunities for showing its nobleness and energy. It surely must be perceived that the idea of immortality, as this idea rises in its generality before the human spirit, is something grander, truer, and more satisfying, than it is in the particular forms by which St. Paul, in the famous fifteenth chapter of the Epistle to the Corinthians, and Plato, in the *Phædo*, endeavour to develop and establish it. Surely we cannot but feel that the argumentation with which the Hebrew apostle goes about to expound this great idea is, after all, confused and inconclusive; and that the reasoning, drawn from analogies of likeness and equality, which is employed upon it by the Greek philosopher, is over-subtle and sterile. Above and beyond the inadequate solutions which Hebraism and Hellenism here attempt, extends the immense and august problem itself, and the human spirit which gave birth to it. And this single illustration may suggest to us how the same thing happens in other cases also.

But meanwhile, by alternations of Hebraism and Hellenism, of a man's intellectual and moral impulses, of the effort to see things as they really are and the effort to win peace by self-conquest, the human spirit proceeds; and each of these two forces has its appointed hours of culmination and seasons of rule. As the great movement of Christianity was a triumph of Hebraism and man's moral impulses, so the great movement which goes by the name of the Renascence* was an uprising and re-instatement of man's intellectual impulses and of Hellenism. We in England, the devoted children of Protestantism, chiefly know the

* I have ventured to give to the foreign word *Renaissance*,—destined to become of more common use amongst us as the movement which it denotes comes, as it will come, increasingly to interest us,—an English form.

Renascence by its subordinate and secondary side of the Reformation. The Reformation has been often called a Hebraising revival, a return to the ardour and sincereness of primitive Christianity. No one, however, can study the development of Protestantism and of Protestant churches without feeling that into the Reformation too,—Hebraising child of the Renascence and offspring of its fervour, rather than its intelligence, as it undoubtedly was,—the subtle Hellenic leaven of the Renascence found its way, and that the exact respective parts, in the Reformation, of Hebraism and of Hellenism, are not easy to separate. But what we may with truth say is, that all which Protestantism was to itself clearly conscious of, all which it succeeded in clearly setting forth in words, had the characters of Hebraism rather than of Hellenism. The Reformation was strong, in that it was an earnest return to the Bible and to doing from the heart the will of God as there written. It was weak, in that it never consciously grasped or applied the central idea of the Renascence,—the Hellenic idea of pursuing, in all lines of activity, the law and science, to use Plato's words, of things as they really are. Whatever direct superiority, therefore, Protestantism had over Catholicism was a moral superiority, a superiority arising out of its greater sincerity and earnestness,—at the moment of its apparition at any rate,—in dealing with the heart and conscience. Its pretensions to an intellectual superiority are in general quite illusory. For Hellenism, for the thinking side in man as distinguished from the acting side, the attitude of mind of Protestantism towards the Bible in no respect differs from the attitude of mind of Catholicism towards the Church. The mental habit of him who imagines that Balaam's ass spoke, in no respect differs from the mental habit of him who imagines that a Madonna of wood or stone winked; and the one, who says that God's Church makes him believe what he believes, and the other, who says that God's Word makes him believe what he believes, are for the philosopher perfectly alike in not really and truly knowing, when they say *God's Church* and *God's Word*, what it is they say, or whereof they affirm.

In the sixteenth century, therefore, Hellenism re-entered the world, and again stood in presence of Hebraism,—a Hebraism renewed and purged. Now, it has not been enough observed, how, in the seventeenth century, a fate befell Hellenism in some respects analogous to that which befell it at the commencement of our era. The Renascence, that great re-awakening of Hellenism, that irresistible return of humanity to nature and to seeing things as they are, which in art, in literature, and in physics, produced such splendid fruits, had, like the anterior Hellenism of the Pagan world, a side of moral weakness, and of relaxation or insensibility of the moral fibre, which in Italy showed itself with the most startling plainness, but which in France, England, and other countries, was very apparent too. Again this loss of spiritual balance, this exclusive preponderance given to man's perceiving and knowing side, this unnatural defect of his feeling and acting side, provoked a reaction. Let us trace that reaction where it most nearly concerns us.

Science has now made visible to everybody the great and pregnant elements of difference which lie in race, and in how signal a manner they make the genius and history of an Indo-European people vary from those of a Semitic people. Hellenism is of Indo-European growth, Hebraism is of Semitic growth; and we English, a nation of Indo-European stock, seem to belong naturally to the movement of Hellenism. But nothing more strongly marks the essential unity of man than the affinities we can perceive, in this point or that, between members of one family of peoples and members of another, and no affinity of this kind is more strongly marked than that likeness in the strength and prominence of the moral fibre, which, notwithstanding immense elements of difference, knits in some special sort the genius and history of us English, and our American descendants across the Atlantic, to the genius and history of the Hebrew people. Puritanism, which has been so great a power in the English nation, and in the strongest part of the English nation, was originally the reaction in the seventeenth century of the conscience and moral sense of our race, against the moral indifference and lax rule of conduct which in the sixteenth century came in with the Renascence. It was a reaction of Hebraism against Hellenism; and it powerfully manifested itself, as was natural, in a people with much of what we call a Hebraising turn, with a signal affinity for the bent which was the master-bent of Hebrew life. Eminently Indo-European by its *humour*, by the power it shows, through this gift, of imaginatively acknowledging the multiform aspects of the problem of life, and of thus getting itself unfixed from its own over-certainty, of smiling at its own over-tenacity, our race has yet (and a great part of its strength lies here), in matters of practical life and moral conduct, a strong share of the assuredness, the tenacity, the intensity of the Hebrews. This turn manifested itself in Puritanism, and has had a great part in shaping our history for the last two hundred years. Undoubtedly it checked and changed amongst us that movement of the Renascence which we see producing in the reign of Elizabeth such wonderful fruits. Undoubtedly it stopped the prominent rule and direct development of that order of ideas which we call by the name of Hellenism, and gave the first rank to a different order of ideas. Apparently, too, as we said of the former defeat of Hellenism, if Hellenism was defeated, this shows that Hellen-

ism was imperfect, and that its ascendency at that moment
would not have been for the world's good.

Yet there is a very important difference between the
defeat inflicted on Hellenism by Christianity eighteen
hundred years ago, and the check given to the Renascence
by Puritanism. The greatness of the difference is well
measured by the difference in force, beauty, significance
and usefulness, between primitive Christianity and Protestantism. Eighteen hundred years ago it was altogether the
hour of Hebraism. Primitive Christianity was legitimately
and truly the ascendent force in the world at that time,
and the way of mankind's progress lay through its full
development. Another hour in man's development began
in the fifteenth century, and the main road of his progress
then lay for a time through Hellenism. Puritanism was no
longer the central current of the world's progress, it was
a side stream crossing the central current and checking it.
The cross and the check may have been necessary and
salutary, but that does not do away with the essential
difference between the main stream of man's advance and
a cross or side stream. For more than two hundred years
the main stream of man's advance has moved towards
knowing himself and the world, seeing things as they are,
spontaneity of consciousness; the main impulse of a great
part, and that the strongest part, of our nation has been
towards strictness of conscience. They have made the
secondary the principal at the wrong moment, and the
principal they have at the wrong moment treated as secondary. This contravention of the natural order has produced,
as such contravention always must produce, a certain confusion and false movement, of which we are now beginning
to feel, in almost every direction, the inconvenience. In all
directions our habitual courses of action seem to be losing
efficaciousness, credit, and control, both with others and

even with ourselves; everywhere we see the beginnings of confusion, and we want a clue to some sound order and authority. This we can only get by going back upon the actual instincts and forces which rule our life, seeing them as they really are, connecting them with other instincts and forces, and enlarging our whole view and rule of life.

CHAPTER V

PORRO UNUM EST NECESSARIUM

THE matter here opened is so large, and the trains of thought to which it gives rise are so manifold, that we must be careful to limit ourselves scrupulously to what has a direct bearing upon our actual discussion. We have found that at the bottom of our present unsettled state, so full of the seeds of trouble, lies the notion of its being the prime right and happiness, for each of us, to affirm himself, and his ordinary self; to be doing, and to be doing freely and as he likes. We have found at the bottom of it the disbelief in right reason as a lawful authority. It was easy to show from our practice and current history that this is so; but it was impossible to show why it is so without taking a somewhat wider sweep and going into things a little more deeply. Why, in fact, should good, well-meaning, energetic, sensible people, like the bulk of our countrymen, come to have such light belief in right reason, and such an exaggerated value for their own independent doing, however crude? The answer is: because of an exclusive and excessive development in them, without due allowance for time, place, and circumstance, of that side of human nature, and that group of human forces, to which we have given the general name of Hebraism. Because they have thought their real and only important homage was owed to a power concerned with their obedience rather than with their intelligence, a power interested in the moral side of their nature almost exclusively. Thus they have been led to regard in themselves, as the one thing needful, *strictness of conscience*, the staunch adherence to some fixed law of doing we have got

already, instead of *spontaneity of consciousness*, which tends
continually to enlarge our whole law of doing. They have
fancied themselves to have in their religion a sufficient
basis for the whole of their life fixed and certain for ever,
a full law of conduct and a full law of thought, so far as
thought is needed, as well; whereas what they really have
is a law of conduct, a law of unexampled power for
enabling them to war against the law of sin in their members and not to serve it in the lusts thereof. The book
which contains this invaluable law they call the Word of
God, and attribute to it, as I have said, and as, indeed, is
perfectly well known, a reach and sufficiency co-extensive
with all the wants of human nature.

This might, no doubt, be so, if humanity were not the
composite thing it is, if it had only, or in quite overpowering eminence, a moral side, and the group of instincts and powers which we call moral. But it has besides, and in notable eminence, an intellectual side, and the
group of instincts and powers which we call intellectual.
No doubt, mankind makes in general its progress in a
fashion which gives at one time full swing to one of these
groups of instincts, at another time to the other; and man's
faculties are so intertwined, that when his moral side, and
the current of force which we call Hebraism, is uppermost, this side will manage somehow to provide, or appear
to provide, satisfaction for his intellectual needs; and when
his intellectual side, and the current of force which we call
Hellenism, is uppermost, this again will provide, or appear
to provide, satisfaction for men's moral needs. But sooner
or later it becomes manifest that when the two sides of
humanity proceed in this fashion of alternate preponderance, and not of mutual understanding and balance, the side
which is uppermost does not really provide in a satisfactory
manner for the needs of the side which is undermost, and

a state of confusion is, sooner or later, the result. The Hellenic half of our nature, bearing rule, makes a sort of provision for the Hebrew half, but it turns out to be an inadequate provision; and again the Hebrew half of our nature, bearing rule, makes a sort of provision for the Hellenic half, but this, too, turns out to be an inadequate provision. The true and smooth order of humanity's development is not reached in either way. And therefore, while we willingly admit with the Christian apostle that the world by wisdom,—that is, by the isolated preponderance of its intellectual impulses,—knew not God, or the true order of things, it is yet necessary, also, to set up a sort of converse to this proposition, and to say likewise (what is equally true) that the world by Puritanism knew not God. And it is on this converse of the apostle's proposition that it is particularly needful to insist in our own country just at present.

Here, indeed, is the answer to many criticisms which have been addressed to all that we have said in praise of sweetness and light. Sweetness and light evidently have to do with the bent or side in humanity which we call Hellenic. Greek intelligence has obviously for its essence the instinct for what Plato calls the true, firm, intelligible law of things; the law of light, of seeing things as they are. Even in the natural sciences, where the Greeks had not time and means adequately to apply this insinct, and where we have gone a great deal further than they did, it is this instinct which is the root of the whole matter and the ground of all our success; and this instinct the world has mainly learnt of the Greeks, inasmuch as they are humanity's most signal manifestation of it. Greek art, again, Greek beauty, have their root in the same impulse to see things as they really are, inasmuch as Greek art and beauty rest on fidelity to nature,—the *best* nature,—and on a delicate

discrimination of what this best nature is. To say we work
for sweetness and light, then, is only another way of saying
that we work for Hellenism. But, oh! cry many people,
sweetness and light are not enough; you must put strength
or energy along with them, and make a kind of trinity of
strength, sweetness and light, and then, perhaps, you may
do some good. That is to say, we are to join Hebraism,
strictness of the moral conscience, and manful walking by
the best light we have, together with Hellenism, inculcate
both, and rehearse the praises of both.

Or, rather, we may praise both in conjunction, but we
must be careful to praise Hebraism most. "Culture," says
an acute, though somewhat rigid critic, Mr. Sidgwick,
"diffuses sweetness and light. I do not undervalue these
blessings, but religion gives fire and strength, and the
world wants fire and strength even more than sweetness
and light." By religion, let me explain, Mr. Sidgwick here
means particularly that Puritanism on the insufficiency of
which I have been commenting and to which he says I am
unfair. Now, no doubt, it is possible to be a fanatical
partisan of light and the instincts which push us to it, a
fanatical enemy of strictness of moral conscience and the
instincts which push us to it. A fanaticism of this sort
deforms and vulgarises the well-known work, in some
respects so remarkable, of the late Mr. Buckle. Such a
fanaticism carries its own mark with it, in lacking sweetness; and its own penalty, in that, lacking sweetness, it
comes in the end to lack light too. And the Greeks,—the
great exponents of humanity's bent for sweetness and light
united, of its perception that the truth of things must be at
the same time beauty,—singularly escaped the fanaticism
which we moderns, whether we Hellenise or whether we
Hebraise, are so apt to show. They arrived,—though failing,
as has been said, to give adequate practical satisfaction to

the claims of man's moral side,—at the idea of a compre-
hensive adjustment of the claims of both the sides in man,
the moral as well as the intellectual, of a full estimate of
both, and of a reconciliation of both; an idea which is
philosophically of the greatest value, and the best of lessons
for us moderns. So we ought to have no difficulty in con-
ceding to Mr. Sidgwick that manful walking by the best
light one has,—fire and strength as he calls it,—has its
high value as well as culture, the endeavour to see things in
their truth and beauty, the pursuit of sweetness and light.
But whether at this or that time, and to this or that set of
persons, one ought to insist most on the praises of fire and
strength, or on the praises of sweetness and light, must
depend, one would think, on the circumstances and needs
of that particular time and those particular persons. And
all that we have been saying, and indeed any glance at the
world around us, shows that with us, with the most respectable and strongest part of us, the ruling force is now, and long
has been, a Puritan force,—the care for fire and strength,
strictness of conscience, Hebraism, rather than the care for
sweetness and light, spontaneity of consciousness, Hellenism.

Well, then, what is the good of our now rehearsing the
praises of fire and strength to ourselves, who dwell too exclusively on them already? When Mr. Sidgwick says so
broadly, that the world wants fire and strength even more
than sweetness and light, is he not carried away by a turn
for broad generalisation? does he not forget that the
world is not all of one piece, and every piece with the same
needs at the same time? It may be true that the Roman
world at the beginning of our era, or Leo the Tenth's
Court at the time of the Reformation, or French society in
the eighteenth century, needed fire and strength even more
than sweetness and light. But can it be said that the Barbarians who overran the empire needed fire and strength

even more than sweetness and light; or that the Puritans needed them more; or that Mr. Murphy, the Birmingham lecturer, and the Rev. W. Cattle and his friends, need them more?

The Puritan's great danger is that he imagines himself in possession of a rule telling him the *unum necessarium*, or one thing needful, and that he then remains satisfied with a very crude conception of what this rule really is and what it tells him, thinks he has now knowledge and henceforth needs only to act, and, in this dangerous state of assurance and self-satisfaction, proceeds to give full swing to a number of the instincts of his ordinary self. Some of the instincts of his ordinary self he has, by the help of his rule of life, conquered; but others which he has not conquered by this help he is so far from perceiving to need subjugation, and to be instincts of an inferior self, that he even fancies it to be his right and duty, in virtue of having conquered a limited part of himself, to give unchecked swing to the remainder. He is, I say, a victim of Hebraism, of the tendency to cultivate strictness of conscience rather than spontaneity of consciousness. And what he wants is a larger conception of human nature, showing him the number of other points at which his nature must come to its best, besides the points which he himself knows and thinks of. There is no *unum necessarium*, or one thing needful, which can free human nature from the obligation of trying to come to its best at all these points. The real *unum necessarium* for us is to come to our best at all points. Instead of our "one thing needful," justifying in us vulgarity, hideousness, ignorance, violence,—our vulgarity, hideousness, ignorance, violence, are really so many touchstones which try our one thing needful, and which prove that in the state, at any rate, in which we ourselves have it, it is not all we want. And as the force which encourages us to stand staunch and fast by the rule and ground we have is Hebraism, so the force which encourages us to go back upon this rule, and to try the very ground on which we appear to stand, is Hellenism, —a turn for giving our consciousness free play and enlarging its range. And what I say is, not that Hellenism is always for everybody more wanted than Hebraism, but that for the Rev. W. Cattle at this particular moment, and for the great majority of us his fellow-countrymen, it is more wanted.

Nothing is more striking than to observe in how many ways a limited conception of human nature, the notion of a one thing needful, a one side in us to be made uppermost, the disregard of a full and harmonious development of ourselves, tells injuriously on our thinking and acting. In the first place, our hold upon the rule or standard to which we look for our one thing needful, tends to become less and less near and vital, our conception of it more and more mechanical, and more and more unlike the thing itself as it was conceived in the mind where it originated. The dealings of Puritanism with the writings of St. Paul afford a noteworthy illustration of this. Nowhere so much as in the writings of St. Paul, and in that great apostle's greatest work, the Epistle to the Romans, has Puritanism found what seemed to furnish it with the one thing needful, and to give it canons of truth absolute and final. Now all writings, as has been already said, even the most precious writings and the most fruitful, must inevitably, from the very nature of things, be but contributions to human thought and human development, which extend wider than they do. Indeed, St. Paul, in the very Epistle of which we are speaking, shows, when he asks, "Who hath known the mind of the Lord?"—who hath known, that is, the true and divine order of things in its entirety,—that he himself acknowledges this fully. And we have already pointed out in another Epistle of St. Paul a great and vital

idea of the human spirit,—the idea of immortality,—
transcending and overlapping, so to speak, the expositor's
power to give it adequate definition and expression.

But quite distinct from the question whether St. Paul's
expression, or any man's expression, can be a perfect and
final expression of truth, comes the question whether we
rightly seize and understand his expression as it exists. Now,
perfectly to seize another man's meaning, as it stood in his
own mind, is not easy; especially when the man is separated
from us by such differences of race, training, time, and
circumstances as St. Paul. But there are degrees of near-
ness in getting at a man's meaning; and though we cannot
arrive quite at what St. Paul had in his mind, yet we may
come near it. And who, that comes thus near it, must not
feel how terms which St. Paul employs, in trying to follow
with his analysis of such profound power and originality
some of the most delicate, intricate, obscure, and contra-
dictory workings and states of the human spirit, are detached
and employed by Puritanism, not in the connected and
fluid way in which St. Paul employs them, and for which
alone words are really meant, but in an isolated, fixed,
mechanical way, as if they were talismans; and how all
trace and sense of St. Paul's true movement of ideas, and
sustained masterly analysis, is thus lost? Who, I say, that
has watched Puritanism,—the force which so strongly
Hebraises, which so takes St. Paul's writings as something
absolute and final, containing the one thing needful,—
handle such terms as *grace*, *faith*, *election*, *righteousness*, but
must feel, not only that these terms have for the mind of
Puritanism a sense false and misleading, but also that this
sense is the most monstrous and grotesque caricature of the
sense of St. Paul, and that his true meaning is by these
worshippers of his words altogether lost?

Or to take another eminent example, in which not

Puritanism only, but, one may say, the whole religious world, by their mechanical use of St. Paul's writings, can be shown to miss or change his real meaning. The whole religious world, one may say, use now the word *resurrection*, —a word which is so often in their thoughts and on their lips, and which they find so often in St. Paul's writings,— in one sense only. They use it to mean a rising again after the physical death of the body. Now it is quite true that St. Paul speaks of resurrection in this sense, that he tries to describe and explain it, and that he condemns those who doubt and deny it. But it is true, also, that in nine cases out of ten where St. Paul thinks and speaks of resurrection, he thinks and speaks of it in a sense different from this;—in the sense of a rising to a new life before the physical death of the body, and not after it. The idea on which we have already touched, the profound idea of being baptized into the death of the great exemplar of self-devotion and self-annulment, of repeating in our own person, by virtue of identification with our exemplar, his course of self-devotion and self-annulment, and of thus coming, within the limits of our present life, to a new life, in which, as in the death going before it, we are identified with our exemplar,—this is the fruitful and original conception of being *risen with Christ* which possesses the mind of St. Paul, and this is the central point round which, with such incomparable emotion and eloquence, all his teaching moves. For him, the life after our physical death is really in the main but a consequence and continuation of the inexhaustible energy of the new life thus originated on this side the grave. This grand Pauline idea of Christian resurrection is worthily rehearsed in one of the noblest collects of the Prayer-Book, and is destined, no doubt, to fill a more and more important place in the Christianity of the future. But meanwhile, almost as signal as the essentialness of this characteristic idea in

7   WA

St. Paul's teaching, is the completeness with which the worshippers of St. Paul's words as an absolute final expression of saving truth have lost it, and have substituted for the apostle's living and near conception of a resurrection now, their mechanical and remote conception of a resurrection hereafter.

In short, so fatal is the notion of possessing, even in the most precious words or standards, the one thing needful, of having in them, once for all, a full and sufficient measure of light to guide us, and of there being no duty left for us except to make our practice square exactly with them,— so fatal, I say, is this notion to the right knowledge and comprehension of the very words or standards we thus adopt, and to such strange distortions and perversions of them does it inevitably lead, that whenever we hear that commonplace which Hebraism, if we venture to inquire what a man knows, is so apt to bring out against us, in disparagement of what we call culture, and in praise of a man's sticking to the one thing needful,—*he knows*, says Hebraism, *his Bible!*—whenever we hear this said, we may, without any elaborate defence of culture, content ourselves with answering simply: "No man, who knows nothing else, knows even his Bible."

Now the force which we have so much neglected, Hellenism, may be liable to fail in moral strength and earnestness, but by the law of its nature,—the very same law which makes it sometimes deficient in intensity when intensity is required,—it opposes itself to the notion of cutting our being in two, of attributing to one part the dignity of dealing with the one thing needful, and leaving the other part to take its chance, which is the bane of Hebraism. Essential in Hellenism is the impulse to the development of the whole man, to connecting and harmonising all parts of him, perfecting all, leaving none to take their chance.

The characteristic bent of Hellenism, as has been said, is to find the intelligible law of things, to see them in their true nature and as they really are. But many things are not seen in their true nature and as they really are, unless they are seen as beautiful. Behaviour is not intelligible, does not account for itself to the mind and show the reason for its existing, unless it is beautiful. The same with discourse, the same with song, the same with worship, all of them modes in which man proves his activity and expresses himself. To think that when one produces in these what is mean, or vulgar, or hideous, one can be permitted to plead that one has that within which passes show; to suppose that the possession of what benefits and satisfies one part of our being can make allowable either discourse like Mr. Murphy's and the Rev. W. Cattle's, or poetry like the hymns we all hear, or places of worship like the chapels we all see,—this it is abhorrent to the nature of Hellenism to concede. And to be, like our honoured and justly honoured Faraday, a great natural philosopher with one side of his being and a Sandemanian with the other, would to Archimedes have been impossible.

It is evident to what a many-sided perfecting of man's powers and activities this demand of Hellenism for satisfaction to be given to the mind by everything which we do, is calculated to impel our race. It has its dangers, as has been fully granted. The notion of this sort of equipollency in man's modes of activity may lead to moral relaxation; what we do not make our one thing needful, we may come to treat not enough as if it were needful, though it is indeed very needful and at the same time very hard. Still, what side in us has not its dangers, and which of our impulses can be a talisman to give us perfection outright, and not merely a help to bring us towards it? Has not Hebraism, as

we have shown, its dangers as well as Hellenism? or have
we used so excessively the tendencies in ourselves to which
Hellenism makes appeal, that we are now suffering from
it? Are we not, on the contrary, now suffering because we
have not enough used these tendencies as a help towards
perfection?

For we see whither it has brought us, the long exclusive
predominance of Hebraism,—the insisting on perfection in
one part of our nature and not in all; the singling out the
moral side, the side of obedience and action, for such in-
tent regard; making strictness of the moral conscience so
far the principal thing, and putting off for hereafter and for
another world the care for being complete at all points,
the full and harmonious development of our humanity.
Instead of watching and following on its ways the desire
which, as Plato says, "for ever through all the universe
tends towards that which is lovely," we think that the
world has settled its accounts with this desire, knows what
this desire wants of it, and that all the impulses of our
ordinary self which do not conflict with the terms of this
settlement, in our narrow view of it, we may follow un-
restrainedly, under the sanction of some such text as "Not
slothful in business," or, "Whatsoever thy hand findeth to
do, do it with all thy might," or something else of the same
kind. And to any of these impulses we soon come to give
that same character of a mechanical, absolute law, which
we give to our religion; we regard it, as we do our religion, as an object for strictness of conscience, not for
spontaneity of consciousness; for unremitting adherence on
its own account, not for going back upon, viewing in its
connection with other things, and adjusting to a number
of changing circumstances. We treat it, in short, just as we
treat our religion,—as machinery. It is in this way that the
Barbarians treat their bodily exercises, the Philistines their

business, Mr. Spurgeon his voluntaryism, Mr. Bright the assertion of personal liberty, Mr. Beales the right of meeting in Hyde Park. In all those cases what is needed is a freer play of consciousness upon the object of pursuit; and in all of them Hebraism, the valuing staunchness and earnestness more than this free play, the entire subordination of thinking to doing, has led to a mistaken and misleading treatment of things.

The newspapers a short time ago contained an account of the suicide of a Mr. Smith, secretary to some insurance company, who, it was said, "laboured under the apprehension that he would come to poverty, and that he was eternally lost." And when I read these words, it occurred to me that the poor man who came to such a mournful end was, in truth, a kind of type,—by the selection of his two grand objects of concern, by their isolation from everything else, and their juxtaposition to one another,—of all the strongest, most respectable, and most representative part of our nation. "He laboured under the apprehension that he would come to poverty, and that he was eternally lost." The whole middle class have a conception of things,—a conception which makes us call them Philistines,—just like that of this poor man; though we are seldom, of course, shocked by seeing it take the distressing, violently morbid, and fatal turn, which it took with him. But how generally, with how many of us, are the main concerns of life limited to these two: the concern for making money, and the concern for saving our souls! And how entirely does the narrow and mechanical conception of our secular business proceed from a narrow and mechanical conception of our religious business! What havoc do the united conceptions make of our lives! It is because the second-named of these two master-concerns presents to us the one thing needful in so fixed, narrow, and mechanical a way,

that so ignoble a fellow master-concern to it as the
first-named becomes possible; and, having been once
admitted, takes the same rigid and absolute character as
the other.

Poor Mr. Smith had sincerely the nobler master-concern as well as the meaner,—the concern for saving his
soul (according to the narrow and mechanical conception
which Puritanism has of what the salvation of the soul is),
as well as the concern for making money. But let us
remark how many people there are, especially outside the
limits of the serious and conscientious middle class to
which Mr. Smith belonged, who take up with a meaner
master-concern,—whether it be pleasure, or field-sports,
or bodily exercises, or business, or popular agitation,—
who take up with one of these exclusively, and neglect
Mr. Smith's nobler master-concern, because of the mechanical form which Hebraism has given to this noble
master-concern. Hebraism makes it stand, as we have
said, as something talismanic, isolated, and all-sufficient,
justifying our giving our ordinary selves free play in bodily
exercises, or business, or popular agitation, if we have
made our account square with this master-concern; and,
if we have not, rendering other things indifferent, and
our ordinary self all we have to follow, and to follow
with all the energy that is in us, till we do. Whereas the
idea of perfection at all points, the encouraging in ourselves spontaneity of consciousness, the letting a free
play of thought live and flow around all our activity, the
indisposition to allow one side of our activity to stand as so
all-important and all-sufficing that it makes other sides indifferent,—this bent of mind in us may not only check us
in following unreservedly a mean master-concern of any
kind, but may even, also, bring new life and movement
into that side of us with which alone Hebraism concerns

itself, and awaken a healthier and less mechanical activity there. Hellenism may thus actually serve to further the designs of Hebraism.

Undoubtedly it thus served in the first days of Christianity. Christianity, as has been said, occupied itself, like Hebraism, with the moral side of man exclusively, with his moral affections and moral conduct; and so far it was but a continuation of Hebraism. But it transformed and renewed Hebraism by criticising a fixed rule, which had become mechanical, and had thus lost its vital motive-power; by letting the thought play freely around this old rule, and perceive its inadequacy; by developing a new motive-power, which men's moral consciousness could take living hold of, and could move in sympathy with. What was this but an importation of Hellenism, as we have defined it, into Hebraism? St. Paul used the contradiction between the Jew's profession and practice, his short-comings on that very side of moral affection and moral conduct which the Jew and St. Paul, both of them, regarded as all in all ("Thou that sayest a man should not steal, dost thou steal? thou that sayest a man should not commit adultery, dost thou commit adultery?"), for a proof of the inadequacy of the old rule of life in the Jew's mechanical conception of it; and tried to rescue him by making his consciousness play freely around this rule,—that is, by a, so far, Hellenic treatment of it. Even so we too, when we hear so much said of the growth of commercial immorality in our serious middle class, of the melting away of habits of strict probity before the temptation to get quickly rich and to cut a figure in the world; when we see, at any rate, so much confusion of thought and of practice in this great representative class of our nation,—may we not be disposed to say, that this confusion shows that his new motive-power of grace and imputed righteousness has become to the Puritan as mechanical, and with as ineffective a hold upon his practice, as the old motive-power of the law was to the Jew? and that the remedy is the same as that which St. Paul employed,—an importation of what we have called Hellenism into his Hebraism, a making his consciousness flow freely round his petrified rule of life and renew it? Only with this difference: that whereas St. Paul imported Hellenism within the limits of our moral part only, this part being still treated by him as all in all; and whereas he well-nigh exhausted, one may say, and used to the very uttermost, the possibilities of fruitfully importing it on that side exclusively; we ought to try and import it,—guiding ourselves by the ideal of a human nature harmoniously perfect in all points,—into all the lines of our activity. Only by so doing can we rightly quicken, refresh, and renew those very instincts, now so much baffled, to which Hebraism makes appeal.

But if we will not be warned by the confusion visible enough at present in our thinking and acting, that we are in a false line in having developed our Hebrew side so exclusively, and our Hellenic side so feebly and at random, in loving fixed rules of action so much more than the intelligible law of things, let us listen to a remarkable testimony which the opinion of the world around us offers. All the world now sets great and increasing value on three objects which have long been very dear to us, and pursues them in its own way, or tries to pursue them. These three objects are industrial enterprise, bodily exercises, and freedom. Certainly we have, before and beyond our neighbours, given ourselves to these three things with ardent passion and with high success. And this our neighbours cannot but acknowledge; and they must needs, when they themselves turn to these things, have an eye to our example, and take something of our practice.

Now, generally, when people are interested in an object of pursuit, they cannot help feeling an enthusiasm for those who have already laboured successfully at it, and for their success; not only do they study them, they also love and admire them. In this way a man who is interested in the art of war not only acquaints himself with the performance of great generals, but he has an admiration and enthusiasm for them. So, too, one who wants to be a painter or a poet cannot help loving and admiring the great painters or poets, who have gone before him and shown him the way.

But it is strange with how little of love, admiration, or enthusiasm, the world regards us and our freedom, our bodily exercises, and our industrial prowess, much as these things themselves are beginning to interest it. And is not the reason because we follow each of these things in a mechanical manner, as an end in and for itself, and not in reference to a general end of human perfection; and this makes the pursuit of them uninteresting to humanity, and not what the world truly wants? It seems to them mere machinery that we can, knowingly, teach them to worship, —a mere fetish. British freedom, British industry, British muscularity, we work for each of these three things blindly, with no notion of giving each its due proportion and prominence, because we have no ideal of harmonious human perfection before our minds, to set our work in motion, and to guide it. So the rest of the world, desiring industry, or freedom, or bodily strength, yet desiring these not, as we do, absolutely, but as means to something else, imitate, indeed, of our practice what seems useful for them, but us, whose practice they imitate, they seem to entertain neither love nor admiration for.

Let us observe, on the other hand, the love and enthusiasm excited by others who have laboured for these very things. Perhaps of what we call industrial enterprise it is not easy to find examples in former times; but let us consider how Greek freedom and Greek gymnastics have attracted the love and praise of mankind, who give so little love and praise to ours. And what can be the reason of this difference? Surely because the Greeks pursued freedom and pursued gymnastics not mechanically, but with constant reference to some ideal of complete human perfection and happiness. And therefore, in spite of faults and failures they interest and delight by their pursuit of them all the rest of mankind, who instinctively feel that only as things are pursued with reference to this ideal are they valuable.

Here again, therefore, as in the confusion into which the thought and action of even the steadiest class amongst us is beginning to fall, we seem to have an admonition that we have fostered our Hebraising instincts, our preference of earnestness of doing to delicacy and flexibility of thinking, too exclusively, and have been landed by them in a mechanical and unfruitful routine. And again we seem taught that the development of our Hellenising instincts, seeking ardently the intelligible law of things, and making a stream of fresh thought play freely about our stock notions and habits, is what is most wanted by us at present.

Well, then, from all sides, the more we go into the matter, the currents seem to converge, and together to bear us along towards culture. If we look at the world outside us we find a disquieting absence of sure authority. We discover that only in right reason can we get a source of sure authority; and culture brings us towards right reason. If we look at our own inner world, we find all manner of confusion arising out of the habits of unintelligent routine and one-sided growth, to which a too exclusive worship of fire, strength, earnestness, and action, has brought us. What we want is a fuller harmonious development of our humanity, a free play of thought upon our routine notions, spontaneity of consciousness, sweetness and light; and these are just what culture generates and fosters. Proceeding from this idea of the harmonious perfection of our humanity, and seeking to help itself up towards this perfection by knowing and spreading the best which has been reached in the world —an object not to be gained without books and reading— culture has got its name touched, in the fancies of men, with a sort of air of bookishness and pedantry, cast upon it from the follies of the many bookmen who forget the end in the means, and use their books with no real aim at perfection. We will not stickle for a name, and the name of culture one might easily give up, if only those who decry the frivolous and pedantic sort of culture, but wish at bottom for the same things as we do, would be careful on their part, not, in disparaging and discrediting the false culture, to un-wittingly disparage and discredit, among a people with little natural reverence for it, the true also. But what we are concerned for is the thing, not the name; and the thing, call it by what name we will, is simply the enabling ourselves, whether by reading, observing, or thinking, to come as near as we can to the firm intelligible law of things, and thus to get a basis for a less confused action and a more complete perfection than we have at present.

And now, therefore, when we are accused of preaching up a spirit of cultivated inaction, of provoking the earnest lovers of action, of refusing to lend a hand at uprooting certain definite evils, of despairing to find any lasting truth to minister to the diseased spirit of our time, we shall not be so much confounded and embarrassed what to answer for ourselves. We shall say boldly that we do not at all despair of finding some lasting truth to minister to the diseased spirit of our time; but that we have discovered the best way of finding this to be not so much by lending a hand to our friends and countrymen in their actual operations for the removal of certain definite evils, but rather in getting our friends and countrymen to seek culture, to let their consciousness play freely round their present operations and the stock notions on which they are founded, show what these are like, and how related to the intelligible law of things, and auxiliary to true human perfection.

CHAPTER VI

OUR LIBERAL PRACTITIONERS

But an unpretending writer, without a philosophy based on inter-dependent, subordinate, and coherent principles, must not presume to indulge himself too much in generalities. He must keep close to the level ground of common fact, the only safe ground for understandings without a scientific equipment. Therefore, since I have spoken so slightingly of the practical operations in which my friends and countrymen are at this moment engaged for the removal of certain definite evils, I am bound to take, before concluding, some of those operations and to make them, if I can, show the truth of what I have advanced.

Probably I could hardly give a greater proof of my confessed inexpertness in reasoning and arguing, than by taking, for my first example of an operation of this kind, the proceedings for the disestablishment of the Irish Church, which we are now witnessing. It seems so clear that this is surely one of those operations for the uprooting of a certain definite evil in which one's Liberal friends engage, and have a right to complain, and to get impatient, and to reproach one with delicate Conservative scepticism and cultivated inaction, if one does not lend a hand to help them. This does, indeed, seem evident; and yet this operation comes so prominently before us at this moment,—it so challenges everybody's regard,—that one seems cowardly in blinking it. So let us venture to try and see whether this conspicuous operation is one of those round which we need to let our consciousness play freely and reveal what manner of spirit we are of in doing it; or whether it is one which by no means admits the application of this doctrine of ours, and one to which we ought to lend a hand immediately.

I

Now it seems plain that the present Church-establishment in Ireland is contrary to reason and justice, in so far as the Church of a very small minority of the people there takes for itself all the Church-property of the Irish people. And one would think, that property, assigned for the purpose of providing for a people's religious worship when that worship was one, the State should, when that worship is split into several forms, apportion between those several forms. But the apportionment should be made with due regard to circumstances, taking account only of great differences, which are likely to be lasting, and of considerable communions, which are likely to represent profound and widespread religious characteristics. It should overlook petty differences, which have no serious reason for lasting, and inconsiderable communions, which can hardly be taken to express any broad and necessary religious lineaments of our common nature. This is just in accordance with that maxim about the State which we have more than once used: *The State is of the religion of all its citizens without the fanaticism of any of them.* Those who deny this, either think so poorly of the State that they do not like to see religion condescend to touch the State, or they think so poorly of religion that they do not like to see the State condescend to touch religion. But no good statesman will easily think thus unworthily either of the State or of religion.

Our statesmen of both parties were inclined, one may say, to follow the natural line of the State's duty, and to make in Ireland some fair apportionment of Church-property between large and radically divided religious communions in that country. But then it was discovered that in Great Britain the national mind, as it is called, is grown averse to endowments for religion and will make no new ones; and though this in itself looks general and solemn enough, yet there were found political philosophers, like Mr. Baxter and Mr. Charles Buxton, to give it a look of more generality and more solemnity still, and to elevate, by their dexterous command of powerful and beautiful language, this supposed edict of the British national mind into a sort of formula for expressing a great law of religious transition and progress for all the world.

But we, who, having no coherent philosophy, must not let ourselves philosophise, only see that the English and Scotch Nonconformists have a great horror of establishments and endowments for religion, which, they assert, were forbidden by Jesus Christ when he said: "My kingdom is not of this world;" and that the Nonconformists will be delighted to aid statesmen in disestablishing any church, but will suffer none to be established or endowed if they can help it. Then we see that the Nonconformists make the strength of the Liberal majority in the House of Commons; and that, therefore, the leading Liberal statesmen, to get the support of the Nonconformists, forsake the notion of fairly apportioning Church-property in Ireland among the chief religious communions, declare that the national mind has decided against new endowments, and propose simply to disestablish and disendow the present establishment in Ireland without establishing or endowing any other. The actual power, in short, by virtue of which the Liberal party in the House of Commons is now trying to disestablish the Irish Church, is not the power of reason and justice, it is the power of the Nonconformists' antipathy to Church establishments.

Clearly it is this; because Liberal statesmen, relying on

the power of reason and justice to help them, proposed
something quite different from what they now propose;
and they proposed what they now propose, and talked of the
decision of the national mind, because they had to rely on
the English and Scotch Nonconformists. And clearly the
Nonconformists are actuated by antipathy to establishments, not by antipathy to the injustice and irrationality of
the present appropriation of Church-property in Ireland;
because Mr. Spurgeon, in his eloquent and memorable
letter, expressly avowed that he would sooner leave things
as they are in Ireland, that is, he would sooner let the injustice and irrationality of the present appropriation continue, than do anything to set up the Roman image,—that
is, than give the Catholics their fair and reasonable share of
Church-property. Most indisputably, therefore, we may
affirm that the real moving power by which the Liberal
party are now operating the overthrow of the Irish establishment is the antipathy of the Nonconformists to Church-
establishments, and not the sense of reason or justice, except
so far as reason and justice may be contained in this antipathy. And thus the matter stands at present.

Now surely we must all see many inconveniences in
performing the operation of uprooting this evil, the Irish
Church-establishment, in this particular way. As was said
about industry and freedom and gymnastics, we shall never
awaken love and gratitude by this mode of operation; for it
is pursued, not in view of reason and justice and human
perfection and all that enkindles the enthusiasm of men, but
it is pursued in view of a certain stock notion, or fetish, of
the Nonconformists, which proscribes Church-establishments. And yet, evidently, one of the main benefits to be
got by operating on the Irish Church is to win the affections
of the Irish people. Besides this, an operation performed in
virtue of a mechanical rule, or fetish, like the supposed

decision of the English national mind against new endowments, does not easily inspire respect in its adversaries, and make their opposition feeble and hardly to be persisted in, as an operation evidently done in virtue of reason and justice might. For reason and justice have in them something persuasive and irresistible; but a fetish or mechanical maxim, like this of the Nonconformists, has in it nothing at all to conciliate either the affections or the understanding. Nay, it provokes the counter-employment of other fetishes or mechanical maxims on the opposite side, by which the confusion and hostility already prevalent are heightened. Only in this way can be explained the apparition of such fetishes as are beginning to be set up on the Conservative side against the fetish of the Nonconformists:—*The Constitution in danger! The bulwark of British freedom menaced! The lamp of the Reformation put out! No Popery!*—and so on. To elevate these against an operation relying on reason and justice to back it, is not so easy, or so tempting to human infirmity, as to elevate them against an operation relying on the Nonconformists' antipathy to Church-establishments to back it. For after all, *No Popery!* is a rallying cry which touches the human spirit quite as vitally as *No Church-establishments!*—that is to say, neither the one nor the other, in themselves, touch the human spirit vitally at all.

Ought the believers in action, then, to be so impatient with us, if we say, that even for the sake of this operation of theirs itself and its satisfactory accomplishment, it is more important to make our consciousness play freely round the stock notion or habit on which their operation relies for aid, than to lend a hand to it straight away? Clearly they ought not; because nothing is so effectual for operating as reason and justice, and a free play of thought will either disengage the reason and justice lying hid in the Nonconformist fetish, and make them effectual, or else it will help to get this fetish out of the way, and to let statesmen go freely where reason and justice take them.

So, suppose we take this absolute rule, this mechanical maxim of Mr. Spurgeon and the Nonconformists, that Church-establishments are bad things because Jesus Christ said: "My kingdom is not of this world." Suppose we try and make our consciousness bathe and float this piece of petrifaction,—for such it now is,—and bring it within the stream of the vital movement of our thought, and into relation with the whole intelligible law of things. An enemy and a disputant might probably say that much of the machinery which Nonconformists themselves employ,—the Liberation Society which exists already, and the Nonconformist Union which Mr. Spurgeon desires to see existing,— come within the scope of Christ's words as well as Church-establishments. This, however, is merely a negative and contentious way of dealing with the Nonconformist maxim; whereas what we desire is to bring this maxim within the positive and vital movement of our thought. We say, therefore, that Jesus Christ's words mean that his religion is a force of inward persuasion acting on the soul, and not a force of outward constraint acting on the body; and if the Nonconformist maxim against Church-establishments and Church-endowments has warrant given to it from what Christ thus meant, then their maxim is good, even though their own practice in the matter of the Liberation Society may be at variance with it.

And here we cannot but remember what we have formerly said about religion, Miss Cobbe, and the British College of Health in the New Road. In religion there are two parts, the part of thought and speculation, and the part of worship and devotion. Jesus Christ certainly meant his religion, as a force of inward persuasion acting on the soul, to employ both parts as perfectly as possible. Now thought and speculation is eminently an individual matter, and worship and devotion is eminently a collective matter. It does not help me to think a thing more clearly that thousands of other people are thinking the same; but it does help me to worship with more emotion that thousands of other people are worshipping with me. The consecration of common consent, antiquity, public establishment, long-used rites, national edifices, is everything for religious worship. "Just what makes worship impressive," says Joubert, "is its publicity, its external manifestation, its sound, its splendour, its observance universally and visibly holding its sway through all the details both of our outward and of our inward life." Worship, therefore, should have in it as little as possible of what divides us, and should be as much as possible a common and public act; as Joubert says again: "The best prayers are those which have nothing distinct about them, and which are thus of the nature of simple adoration." For, "the same devotion," as he says in another place, "unites men far more than the same thought and knowledge." Thought and knowledge, as we have said before, is eminently something individual, and of our own; the more we possess it as strictly of our own, the more power it has on us. Man worships best, therefore, with the community; he philosophises best alone.

So it seems that whoever would truly give effect to Jesus Christ's declaration that his religion is a force of inward persuasion acting on the soul, would leave our thought on the intellectual aspects of Christianity as individual as possible, but would make Christian worship as collective as possible. Worship, then, appears to be eminently a matter for public and national establishment; for even Mr. Bright, who, when he stands in Mr. Spurgeon's great Tabernacle, is so ravished with admiration, will hardly say that the great Tabernacle and its worship are in themselves, as a temple and service of religion, so impressive and affecting as the public and national Westminster Abbey, or Notre Dame, with their worship. And when, immediately after the great Tabernacle, one comes plump down to the mass of private and individual establishments of religious worship, establishments falling, like the British College of Health in the New Road, conspicuously short of what a public and national establishment might be, then one cannot but feel that Jesus Christ's command to make his religion a force of persuasion to the soul, is, so far as one main source of persuasion is concerned, altogether set at nought.

But perhaps the Nonconformists worship so unimpressively because they philosophise so keenly; and one part of religion, the part of public national worship, they have subordinated to the other part, the part of individual thought and knowledge. This, however, their organisation in congregations forbids us to admit. They are members of congregations, not isolated thinkers; and a free play of individual thought is at least as much impeded by membership of a small congregation as by membership of a great Church. Thinking by batches of fifties is to the full as fatal to free thought as thinking by batches of thousands. Accordingly, we have had occasion already to notice that Nonconformity does not at all differ from the Established Church by having worthier or more philosophical ideas about God, and the ordering of the world, than the Established Church has. It has very much the same ideas about these as the Established Church has, but it differs from the Established Church in that its worship is a much less collective and national affair.

So Mr. Spurgeon and the Nonconformists seem to have misapprehended the true meaning of Christ's words, *My kingdom is not of this world.* Because, by these words, Christ meant that his religion was to work on the soul. And of the two parts of the soul on which religion works,—the thinking and speculative part, and the feeling and imaginative part,—Nonconformity satisfies the first no better than the Established Churches, which Christ by these words is supposed to have condemned, satisfy it; and the second part it satisfies even worse than the Established Churches. And thus the balance of advantage seems to rest with the Established Churches; and they seem to have apprehended and applied Christ's words, if not with perfect adequacy, at least, less inadequately than the Nonconformists.

Might it not, then, be urged with great force that the way to do good, in presence of this operation for uprooting the Church-establishment in Ireland by the power of the Nonconformists' antipathy to publicly establishing or endowing religious worship, is not by lending a hand straight away to the operation, and Hebraising,—that is, in this case, taking an uncritical interpretation of certain Bible words as our absolute rule of conduct,—with the Nonconformists! It may be very well for born Hebraisers, like Mr. Spurgeon, to Hebraise; but for Liberal statesmen to Hebraise is surely unsafe, and to see poor old Liberal hacks Hebraising, whose real self belongs to a kind of negative Hellenism,—a state of moral indifferency without intellectual ardour,—is even painful. And when, by our Hebraising, we neither do what the better mind of statesmen prompted them to do, nor win the affections of the people we want to conciliate, nor yet reduce the opposition of our adversaries but rather heighten it, surely it may not be unreasonable to Hellenise a little, to let our thought and consciousness play freely about our proposed operation and its motives, dissolve these motives if they are unsound,— which certainly they have some appearance, at any rate, of being,—and create in their stead, if they are, a set of sounder and more persuasive motives conducting to a more solid

operation. May not the man who promotes this be giving
the best help towards finding some lasting truth to minister
to the diseased spirit of his time, and does he really deserve
that the believers in action should grow impatient with
him?

II

But now to take another operation which does not at
this moment so excite people's feelings as the disestablishment of the Irish Church, but which, I suppose, would
also be called exactly one of those operations of simple,
practical, common-sense reform, aiming at the removal of
some particular abuse, and rigidly restricted to that object,
to which a Liberal ought to lend a hand, and deserves that
other Liberals should grow impatient with him if he does
not. This operation I had the great advantage of, with my
own ears, hearing discussed in the House of Commons, and
recommended by a powerful speech from that famous
speaker, Mr. Bright. So that the effeminate horror which,
it is alleged, I have of practical reforms of this kind, was put
to a searching test; and if it survived, it must have, one
would think, some reason or other to support it, and can
hardly quite merit the stigma of its present name.

The operation I mean was that which the Real Estate
Intestacy Bill aimed at accomplishing, and the discussion on
this bill I heard in the House of Commons. The bill
proposed, as every one knows, to prevent the land of a man
who dies intestate from going, as it goes now, to his eldest
son, and was thought, by its friends and by its enemies, to be
a step towards abating the now almost exclusive possession
of the land of this country by the people whom we call the
Barbarians. Mr. Bright, and other speakers on his side,
seemed to hold that there is a kind of natural law or fitness
of things which assigns to all a man's children a right to

equal shares in the enjoyment of his property after his death; and that if, without depriving a man of an Englishman's prime privilege of doing what he likes by making what will he chooses, you provide that when he makes none his land shall be divided among his family, then you give the sanction of the law to the natural fitness of things, and inflict a sort of check on the present violation of this by the Barbarians.

It occurred to me, when I saw Mr. Bright and his friends proceeding in this way, to ask myself a question. If the almost exclusive possession of the land of this country by the Barbarians is a bad thing, is this practical operation of the Liberals, and the stock notion, on which it seems to rest, about the natural right of children to share equally in the enjoyment of their father's property after his death, the best and most effective means of dealing with it? Or is it best dealt with by letting one's thought and consciousness play freely and naturally upon the Barbarians, this Liberal operation, and the stock notion at the bottom of it, and trying to get as near as we can to the intelligible law of things as to each of them?

Now does any one, if he simply and naturally reads his consciousness, discover that he has any rights at all? For my part, the deeper I go in my own consciousness, and the more simply I abandon myself to it, the more it seems to tell me that I have no rights at all, only duties; and that men get this notion of rights from a process of abstract reasoning, inferring that the obligations they are conscious of towards others, others must be conscious of towards them, and not from any direct witness of consciousness at all. But it is obvious that the notion of a right, arrived at in this way, is likely to stand as a formal and petrified thing, deceiving and misleading us; and that the notions got directly from our consciousness ought to be brought to bear upon it, and to control it. So it is unsafe and misleading to say that our children have rights against us; what is true and safe to say is, that we have duties towards our children. But who will find among these natural duties, set forth to us by our consciousness, the obligation to leave to all our children an equal share in the enjoyment of our property? Or, though consciousness tells us we ought to provide for our children's welfare, whose consciousness tells him that the enjoyment of property is in itself welfare? Whether our children's welfare is best served by their all sharing equally in our property, depends on circumstances and on the state of the community in which we live. With this equal sharing, society could not, for example, have organised itself afresh out of the chaos left by the fall of the Roman Empire; and to have an organised society to live in is more for a child's welfare than to have an equal share of his father's property.

So we see how little convincing force the stock notion on which the Real Estate Intestacy Bill was based,—the notion that in the nature and fitness of things all a man's children have a right to an equal share in the enjoyment of what he leaves,—really has; and how powerless, therefore, it must of necessity be to persuade and win any one who has habits and interests which disincline him to it. On the other hand, the practical operation proposed relies entirely, if it is to be effectual in altering the present practice of the Barbarians, on the power of truth and persuasiveness in the notion which it seeks to consecrate; for it leaves to the Barbarians full liberty to continue their present practice, to which all their habits and interests incline them, unless the promulgation of a notion, which we have seen to have no vital efficacy and hold upon our consciousness, shall hinder them.

Are we really to adorn an operation of this kind, merely

because it proposes to *do* something, with all the favourable epithets of simple, practical, common-sense, definite; to enlist on its side all the zeal of the believers in action, and to call indifference to it an effeminate horror of useful reforms? It seems to me quite easy to show that a free disinterested play of thought on the Barbarians and their land-holding is a thousand times more really practical, a thousand times more likely to lead to some effective result, than an operation such as that of which we have been now speaking. For if, casting aside the impediments of stock notions and mechanical action, we try to find the intelligible law of things respecting a great land-owning class such as we have in this country, does not our consciousness readily tell us that whether the perpetuation of such a class is for its own real good and for the real good of the community, depends on the actual circumstances of this class and of the community? Does it not readily tell us that wealth, power, and consideration are,—and above all when inherited and not earned,—in themselves trying and dangerous things? as Bishop Wilson excellently says: "Riches are almost always abused without a very extraordinary grace." But this extraordinary grace was in great measure supplied by the circumstances of the feudal epoch, out of which our land-holding class, with its rules of inheritance, sprang. The labour and contentions of a rude, nascent, and struggling society supplied it. These perpetually were trying, chastising, and forming the class whose predominance was then needed by society to give it points of cohesion, and was not so harmful to themselves because they were thus sharply tried and exercised. But in a luxurious, settled, and easy society, where wealth offers the means of enjoyment a thousand times more, and the temptation to abuse them is thus made a thousand times greater, the exercising discipline is at the same time taken away, and the feudal class is left exposed to the full operation of the natural law well put by the French moralist: *Pouvoir sans savior est fort dangereux.* And, for my part, when I regard the young people of this class, it is above all by the trial and shipwreck made of their own welfare by the circumstances in which they live that I am struck. How far better it would have been for nine out of every ten among them, if they had had their own way to make in the world, and not been tried by a condition for which they had not the extraordinary grace requisite!

This, I say, seems to be what a man's consciousness, simply consulted, would tell him about the actual welfare of our Barbarians themselves. Then, as to the effect upon the welfare of the community, how can that be salutary, if a class which, by the very possession of wealth, power and consideration, becomes a kind of ideal or standard for the rest of the community, is tried by ease and pleasure more than it can well bear, and almost irresistibly carried away from excellence and strenuous virtue? This must certainly be what Solomon meant when he said: "As he who putteth a stone in a sling, so is he that giveth honour to a fool."

For any one can perceive how this honouring of a false ideal, not of intelligence and strenuous virtue, but of wealth and station, pleasure and ease, is as a stone from a sling to kill in our great middle class, in us who are called Philistines, the desire before spoken of, which by nature for ever carries all men towards that which is lovely; and to leave instead of it only a blind deteriorating pursuit, for ourselves also, of the false ideal. And in those among us Philistines whom the desire does not wholly abandon, yet, having no excellent ideal set forth to nourish and to steady it, it meets with that natural bent for the bathos which together with this desire itself is implanted at birth in the breast of man, and is by that force twisted awry, and borne at random hither and thither, and at last flung upon those grotesque and hideous forms of popular religion which the more respectable part among us Philistines mistake for the true goal of man's desire after all that is lovely. And for the Populace this false ideal is a stone which kills the desire before it can even arise; so impossible and unattainable for them do the conditions of that which is lovely appear according to this ideal to be made, so necessary to the reaching of them by the few seems the falling short of them by the many. So that, perhaps, of the actual vulgarity of our Philistines and brutality of our Populace, the Barbarians and their feudal habits of succession, enduring out of their due time and place, are involuntarily the cause in a great degree; and they hurt the welfare of the rest of the community at the same time that, as we have seen, they hurt their own.

But must not, now, the working in our minds of considerations like these, to which culture, that is, the disinterested and active use of reading, reflection, and observation, in the endeavour to know the best that can be known, carries us, be really much more effectual to the dissolution of feudal habits and rules of succession in land than an operation like the Real Estate Intestacy Bill, and a stock notion like that of the natural right of all a man's children to an equal share in the enjoyment of his property; since we have seen that this mechanical maxim is unsound, and that, if it is unsound, the operation relying upon it cannot possibly be effective? If truth and reason have, as we believe, any natural irresistible effect on the mind of man, it must. These considerations, when culture has called them forth and given them free course in our minds, will live and work. They will work gradually, no doubt, and will not bring us ourselves to the front to sit in high place and put them into effect; but so they will be all the more beneficial. Everything teaches us how gradually nature would have all profound changes brought about; and we can even see, too, where the absolute abrupt stoppage of feudal habits has worked harm. And appealing to the sense of truth and reason, these considerations will, without doubt, touch and move all those of even the Barbarians themselves, who are (as are some of us Philistines also, and some of the Populace) beyond their fellows quick of feeling for truth and reason. For indeed this is just one of the advantages of sweetness and light over fire and strength, that sweetness and light make a feudal class quietly and gradually drop its feudal habits because it sees them at variance with truth and reason, while fire and strength are for tearing them passionately off, because this class applauded Mr. Lowe when he called, or was supposed to call, the working class drunken and venal.

III

But when once we have begun to recount the practical operations by which our Liberal friends work for the removal of definite evils, and in which if we do not join them they are apt to grow impatient with us, how can we pass over that very interesting operation,—the attempt to enable a man to marry his deceased wife's sister? This operation, too, like that for abating the feudal customs of succession in land, I have had the advantage of myself seeing and hearing my Liberal friends labour at.

I was lucky enough to be present when Mr. Chambers brought forward in the House of Commons his bill for enabling a man to marry his deceased wife's sister, and I heard the speech which Mr. Chambers then made in support of his bill. His first point was that God's law,—the name he always gave to the Book of Leviticus,—did not really forbid a man to marry his deceased wife's sister. God's law not forbidding it, the Liberal maxim, that a man's prime right and happiness is to do as he likes, ought at once to come into force, and to annul any such check upon the assertion of personal liberty as the prohibition to marry one's deceased wife's sister. A distinguished Liberal supporter of Mr. Chambers, in the debate which followed the introduction of the bill, produced a formula of much beauty and neatness for conveying in brief the Liberal notions on this head: "Liberty," said he, "is the law of human life." And, therefore, the moment it is ascertained that God's law, the Book of Leviticus, does not stop the way, man's law, the law of liberty, asserts its right, and makes us free to marry our deceased wife's sister.

And this exactly falls in with what Mr. Hepworth Dixon, who may almost be called the Colenso of love and marriage—such a revolution does he make in our ideas on these matters, just as Dr. Colenso does in our ideas on religion,—tells us of the notions and proceedings of our kinsmen in America. With that affinity of genius to the Hebrew genius which we have already noticed, and with the strong belief of our race that liberty is the law of human life, so far as that fixed, perfect, and paramount rule of conscience, the Bible, does not expressly control it, our American kinsmen go again, Mr. Hepworth Dixon tells us, to their Bible, the Mormons to the patriarchs and the Old Testament, Brother Noyes to St. Paul and the New, and having never before read anything else but their Bible, they now read their Bible over again, and make all manner of great discoveries there. All these discoveries are favourable to liberty, and in this way is satisfied that double craving so characteristic of our Philistine, and so eminently exemplified in that crowned Philistine, Henry the Eighth,—the craving for forbidden fruit and the craving for legality.

Mr. Hepworth Dixon's eloquent writings give currency, over here, to these important discoveries; so that now, as

regards love and marriage, we seem to be entering, with all
our sails spread, upon what Mr. Hepworth Dixon, its apostle
and evangelist, calls a Gothic Revival, but what one of the
many newspapers that so greatly admire Mr. Hepworth
Dixon's lithe and sinewy style and form their own style
upon it, calls, by a yet bolder and more striking figure,
"a great sexual insurrection of our Anglo-Teutonic race."
For this end we have to avert our eyes from everything
Hellenic and faniciful, and to keep them steadily fixed
upon the two cardinal points of the Bible and liberty. And
one of those practical operations in which the Liberal party
engage, and in which we are summoned to join them,
directs itself entirely, as we have seen, to these cardinal
points, and may almost be regarded, perhaps, as a kind of
first instalment, or public and parliamentary pledge, of the
great sexual insurrection of our Anglo-Teutonic race.

But here, as elsewhere, what we seek is the Philistine's
perfection, the development of his best self, not mere liberty
for his ordinary self. And we no more allow absolute
validity to his stock maxim, *Liberty is the law of human life*,
than we allow it to the opposite maxim, which is just as
true, *Renouncement is the law of human life*. For we know
that the only perfect freedom is, as our religion says, a
service; not a service to any stock maxim, but an elevation
of our best self, and a harmonising in subordination to this,
and to the idea of a perfected humanity, all the multitudinous, turbulent, and blind impulses of our ordinary selves.
Now, the Philistine's great defect being a defect in delicacy
of perception, to cultivate in him this delicacy, to render it
independent of external and mechanical rule, and a law to
itself, is what seems to make most for his perfection, his
true humanity. And his true humanity, and therefore his
happiness, appears to lie much more, so far as the relations
of love and marriage are concerned, in becoming alive to

the finer shades of feeling which arise within these relations, in being able to enter with tact and sympathy into the subtle instinctive propensions and repugnances of the person with whose life his own life is bound up, to make them his own, to direct and govern in harmony with them the arbitrary range of his personal action, and thus to enlarge his spiritual and intellectual life and liberty, than in remaining insensible to these finer shades of feeling and this delicate sympathy, in giving unchecked range, so far as he can, to his mere personal action, in allowing no limits or government to this except such as a mechanical external law imposes, and in thus really narrowing, for the satisfaction of his ordinary self, his spiritual and intellectual life and liberty.

Still more must this be so, when his fixed eternal rule, his God's law, is supplied to him from a source which is less fit, perhaps, to supply final and absolute instructions on this particular topic of love and marriage than on any other relation of human life. Bishop Wilson, who is full of examples of that fruitful Hellenising within the limits of Hebraism itself, of that renewing of the stiff and stark notions of Hebraism by turning upon them a stream of fresh thought and consciousness, which we have already noticed in St. Paul,—Bishop Wilson gives an admirable lesson to rigid Hebraisers, like Mr. Chambers, asking themselves: Does God's law (that is, the Book of Leviticus) forbid us to marry our wife's sister?—Does God's law (that is, again, the Book of Leviticus) allow us to marry our wife's sister?— when he says: "Christian duties are founded on reason, not on the sovereign authority of God commanding what he pleases; God cannot command us what is not fit to be believed or done, all his commands being founded in the necessities of our nature." And, immense as is our debt to the Hebrew race and its genius, incomparable as is its

authority on certain profoundly important sides of our
human nature, worthy as it is to be described as having
uttered, for those sides, the voice of the deepest necessities of
our nature, the statutes of the divine and eternal order of
things, the law of God,—who, that is not manacled and
hoodwinked by his Hebraism, can believe that, as to love
and marriage, our reason and the necessities of our humanity
have their true, sufficient, and divine law expressed for
them by the voice of any Oriental and polygamous nation
like the Hebrews? Who, I say, will believe, when he really
considers the matter, that where the feminine nature, the
feminine ideal, and our relations to them, are brought into
question, the delicate and apprehensive genius of the Indo-
European race, the race which invented the Muses, and
chivalry, and the Madonna, is to find its last word on this
question in the institutions of a Semitic people, whose
wisest king had seven hundred wives and three hundred
concubines?

IV

If here again, therefore, we seem to minister better to
the diseased spirit of our time by leading it to think about
the operation our Liberal friends have in hand, than by
lending a hand to this operation ourselves, let us see, before
we dismiss from our view the practical operations of our
Liberal friends, whether the same thing does not hold good
as to their celebrated industrial and economical labours also.
Their great work of this kind is, of course, their free-trade
policy. This policy, as having enabled the poor man to eat
untaxed bread, and as having wonderfully augmented trade,
we are accustomed to speak of with a kind of thankful
solemnity. It is chiefly on their having been our leaders
in this policy that Mr. Bright founds for himself and his
friends the claim, so often asserted by him, to be considered

guides of the blind, teachers of the ignorant, benefactors slowly and laboriously developing in the Conservative party and in the country that which Mr. Bright is fond of calling *the growth of intelligence*,—the object, as is well known, of all the friends of culture also, and the great end and aim of the culture that we preach.

Now, having first saluted free-trade and its doctors with all respect, let us see whether even here, too, our Liberal friends do not pursue their operations in a mechanical way, without reference to any firm intelligible law of things, to human life as a whole, and human happiness; and whether it is not more for our good, at this particular moment at any rate, if, instead of worshipping free-trade with them Hebraistically, as a kind of fetish, and helping them to pursue it as an end in and for itself, we turn the free stream of our thought upon their treatment of it, and see how this is related to the intelligible law of human life, and to national well-being and happiness. In short, suppose we Hellenise a little with free-trade, as we Hellenised with the Real Estate Intestacy Bill, and with the disestablishment of the Irish Church by the power of the Nonconformists' antipathy to religious establishments and endowments, and see whether what our reprovers beautifully call ministering to the diseased spirit of our time is best done by the Hellenising method of proceeding, or by the other.

But first let us understand how the policy of free-trade really shapes itself for our Liberal friends, and how they practically employ it as an instrument of national happiness and salvation. For as we said that it seemed clearly right to prevent the Church-property of Ireland from being all taken for the benefit of the Church of a small minority, so it seems clearly right that the poor man should eat untaxed bread, and, generally, that restrictions and regulations which, for the supposed benefit of some particular

8   W A

person or class of persons, make the price of things artificially high here, or artificially low there, and interfere with the natural flow of trade and commerce, should be done away with. But in the policy of our Liberal friends free-trade means more than this, and is specially valued as a stimulant to the production of wealth, as they call it, and to the increase of the trade, business, and population of the country. We have already seen how these things,—trade, business, and population,—are mechanically pursued by us as ends precious in themselves, and are worshipped as what we call fetishes; and Mr. Bright, I have already said, when he wishes to give the working class a true sense of what makes glory and greatness, tells it to look at the cities it has built, the railroads it has made, the manufactures it has produced. So to this idea of glory and greatness the free-trade which our Liberal friends extol so solemnly and devoutly has served,—to the increase of trade, business, and population; and for this it is prized. Therefore, the untaxing of the poor man's bread has, with this view of national happiness, been used not so much to make the existing poor man's bread cheaper or more abundant, but rather to create more poor men to eat it; so that we cannot precisely say that we have fewer poor men than we had before free-trade, but we can say with truth that we have many more centres of industry, as they are called, and much more business, population, and manufactures. And if we are sometimes a little troubled by our multitude of poor men, yet we know the increase of manufactures and population to be such a salutary thing in itself, and our free-trade policy begets such an admirable movement, creating fresh centres of industry and fresh poor men here, while we were thinking about our poor men there, that we are quite dazzled and borne away, and more and more industrial movement is called for, and our social progress seems to become one triumphant and enjoyable course of what is sometimes called, vulgarly, outrunning the constable.

If, however, taking some other criterion of man's well-being than the cities he has built and the manufactures he has produced, we persist in thinking that our social progress would be happier if there were not so many of us so very poor, and in busying ourselves with notions of in some way or other adjusting the poor man and business one to the other, and not multiplying the one and the other mechanically and blindly, then our Liberal friends, the appointed doctors of free-trade, take us up very sharply. "Art is long," says the *Times*, "and life is short; for the most part we settle things first and understand them afterwards. Let us have as few theories as possible; what is wanted is not the light of speculation. If nothing worked well of which the theory was not perfectly understood, we should be in sad confusion. The relations of labour and capital, we are told, are not understood, yet trade and commerce, on the whole, work satisfactorily." I quote from the *Times* of only the other day. But thoughts like these, as I have often pointed out, are thoroughly British thoughts, and we have been familiar with them for years.

Or, if we want more of a philosophy of the matter than this, our free-trade friends have two axioms for us, axioms laid down by their justly esteemed doctors, which they think ought to satisfy us entirely. One is, that, other things being equal, the more population increases, the more does production increase to keep pace with it; because men by their numbers and contact call forth all manner of activities and resources in one another and in nature, which, when men are few and sparse, are never developed. The other is, that, although population always tends to equal the means of subsistence, yet people's notions of what subsistence is enlarge as civilisation advances, and take in a number of

things beyond the bare necessaries of life; and thus, therefore, is supplied whatever check on population is needed.
But the error of our friends is, perhaps, that they apply
axioms of this sort as if they were self-acting laws which will
put themselves into operation without trouble or planning
on our part, if we will only pursue free-trade, business,
and population zealously and staunchly. Whereas the real
truth is, that, however the case might be under other
circumstances, yet in fact, as we now manage the matter,
the enlarged conception of what is included in *subsistence*
does not operate to prevent the bringing into the world of
numbers of people who but just attain to the barest necessaries of life or who even fail to attain to them; while,
again, though production may increase as population
increases, yet it seems that the production may be of such a
kind, and so related, or rather non-related, to population,
that the population may be little the better for it.

For instance, with the increase of population since
Queen Elizabeth's time the production of silk-stockings
has wonderfully increased, and silk-stockings have become
much cheaper, and procurable in greater abundance by
many more people, and tend perhaps, as population and
manufactures increase, to get cheaper and cheaper, and at
last to become, according to Bastiat's favourite image, a
common free property of the human race, like light and air.
But bread and bacon have not become much cheaper with
the increase of population since Queen Elizabeth's time,
nor procurable in much greater abundance by many more
people; neither do they seem at all to promise to become,
like light and air, a common free property of the human
race. And if bread and bacon have not kept pace with our
population, and we have many more people in want of them
now than in Queen Elizabeth's time, it seems vain to tell us
that silk-stockings have kept pace with our population, or

even more than kept pace with it, and that we are to get our comfort out of that.

In short, it turns out that our pursuit of free-trade, as of so many other things, has been too mechanical. We fix upon some object, which in this case is the production of wealth, and the increase of manufactures, population, and commerce through free-trade, as a kind of one thing needful or end in itself; and then we pursue it staunchly and mechanically, and say that it is our duty to pursue it staunchly and mechanically, not to see how it is related to the whole intelligible law of things and to full human perfection, or to treat it as the piece of machinery, of varying value as its relations to the intelligible law of things vary, which it really is.

So it is of no use to say to the *Times*, and to our Liberal friends rejoicing in the possession of their talisman of free-trade, that about one in nineteen of our population is a pauper, and that, this being so, trade and commerce can hardly be said to prove by their satisfactory working that it matters nothing whether the relations between labour and capital are understood or not; nay, that we can hardly be said not to be in sad confusion. For here our faith in the staunch mechanical pursuit of a fixed object comes in, and covers itself with that imposing and colossal necessitarianism of the *Times* which we have before noticed. And this necessitarianism, taking for granted that an increase in trade and population is a good in itself, one of the chiefest of goods, tells us that disturbances of human happiness caused by ebbs and flows in the tide of trade and business, which, on the whole, steadily mounts, are inevitable and not to be quarrelled with. This firm philosophy I seek to call to mind when I am in the East of London, whither my avocations often lead me; and, indeed, to fortify myself against the depressing sights which on these occasions assail us, I have transcribed from the *Times* one strain of this kind, full of the finest economical doctrine, and always carry it about with me. The passage is this:—

"The East End is the most commercial, the most industrial, the most fluctuating region of the metropolis. It is always the first to suffer; for it is the creature of prosperity, and falls to the ground the instant there is no wind to bear it up. The whole of that region is covered with huge docks, shipyards, manufactories, and a wilderness of small houses, all full of life and happiness in brisk times, but in dull times withered and lifeless, like the deserts we read of in the East. Now their brief spring is over. There is no one to blame for this; it is the result of Nature's simplest laws!" We must all agree that it is impossible that anything can be firmer than this, or show a surer faith in the working of free-trade, as our Liberal friends understand and employ it.

But, if we still at all doubt whether the indefinite multiplication of manufactories and small houses can be such an absolute good in itself as to counterbalance the indefinite multiplication of poor people, we shall learn that this multiplication of poor people, too, is an absolute good in itself, and the result of divine and beautiful laws. This is indeed a favourite thesis with our Philistine friends, and I have already noticed the pride and gratitude with which they receive certain articles in the *Times*, dilating in thankful and solemn language on the majestic growth of our population. But I prefer to quote now, on this topic, the words of an ingenious young Scotch writer, Mr. Robert Buchanan, because he invests with so much imagination and poetry this current idea of the blessed and even divine character which the multiplying of population is supposed in itself to have. "We move to multiplicity," says Mr. Robert Buchanan. "If there is one quality which seems God's, and his exclusively, it seems that divine philoprogenitiveness, that passionate love of distribution and expansion into living forms. Every animal added seems a new ecstasy to the Maker; every life added, a new embodiment of his love. He would *swarm* the earth with beings. There are never enough. Life, life, life,—faces gleaming, hearts beating, must fill every cranny. Not a corner is suffered to remain empty. The whole earth breeds, and God glories."

It is a little unjust, perhaps, to attribute to the Divinity exclusively this philoprogenitiveness, which the British Philistine, and the poorer class of Irish, may certainly claim to share with him; yet how inspiriting is here the whole strain of thought! and these beautiful words, too, I carry about with me in the East of London, and often read them there. They are quite in agreement with the popular language one is accustomed to hear about children and large families, which describes children as *sent*. And a line of poetry, which Mr. Robert Buchanan throws in presently after the poetical prose I have quoted,—

'Tis the old story of the fig-leaf time—

this fine line, too, naturally connects itself, when one is in the East of London, with the idea of God's desire to *swarm* the earth with beings; because the swarming of the earth with beings does indeed, in the East of London, so seem to revive *the old story of the fig-leaf time*, such a number of the people one meets there having hardly a rag to cover them; and the more the swarming goes on, the more it promises to revive this old story. And when the story is perfectly revived, the swarming quite completed, and every cranny choke full, then, too, no doubt, the faces in the East of London will be gleaming faces, which Mr. Robert Buchanan says it is God's desire they should be, and which every one must perceive they are not at present, but, on the contrary, very miserable.

But to prevent all this philosophy and poetry from quite running away with us, and making us think with the *Times*, and our practical Liberal free-traders, and the British Philistines generally, that the increase of houses and manufactories, or the increase of population, are absolute goods in themselves, to be mechanically pursued, and to be worshipped like fetishes,—to prevent this, we have got that notion of ours immovably fixed, of which I have long ago spoken, the notion that culture, or the study of perfection, leads us to conceive of no perfection as being real which is not a *general* perfection, embracing all our fellow-men with whom we have to do. Such is the sympathy which binds humanity together, that we are indeed, as our religion says, members of one body, and if one member suffer, all the members suffer with it. Individual perfection is impossible so long as the rest of mankind are not perfected along with us. "The *multitude* of the wise is the welfare of the world," says the Wise Man. And to this effect that excellent and often quoted guide of ours, Bishop Wilson, has some striking words:—"It is not," says he, "so much our neighbour's interest as our own that we love him." And again he says: "Our salvation does in some measure depend upon that of others." And the author of the *Imitation* puts the same thing admirably when he says:—"*Obscurior etiam via ad cœlum videbatur quando tam pauci regnum cœlorum quærere curabant;* the fewer there are who follow the way to perfection, the harder that way is to find." So all our fellow-men, in the East of London and elsewhere, we must take along with us in the progress towards perfection, if we ourselves really, as we profess, want to be perfect; and we must not let the worship of any fetish, any machinery, such as manufactures or population,—which are not, like perfection, absolute goods in themselves, though we think them so,—create for us such a multitude of miserable, sunken, and ignorant human beings, that to carry them all along with us is impossible, and perforce they must for the most part be left by us in their degradation and wretchedness. But evidently the conception of free-trade, on which our Liberal friends vaunt themselves, and in which they think they have found the secret of national prosperity,—evidently, I say, the mere unfettered pursuit of the production of wealth, and the mere mechanical multiplying, for this end, of manufactures and population, threatens to create for us, if it has not created already, those vast, miserable, unmanageable masses of sunken people,—one pauper at the present moment, for every nineteen of us,—to the existence of which we are, as we have seen, absolutely forbidden to reconcile ourselves, in spite of all that the philosophy of the *Times* and the poetry of Mr. Robert Buchanan may say to persuade us.

And though Hebraism, following its best and highest instinct,—identical, as we have seen, with that of Hellenism in its final aim, the aim of perfection,—teaches us this very clearly; and though from Hebraising counsellors,— the Bible, Bishop Wilson, the author of the *Imitation*,—I have preferred (as well I may, for from this rock of Hebraism we are all hewn!) to draw the texts which we use to bring home to our minds this teaching; yet Hebraism in general seems powerless, almost as powerless as our free-trading Liberal friends, to deal efficaciously with our ever-accumulating masses of pauperism, and to prevent their accumulating still more. Hebraism builds churches, indeed, for these masses, and sends missionaries among them; above all, it sets itself against the social necessitarianism of the *Times*, and refuses to accept their degradation as inevitable.

But with regard to their ever-increasing accumulation, it seems to be led to the very same conclusions, though from a point of view of its own, as our free-trading Liberal friends. Hebraism, with that mechanical and misleading use of the letter of Scripture on which we have already commented, is governed by such texts as: *Be fruitful and multiply*, the edict of God's law, as Mr. Chambers would say; or by the declaration of what he would call God's word in the Psalms, that the man who has a great number of children is thereby made happy. And in conjunction with such texts as these, Hebraism is apt to place another text: *The poor shall never cease out of the land.* Thus Hebraism is conducted to nearly the same notion as the popular mind and as Mr. Robert Buchanan, that children are *sent*, and that the divine nature takes a delight in swarming the East End of London with paupers. Only, when they are perishing in their helplessness and wretchedness, it asserts the Christian duty of succouring them, instead of saying, like the *Times*: "Now their brief spring is over; there is nobody to blame for this; it is the result of Nature's simplest laws!" But, like the *Times*, Hebraism despairs of any help from knowledge and says that "what is wanted is not the light of speculation."

I remember, only the other day, a good man looking with me upon a multitude of children who were gathered before us in one of the most miserable regions of London,—children eaten up with disease, half-sized, half-fed, half-clothed, neglected by their parents, without health, without home, without hope,—said to me: "The one thing really needful is to teach these little ones to succour one another, if only with a cup of cold water; but now, from one end of the country to the other, one hears nothing but the cry for knowledge, knowledge, knowledge!" And yet surely, so long as these children are there in these festering masses, without health, without home, without hope, and so long as their multitude is perpetually swelling, charged with misery they must still be for themselves, charged with misery they must still be for us, whether they help one another with a cup of cold water or no; and the knowledge how to prevent their accumulating is necessary, even to give their moral life and growth a fair chance!

May we not, therefore, say, that neither the true Hebraism of this good man, willing to spend and be spent for these sunken multitudes, nor what I may call the spurious Hebraism of our free-trading Liberal friends,—mechanically worshipping their fetish of the production of wealth and of the increase of manufactures and population, and looking neither to the right nor left so long as this increase goes on,—avail us much here; and that here, again, what we want is Hellenism, the letting our consciousness play freely and simply upon the facts before us, and listening to what it tells us of the intelligible law of things as concerns them? And surely what it tells us is, that a man's children are not really *sent*, any more than the pictures upon his wall, or the horses in his stable are *sent;* and that to bring people into the world, when one cannot afford to keep them and oneself decently and not too precariously, or to bring more of them into the world than one can afford to keep thus, is, whatever the *Times* and Mr. Robert Buchanan may say, by no means an accomplishment of the divine will or a fulfilment of Nature's simplest laws, but is just as wrong, just as contrary to reason and the will of God, as for a man to have horses, or carriages, or pictures, when he cannot afford them, or to have more of them than he can afford; and that, in the one case as in the other, the larger the scale on which the violation of reason's law is practised, and the longer it is persisted in, the greater must be the confusion and final trouble. Surely no laudations of

free-trade, no meetings of bishops and clergy in the East
End of London, no reading of papers and reports, can tell
us anything about our social condition which it more
concerns us to know than that! and not only to know, but
habitually to have the knowledge present, and to act upon it
as one acts upon the knowledge that water wets and fire
burns! And not only the sunken populace of our great
cities are concerned to know it, and the pauper twentieth of
our population; we Philistines of the middle class, too, are
concerned to know it, and all who have to set themselves to
make progress in perfection.

But we all know it already! some one will say; it is the
simplest law of prudence. But how little reality must there
be in our knowledge of it; how little can we be putting it in
practice; how little is it likely to penetrate among the poor
and struggling masses of our population, and to better our
condition, so long as an unintelligent Hebraism of one sort
keeps repeating as an absolute eternal word of God the
psalm-verse which says that the man who has a great many
children is happy; or an unintelligent Hebraism of another
sort—that is to say, a blind following of certain stock
notions as infallible—keeps assigning as an absolute proof
of national prosperity the multiplying of manufactures and
population! Surely, the one set of Hebraisers have to learn
that their psalm-verse was composed at the resettlement of
Jerusalem after the Captivity, when the Jews of Jerusalem
were a handful, an undermanned garrison, and every child
was a blessing; and that the word of God, or the voice of
the divine order of things, declares the possession of a great
many children to be a blessing only when it really is so!
And the other set of Hebraisers, have they not to learn that
if they call their private acquaintances imprudent or un-
lucky when, with no means of support for them or with
precarious means, they have a large family of children, then

they ought not to call the State well managed and prosperous merely because its manufactures and its citizens multiply, if the manufactures, which bring new citizens into existence just as much as if they had actually begotten them, bring more of them into existence than they can maintain, or are too precarious to go on maintaining those whom for a while they maintained?

Hellenism, surely, or the habit of fixing our mind upon the intelligible law of things, is most salutary if it makes us see that the only absolute good, the only absolute and eternal object prescribed to us by God's law, or the divine order of things, is the progress towards perfection,—our own progress towards it and the progress of humanity. And therefore, for every individual man, and for every society of men, the possession and multiplication of children, like the possession and multiplication of horses and pictures, is to be accounted good or bad, not in itself, but with reference to this object and the progress towards it. And as no man is to be excused in having horses or pictures, if his having them hinders his own or others' progress towards perfection and makes them lead a servile and ignoble life, so is no man to be excused for having children if his having them makes him or others lead this. Plain thoughts of this kind are surely the spontaneous product of our consciousness, when it is allowed to play freely and disinterestedly upon the actual facts of our social condition, and upon our stock notions and stock habits in respect to it. Firmly grasped and simply uttered, they are more likely, one cannot but think, to better that condition, and to diminish our formidable rate of one pauper to every nineteen of us, than is the Hebraising and mechanical pursuit of free-trade by our Liberal friends.

V

So that, here as elsewhere, the practical operations of our
Liberal friends, by which they set so much store, and in
which they invite us to join them and to show what Mr.
Bright calls a commendable interest, do not seem to us so
practical for real good as they think; and our Liberal
friends seem to us themselves to need to Hellenise, as we
say, a little,—that is, to examine into the nature of real
good, and to listen to what their consciousness tells them
about it,—rather than to pursue with such heat and confidence their present practical operations. And it is clear
that they have no just cause, so far as regards several
operations of theirs which we have canvassed, to reproach
us with delicate Conservative scepticism. For often by
Hellenising we seem to subvert stock Conservative notions
and usages more effectually than they subvert them by
Hebraising. But, in truth, the free spontaneous play of
consciousness with which culture tries to float our stock
habits of thinking and acting, is by its very nature, as has
been said, disinterested. Sometimes the result of floating
them may be agreeable to this party, sometimes to that; now
it may be unwelcome to our so-called Liberals, now to our
so-called Conservatives; but what culture seeks is, above all,
to *float* them, to prevent their being stiff and stark pieces of
petrifaction any longer. It is mere Hebraising, if we stop
short, and refuse to let our consciousness play freely,
whenever we or our friends do not happen to like what it
discovers to us. This is to make the Liberal party, or the
Conservative party, our one thing needful, instead of human
perfection; and we have seen what mischief arises from
making an even greater thing than the Liberal or the
Conservative party,—the predominance of the moral side
in man,—our one thing needful. But wherever the free

play of our consciousness leads us, we shall follow; believing that in this way we shall tend to make good at all points what is wanting to us, and so shall be brought nearer to our complete human perfection.

Thus we may often, perhaps, praise much that a so-called Liberal thinks himself forbidden to praise, and yet blame much that a so-called Conservative thinks himself forbidden to blame, because these are both of them partisans, and no partisan can afford to be thus disinterested. But we who are not partisans can afford it; and so, after we have seen what Nonconformists lose by being locked up in their New Road forms of religious institution, we can let ourselves see, on the other hand, how their ministers, in a time of movement of ideas like our present time, are apt to be more exempt than the ministers of a great Church establishment from that self-confidence, and sense of superiority to such a movement, which are natural to a powerful hierarchy; and which in Archdeacon Denison, for instance, seem almost carried to such a pitch that they may become, one cannot but fear, his spiritual ruin. But seeing this does not dispose us, therefore, to lock up all the nation in forms of worship of the New Road type; but it points us to the quite new ideal, of combining grand and national forms of worship with an openness and movement of mind not yet found in any hierarchy. So, again, if we see what is called ritualism making conquests in our Puritan middle class, we may rejoice that portions of this class should have become alive to the æsthetical weakness of their position, even although they have not yet become alive to the intellectual weakness of it. In Puritanism, on the other hand, we can respect that idea of dealing sincerely with oneself, which is at once the great force of Puritanism,— Puritanism's great superiority over all products, like ritualism, of our Catholicising tendencies,—and also an idea rich in the latent seeds of intellectual promise. But we do this, without on that account hiding from ourselves that Puritanism has by Hebraising misapplied that idea, has as yet developed none or hardly one of those seeds, and that its triumph at its present stage of development would be baneful.

Everything, in short, confirms us in the doctrine, so unpalatable to the believers in action, that our main business at the present moment is not so much to work away at certain crude reforms of which we have already the scheme in our own mind, as to create, through the help of that culture which at the very outset we began by praising and recommending, a frame of mind out of which the schemes of really fruitful reforms may with time grow. At any rate, we ourselves must put up with our friends' impatience and with their reproaches against cultivated inaction, and must still decline to lend a hand to their practical operations, until we, for our own part at least, have grown a little clearer about the nature of real good, and have arrived nearer to a condition of mind out of which really fruitful and solid operations may spring.

In the meanwhile, since our Liberal friends keep loudly and resolutely assuring us that their actual operations at present are fruitful and solid, let us in each case keep testing these operations in the simple way we have indicated, by letting the natural stream of our consciousness flow over them freely; and if they stand this test successfully, then let us give them our interest, but not else. For example. Our Liberal friends assure us, at the very top of their voices, that their present actual operation for the disestablishment of the Irish Church is fruitful and solid. But what if, on testing it, the truth appears to be, that the statesmen and reasonable people of both parties wished for much the same thing,—the fair apportionment of the church property of Ireland among the principal religious bodies there; but that, behind the statesmen and reasonable people, there was, on one side, a mass of Tory prejudice, and, on the other, a mass of Nonconformist prejudice, to which such an arrangement was unpalatable? Well, the natural way, one thinks, would have been for the statesmen and reasonable people of both sides to have united, and to have allayed and dissipated, so far as they could, the resistance of their respective extremes, and where they could not, to have confronted it in concert. But we see that, instead of this, Liberal statesmen waited to trip up their rivals, if they proposed the arrangement which both knew to be reasonable, by means of the prejudice of their own Nonconformist extreme; and then, themselves proposing an arrangement to flatter this prejudice, made the other arrangement, which they themselves knew to be reasonable, out of the question; and drove their rivals in their turn to blow up with all their might, in the hope of baffling them, a great fire, among their own Tory extreme, of fierce prejudice and religious bigotry,—a fire which, once kindled, may always very easily spread further? If, I say, on testing the present operation of our Liberal friends for the disestablishment of the Irish Church, the truth about it appears to be very much this, then, I think,—even with a triumphant Liberal majority, and with our Liberal friends making impassioned appeals to us to take a commendable interest in their operation and them, and to rally round what Sir Henry Hoare (who may be described, perhaps, as a Barbarian converted to Philistinism, as I, on the other hand, seem to be a Philistine converted to culture) finely calls the conscientiousness of a Gladstone and the intellect of a Bright,—it is rather our duty to abstain, and, instead of lending a hand to the operation of our Liberal friends, to do what we can to abate and dissolve the mass of prejudice, Tory or Nonconformist, which makes so doubtfully begotten and equivocal an operation as the present, producible and possible.

CONCLUSION

A N D so we bring to an end what we had to say in praise of culture, and in evidence of its special utility for the circumstances in which we find ourselves, and the confusion which environs us. Through culture seems to lie our way, not only to perfection, but even to safety. Resolutely refusing to lend a hand to the imperfect operations of our Liberal friends, disregarding their impatience, taunts, and reproaches, firmly bent on trying to find in the intelligible law of things a firmer and sounder basis for future practice than any which we have at present, and believing this search and discovery to be, for our generation and circumstances, of yet more vital and pressing importance than practice itself, we nevertheless may do more, perhaps, we poor disparaged followers of culture, to make the actual present, and the frame of society in which we live, solid and seaworthy, than all which our bustling politicians can do.

For we have seen how much of our disorders and perplexities is due to the disbelief, among the classes and combinations of men, Barbarian or Philistine, which have hitherto governed our society, in right reason, in a paramount best self; to the inevitable decay and break-up of the organisations by which, asserting and expressing in these organisations their ordinary self only, they have so long ruled us; and to their irresolution, when the society, which their conscience tells them they have made and still manage not with right reason but with their ordinary self, is rudely shaken, in offering resistance to its subverters. But for us,—who believe in right reason, in the duty and possibility of extricating and elevating our best self, in the progress of humanity towards perfection,—for us the framework of society, that theatre on which this august drama has to unroll itself, is sacred; and whoever administers it, and however we may seek to remove them from their tenure of administration, yet, while they administer, we steadily and with undivided heart support them in repressing anarchy and disorder; because without order there can be no society, and without society there can be no human perfection.

With me, indeed, this rule of conduct is hereditary. I remember my father, in one of his unpublished letters written more than forty years ago, when the political and social state of the country was gloomy and troubled, and there were riots in many places, goes on, after strongly insisting on the badness and foolishness of the government, and on the harm and dangerousness of our feudal and aristocratical constitution of society, and ends thus: "As for rioting, the old Roman way of dealing with *that* is always the right one; flog the rank and file, and fling the ring-leaders from the Tarpeian Rock!" And this opinion we can never forsake, however our Liberal friends may think a little rioting, and what they call popular demonstrations, useful sometimes to their own interests and to the interests of the valuable practical operations they have in hand, and however they may preach the right of an Englishman to be left to do as far as possible what he likes, and the duty of his government to indulge him and connive as much as possible and abstain from all harshness of repression. And even when they artfully show us operations which are undoubt-edly precious, such as the abolition of the slave-trade, and ask us if, for their sake, foolish and obstinate governments may not wholesomely be frightened by a little disturbance, the good design in view and the difficulty of overcoming opposition to it being considered,—still we say no, and that monster processions in the streets and forcible irruptions into the parks, even in professed support of this good design, ought to be unflinchingly forbidden and repressed; and that far more is lost than is gained by permitting them. Because a State in which law is authoritative and sovereign, a firm and settled course of public order, is requisite if man is to bring to maturity anything precious and lasting now, or to found anything precious and lasting for the future.

Thus, in our eyes, the very framework and exterior order of the State, whoever may administer the State, is sacred; and culture is the most resolute enemy of anarchy, because of the great hopes and designs for the State which culture teaches us to nourish. But as, believing in right reason, and having faith in the progress of humanity towards perfection, and ever labouring for this end, we grow to have clearer sight of the ideas of right reason, and of the elements and helps of perfection, and come gradually to fill the framework of the State with them, to fashion its internal composition and all its laws and institutions conformably to them, and to make the State more and more the expression, as we say, of our best self, which is not manifold, and vulgar, and unstable, and contentious, and ever-varying, but one, and noble, and secure, and peaceful, and the same for all mankind,—with what aversion shall we not *then* regard anarchy, with what firmness shall we not check it, when there is so much that is so precious which it will endanger!

So that, for the sake of the present, but far more for the sake of the future, the lovers of culture are unswervingly and with a good conscience the opposers of anarchy. And not as the Barbarians and Philistines, whose honesty and whose sense of humour make them shrink, as we have seen, from treating the State as too serious a thing, and from giving it too much power;—for indeed the only State they know of, and think they administer, is the expression of their ordinary self. And though the headstrong and violent extreme among them might gladly arm this with full authority, yet their virtuous mean is, as we have said, pricked in conscience at doing this; and so our Barbarian Secretaries of State let the Park railings be broken down, and our Philistine Alderman-Colonels let the London roughs rob and beat the bystanders. But we, beholding in the State no expression of our ordinary self, but even already, as it were, the appointed frame and prepared vessel of our best self, and, for the future, our best self's powerful, beneficent and sacred expression and organ,—we are willing and resolved, even now, to strengthen against anarchy the trembling hands of our Barbarian Home Secretaries and the feeble knees of our Philistine Alderman-Colonels; and to tell them, that it is not really in behalf of their own ordinary self that they are called to protect the Park railings, and to suppress the London roughs, but in behalf of the best self both of themselves and of all of us in the future.

Nevertheless, though for resisting anarchy the lovers of culture may prize and employ fire and strength, yet they must, at the same time, bear constantly in mind that it is not at this moment true, what the majority of people tell us, that the world wants fire and strength more than sweetness and light, and that things are for the most part to be settled first and understood afterwards. We have seen how much of our present perplexities and confusion this untrue notion of the majority of people amongst us has caused, and tends to perpetuate. Therefore the true business of the friends of culture now is, to dissipate this false notion, to spread the belief in right reason and in a firm intelligible law of things, and to get men to allow their thought and con-sciousness to play on their stock notions and habits disin-

terestedly and freely; to get men to try, in preference to
staunchly acting with imperfect knowledge, to obtain some
sounder basis of knowledge on which to act. This is
what the friends and lovers of culture have to do, however
the believers in action may grow impatient with us for
saying so, and may insist on our lending a hand to their
practical operations and showing a commendable interest
in them.

To this insistence we must indeed turn a deaf ear. But
neither, on the other hand, must the friends of culture
expect to take the believers in action by storm, or to be
visibly and speedily important, and to rule and cut a
figure in the world. Aristotle says that those for whom alone
ideas and the pursuit of the intelligible law of things can, in
general, have much attraction, are principally the young,
filled with generous spirit and with a passion for perfection;
but the mass of mankind, he says, follow seeming goods
for real, bestowing hardly a thought upon true sweetness
and light;—"and to *their* lives," he adds mournfully, "who
can give another and a better rhythm?"   But, although
those chiefly attracted by sweetness and light will probably
always be the young and enthusiastic, and culture must not
hope to take the mass of mankind by storm, yet we will not
therefore, for our own day and for our own people, admit
and rest in the desponding sentence of Aristotle. For is not
this the right crown of the long discipline of Hebraism, and
the due fruit of mankind's centuries of painful schooling in
self-conquest, and the just reward, above all, of the strenuous energy of our own nation and kindred in dealing
honestly with itself and walking steadfastly according to the
best light it knows,—that when in the fulness of time it
has reason and beauty offered to it, and the law of things as
they really are, it should at last walk by this true light with
the same staunchness and zeal with which it formerly

walked by its imperfect light? And thus man's two great natural forces, Hebraism and Hellenism, will no longer be dissociated and rival, but will be a joint force of right thinking and strong doing to carry him on towards perfection. This is what the lovers of culture may perhaps dare to augur for such a nation as ours.

Therefore, however great the changes to be accomplished, and however dense the array of Barbarians, Philistines, and Populace, we will neither despair on the one hand, nor, on the other, threaten violent revolution and change. But we will look forward cheerfully and hopefully to "a revolution," as the Duke of Wellington said, "by due course of law;" though not exactly such laws as our Liberal friends are now, with their actual lights, fond of offering to us.

But if despondency and violence are both of them forbidden to the believer in culture, yet neither, on the other hand, is public life and direct political action much permitted to him. For it is his business, as we have seen, to get the present believers in action, and lovers of political talking and doing, to make a return upon their own minds, scrutinise their stock notions and habits much more, value their present talking and doing much less; in order that, by learning to think more clearly, they may come at last to act less confusedly. But how shall we persuade our Barbarian to hold lightly to his feudal usages; how shall we persuade our Nonconformist that his time spent in agitating for the abolition of church-establishments would have been better spent in getting worthier ideas than churchmen have of God and the ordering of the world, or his time spent in battling for voluntaryism in education better spent in learning to value and found a public and national culture; how shall we persuade, finally, our Alderman-Colonel not to be content with sitting in the hall of judgment or marching at the head of his men of war, without some knowledge how to perform judgment and how to direct men of war,—how, I say, shall we persuade all these of this, if our Alderman-Colonel sees that we want to get his leading-staff and his scales of justice for our own hands; or the Nonconformist, that we want for ourselves his platform; or the Barbarian, that we want for ourselves his pre-eminency and function? Certainly they will be less slow to believe, as we want them to believe, that the intelligible law of things has in itself something desirable and precious, and that all place, function, and bustle are hollow goods without it, if they see that we ourselves can content ourselves with this law, and find in it our satisfaction, without making it an instrument to give us for ourselves place, function, and bustle.

And although Mr. Sidgwick says that social usefulness really means "losing oneself in a mass of disagreeable, hard, mechanical details," and though all the believers in action are fond of asserting the same thing, yet, as to lose ourselves is not what we want, but to find ourselves through finding the intelligible law of things, this assertion too we shall not blindly accept, but shall sift and try it a little first. And if we see that because the believers in action, forgetting Goethe's maxim, "To act is easy, to think is hard," imagine there is some wonderful virtue in losing oneself in a mass of mechanical details, therefore they excuse themselves from much thought about the clear ideas which ought to govern these details, then we shall give our chief care and pains to seeking out those ideas and to setting them forth; being persuaded that if we have the ideas firm and clear, the mechanical details for their execution will come a great deal more simply and easily than we now suppose. And even in education, where our Liberal friends are now, with much zeal, bringing out their train of practical operations and inviting all men to lend them a hand; and where, since education is the road to culture, we might gladly lend them a hand with their practical operations if we could lend them one anywhere; yet, if we see that any German or Swiss or French law for education rests on very clear ideas about the citizen's claim, in this matter, upon the State, and the State's duty towards the citizen, but has its mechanical details comparatively few and simple, while an English law for the same concern is ruled by no clear idea about the citizen's claim and the State's duty, but has, in compensation, a mass of minute mechanical details about the number of members on a school-committee, and how many shall be a quorum, and how they shall be summoned and how often they shall meet,—then we must conclude that our nation stands in more need of clear ideas on the main matter than of laboured details about the accessories of the matter, and that we do more service by trying to help it to the ideas, than by lending it a hand with the details. So while Mr. Samuel Morley and his friends talk of changing their policy on education not for the sake of modelling it on more sound ideas but "for fear the management of education should be taken out of their hands," we shall not much care for taking the management out of their hands and getting it into ours; but rather we shall try and make them perceive, that to model education on sound ideas is of more importance than to have the management of it in one's own hands ever so fully.

At this exciting juncture, then, while so many of the lovers of new ideas, somewhat weary, as we too are, of the stock performances of our Liberal friends upon the political stage, are disposed to rush valiantly upon this public stage themselves, we cannot at all think that for a wise lover of new ideas this stage is the right one. Plenty of people there will be without us,—country gentlemen in search of a club, demagogues in search of a tub, lawyers in search of a place, industrialists in search of gentility,—who will come from the east and from the west, and will sit down at that Thyesteän banquet of clap-trap which English public life for these many years past has been. And, so long as those old organisations, of which we have seen the insufficiency,—those expressions of our ordinary self, Barbarian or Philistine,—have force anywhere, they will have force in Parliament. There, the man whom the Barbarians send, cannot but be impelled to please the Barbarians' ordinary self, and their natural taste for the bathos: and the man whom the Philistines send cannot but be impelled to please those of the Philistines. Parliamentary Conservatism will and must long mean this, that the Barbarians should keep their heritage; and Parliamentary Liberalism, that the Barbarians should pass away, as they will pass away, and that into their heritage the Philistines should enter. This seems, indeed, to be the true and authentic promise of which our Liberal friends and Mr. Bright believe themselves the heirs, and the goal of that great man's labours. Presently, perhaps, Mr. Odger and Mr. Bradlaugh will be there with their mission to oust both Barbarians and Philistines, and to get the heritage for the Populace.

We, on the other hand, are for giving the heritage neither to the Barbarians nor to the Philistines, nor yet to the Populace; but we are for the transformation of each and all of these according to the law of perfection. Through the length and breadth of our nation a sense,—vague and obscure as yet,—of weariness with the old organisations, of desire for this transformation, works and grows. In the House of Commons the old organisations must inevitably be most enduring and strongest, the transformation must inevitably be longest in showing itself; and it may truly be averred, therefore, that at the present juncture the centre of movement is not in the House of Commons. It is in the fermenting mind of the nation; and his is for the next twenty years the real influence who can address himself to this.

Pericles was perhaps the most perfect public speaker who ever lived, for he was the man who most perfectly combined thought and wisdom with feeling and eloquence. Yet Plato brings in Alcibiades declaring, that men went away from the oratory of Pericles, saying it was very fine, it was very good, and afterwards thinking no more about it; but they went away from hearing Socrates talk, he says, with the point of what he had said sticking fast in their minds, and they could not get rid of it. Socrates has drunk his hemlock and is dead; but in his own breast does not every man carry about with him a possible Socrates, in that power of a disinterested play of consciousness upon his stock notions and habits, of which this wise and admirable man gave all through his lifetime the great example, and which was the secret of his incomparable influence? And he who leads men to call forth and exercise in themselves this power, and who busily calls it forth and exercises it in himself, is at the present moment, perhaps, as Socrates was in his time, more in concert with the vital working of men's minds, and more effectually significant, than any House of Commons' orator, or practical operator in politics.

Everyone is now boasting of what he has done to educate men's minds and to give things the course they are taking. Mr. Disraeli educates, Mr. Bright educates, Mr. Beales educates. We, indeed, pretend to educate no one, for we are still engaged in trying to clear and educate ourselves. But we are sure that the endeavour to reach, through culture, the firm intelligible law of things,—we are sure that the detaching ourselves from our stock notions and habits,—that a more free play of consciousness, an increased desire for sweetness and light, and all the bent which we call Hellenising, is the master-impulse even now of the life of our nation and of humanity,—somewhat obscurely perhaps for this actual moment, but decisively and certainly for the immediate future; and that those who work for this are the sovereign educators.

Docile echoes of the eternal voice, pliant organs of the infinite will, such workers are going along with the essential movement of the world; and this is their strength, and their happy and divine fortune. For if the believers in action, who are so impatient with us and call us effeminate, had had the same good fortune, they would, no doubt, have surpassed us in this sphere of vital influence by all the superiority of their genius and energy over ours. But now we go the way the human race is going, while they abolish the Irish Church by the power of the Nonconformists' antipathy to establishments, or they enable a man to marry his deceased wife's sister.

NOTES

PREFACE

p. 3. **Bishop Wilson:** Thomas Wilson (1663–1755), the famous bp. of Sodor and Man. An article on Keble's *Life* of him in the *Quarterly* for July, 1866, seems first to have awakened Arnold's interest in his *Maxims*, a copy of which he discovered in his father's study at Fox How in the following autumn and read with delight (*Letters*, 1, 341). An edition of the *Maxims* by Prof. Relton appeared in 1898 ("English Theological Library").

votary of the natural sciences: cf. "distinguished physicist" below. Probably Tyndall is meant. Arnold sat next him at a Geological Society dinner on Feb. 21, 1868, and they must have discussed *Culture and Anarchy* which was then appearing in the *Cornhill* (*Letters*, 1, 389).

embargo...recreative religion: there is no reference to this "embargo" in Huxley's *Life and Letters* and I have failed to track it down elsewhere. Huxley was giving lectures at St Martin's Hall in 1854: cf. *Science and Education* by T. H. Huxley, pp. vii, 38.

p. 4. **Marcus Aurelius:** v. Arnold's essay on him in *Ess. Crit.* 1.

Joubert (1754–1824): French religious philosopher whom Arnold compared with Coleridge. **Nicole** (1625–95), one of the Port-royalists, a friend of Pascal and author of *Essaies de Morale*. Arnold's *Ess. Crit.* 1 includes an essay on Joubert, in which the passage referred to is quoted in full (p. 295).

Michelet (1798–1874), whose history of the French Revolution, completed in 1854, was very popular in England at this period.

the *Imitation*, i.e. the *Imitatio Christi* by St Thomas à Kempis.

pp. 6–7. **I say again here...the essential inwardness of the operation is lost sight of:** this is omitted in ed. 2 and its place taken by the sentence, "And the culture we recommend is, above all, an inward operation," the next sentence beginning with "But."

p. 7. **we have freely pointed out...French Academy:**
v. "The literary influence of academies," *Ess. Crit.* 1.

the Corinthian style: cf. "Corinthian leading articles" (p. 8).
Arnold describes "the Corinthian style" in *Ess. Crit.* 1 (pp. 75–6)
thus: "it has glitter without warmth, rapidity without ease,
effectiveness without charm...it has no *soul*; all it exists for is to
get its ends, to make its points, to damage its adversaries, to be
admired, to triumph." It is in short the style of the newspaper
leading article (v. note on Mr G. A. Sala, p. 8).

the One Primeval Language: i.e. a book by a certain
Charles Forster, "a mystification about the Sinaitic inscriptions,
in which he declares he finds the primitive language" (*Ess. Crit.*
1, 59). The same writer excited the derision of Renan and Arnold
by another book which maintained that Mahomet and the Pope
were the little horn and the great horn of the he-goat in *Daniel* viii.
Our modern Baconians and writers on the mathematical properties
of the Pyramids uphold the same national tradition.

p. 8. **Lord Stanhope:** historian, promoter of the copyright
act, and chief mover in the establishment of the National Portrait
Gallery and of the Historical MSS. Commission.

Dean of St. Paul's (omitted in ed. 1): i.e. H. H. Milman,
author of *A History of Christianity* and other Books.

Bishop of Oxford: Samuel Wilberforce, "the greatest prelate
of the age" (cf. Editor's Introduction, p. xvii and note on "the
Oxford Movement," p. 62).

Dean of Westminster: A. P. Stanley, author of the *Life of
Dr Arnold, The Memorials of Canterbury*, etc., a friend of Arnold's,
whose noble "Westminster Abbey" ode was written at his death
in 1881.

Mr. Froude: J. A. Froude, the well-known historian.

Mr. Henry Reeve: at one time on the staff of the *Times* and
later editor of the *Edinburgh Review*, the confidant of ambassadors
and the friend of princes.

Mr. G. A. Sala: a journalist on the staff of the *Daily Telegraph*,
a newspaper at which Arnold was fond of poking fun upon every
possible occasion. Established in 1855 as the first penny paper in
London and boasting of "the largest circulation in the world"
(cf. p. 59), it held a position at this time comparable with that of
the *Daily Mail* to-day. Sala was the type of half-educated, self-

confident and bombastic writer that provoked Arnold to the utmost possible "vivacity"; many pages of *Friendship's Garland* are devoted to him.

pp. 8–10. **It is by a like sort of misunderstanding...be suffered to continue**: omitted in ed. 2, for reasons given in the next note.

p. 8. **Mr. Oscar Browning...in the *Quarterly Review***: v. the review article on Arnold's *Schools and Universities on the Continent* in the *Quarterly* for Oct. 1868 (vol. 9, pp. 473–90). It was anonymous, according to the custom of that journal, but it so clearly emanated from Eton that Arnold would have no difficulty in discovering the name of the author, and in a letter of Oct. 24, 1868, he notes, "There is a vicious article in the new *Quarterly* on my school-book by one of the Eton undermasters, who, like Demetrius the silversmith, seems alarmed for the gains of his occupation." In another letter (Feb. 20, 1869) he writes: "Dr William Smith of the *Quarterly Review* came up to me a day or two ago with his hand held out, saying that he forgave all I had said about him and the *Quarterly*, which he added was a great deal, for the sake of the truth and usefulness of what I had said about the Nonconformists. He said he was born a Nonconformist, was brought up with them, and had seen them all his life, so he was a good judge." After this handsome gesture Arnold could hardly retain the paragraph in ed. 2. The "Eton under-master" who thus dared to cross swords with Arnold, and whom those who read his article will agree that Arnold treated with leniency, later became the famous and fantastic don of King's College, known to many generations of undergraduates. He was born in 1837 and died in 1923. Cf. Editor's Preface, pp. vii–viii.

p. 10. **either of the...mentioned**: ed. 2, having omitted one of the two, reads "any question of an Academy."

the present operation of disestablishing the Irish Church: v. Editor's Introduction, p. xxxi, and ch. vi, pp. 166–74.

we are charged...sects all round: omitted in ed. 2, which, however, adds after "Establishment" the words "possessed with the one desire to help the clergy and to harm the Dissenters."

p. 12. **like Mr. Baxter and Mr. Charles Buxton**: omitted in ed. 2. W. E. Baxter (1825–90), Liberal M.P. for Montrose,

Secretary to the Admiralty, 1868–71. Charles Buxton (1823–/1), Liberal M.P. for East Surrey.

like the Dean of Canterbury: these words are also omitted in ed. 2. The Dean was Dr Henry Alford (1810–71).

help Mr. Baxter. . . in their: in ed. 2 this reads "take part in."

p. 13. the Rev. Edward White (1819–98): a well-known London Congregational minister and friend of Edward Miall (v. note, p. 87). I find no mention of the pamphlet referred to by Arnold in the official *Life of Edward White* by F. A. Freer.

Hooker, Richard (1554–1600): author of *The Laws of Ecclesiastical Polity*, v. below, pp. 23–6.

Barrow, Isaac (1630–77): the great Anglican divine and preacher of the Caroline period. The elder Pitt "when qualifying himself in early life for public speaking, read Barrow's sermons again and again" and recommended his son to do the same.

Butler, Joseph (1692–1752): the famous bishop and philosopher, author of the *Analogy of Religion*. Cf. Arnold's "Bishop Butler and the Zeit-geist" in *Last Essays on Church and Religion*.

Milton, John (1608–74): the poet. Originally intended to take orders but abandoned the idea about 1643.

Baxter, Richard (1615–91): the famous preacher and author of *The Saint's Everlasting Rest*. Was ordained in 1638, but was driven out of the Established Church by the Act of Uniformity, 1662.

Wesley, John (1703–91): the founder of Methodism, was an ordained clergyman of the Church of England and never renounced his orders.

p. 14. a provincialism which has two main types. . . our humanity: omitted in ed. 2.

p. 15. *eigene grosse Erfindungen*: their own great discoveries. Cf. p. 181.

p. 16. open the Universities to everybody: Nonconformists had been admitted to Oxford and Cambridge first by the Universities Acts of 1854–56, but were not entitled to take the M.A. or to be elected to fellowships until the Universities Tests Act of 1871. In 1869 Sir John Coleridge brought in a bill anticipating this act; it passed the Commons but was thrown out by the Lords. Cf. Editor's Introduction, p. xvi n.

in the same case: ed. 1 reads "in the same boat."

p. 17. **Mr. Bright, in a speech at Birmingham about education:** for John Bright (1811–89), v. Editor's Introduction, pp. xxiii, xxvi–xxvii, xxxi. The speech was delivered on Feb. 5, 1868, its subject being "On assistance by Government to Technical Education." Arnold is here unfair in that he misquotes (no doubt quite unconsciously) Bright's words which run as follows: "I believe the people of the United States have offered to the world more valuable *inventions* during the last forty years than all Europe put together" (p. 62, *Public Addresses*, ed. Thorold Rogers, 1879). The word "inventions" destroys the whole point of Arnold's argument.

in culture and totality...provincialism: omitted in ed. 2, which reads instead "even in light and the things of the mind," which if possible renders Arnold's misquotation of Bright even more serious.

M. Renan: i.e. Ernest Renan (1823–92), the great French critic and orientalist, author of *Vie de Jésus* (1863). Arnold's quotation comes from p. vii of the Preface to *Questions Contemporaines* (Paris, 1868).

p. 19. **our race pursues:** ed. 1 reads "we pursue."

as we...reason of things: ed. 1 reads "in our own words, a reference of all our operating to a firm intelligible law of things."

p. 20. **Mr. Spurgeon's Tabernacle:** Spurgeon, the most popular Nonconformist preacher of the period, had erected in 1861 a vast Metropolitan Tabernacle for his congregation at the cost of £31,000.

p. 22. **Mr. Beecher or Brother Noyes:** Henry Ward Beecher (1813–87), the most popular Congregational minister in New York, a strong anti-slavery man, who visited England in 1863. John Humphrey Noyes (1811–86), founder of the "Perfectionists," an American communist sect which formed the Oneida community; v. Nordhoff, *Communistic Societies of U.S.A.*

Mr Ezra Cornell (1807–74): founded in 1868 a university in the town of Ithaca, New York, and heavily endowed it.

who think that spirituality: ed. 1 reads "who think that culture."

p. 23. **the Dean of Westminster:** v. note, p. 8.

trained in the same school: i.e. under Thomas Arnold at Rugby.

p. 24. **had first been made** (ed. 2): ed. 1 misprints "had just been made."

p. 25. **Mr. Binney:** Thomas Binney (1798–1874), distinguished Nonconformist divine and preacher, with whom it was "a matter of deep, serious, religious conviction that the established church is a great national evil" (*D.N.B.*).

pp. 27–28. **Presbyterian:** ed. 1 reads "Presbyterian or Congregational." Arnold deleted "or Congregational" in ed. 2 and substituted "Presbyterian" for "Congregational" 8 lines further down in order no doubt to avoid raising problems incident to a suggested combination of an episcopal and a congregational church system.

p. 28. **while their latitudinarian friends make light of it:** omitted in ed. 2.

Lord Bolingbroke (1678–1751): the well-known statesman and political writer of the time of Queen Anne to George II.

p. 29. **M. Albert Réville** (1826–1906): a French Protestant theologian and historian, with very "advanced" views for his age. An attack in 1886 upon his *Prolegomena to the History of Religion* by Gladstone precipitated the famous controversy between the latter and Huxley on the book of Genesis (Huxley, *Life*, II, 425).

p. 30. **Socinian:** i.e. Unitarian. Laelius and Faustus Socinus were 16th century Italian precursors of modern Unitarianism.

Luther—whom we have called a Philistine of genius: v. *Celtic Literature*, § vi (ed. 1867, p. 140). For "Philistine" v. note, p. 100 below.

pp. 30–33. **All this is true...for the sake of which it chose it:** in the 2nd ed. Arnold contracted these three pages into one brief paragraph of about a dozen lines.

p. 30. **Mr. Greg:** W. R. Greg (1809–81), Lancashire mill-owner and writer of essays, critical of Christianity and politically pessimistic. In Jan. 1863, Arnold wrote an article in *Macmillan's Magazine* entitled "The Bishop and the Philosopher," comparing Bishop Colenso with Spinoza (reprinted in part in "Spinoza and the Bible," *Ess. Crit.* 1) to which Greg replied in an article called "Truth *versus* Edification," reprinted in *Literary and Social Judgments*, 1868.

p. 31. **Benthamism**: cf note, p. 66.

Mialism: the doctrines of Edward Miall (cf. note, p. 87), the leader of the movement for disestablishment.

Sir Henry Wotton: (1568–1639), diplomatist and poet. Arnold probably quotes from *The State of Christendom* (published 1657).

Father Jackson: i.e. Thomas Jackson (1783–1873), Wesleyan minister and itinerant preacher, author of *Life of Charles Wesley*, etc.

p. 32. **Lacordaire** (1802–61): a great French preacher and educationalist, head master of the school at Sorèze, a visit to which Arnold describes in *A French Eton*.

pp. 34–35. **For instance...culture to tell them the contrary**: this is rearranged and slightly abridged in the 2nd ed. and the reference to Baxter, Buxton and the Dean of Canterbury omitted.

pp. 35–36. **with our pauperism...population**: ed. 2 reads "with our social condition what it is."

p. 36. **the one pure and Christ-ordained way**: ed. 2 reads "the one true way."

rather indifferent: ed. 1 reads "pliant and easy."

one concern of our actual: ed. 1 reads "bane of."

p. 37. **the reformed constituencies**: *v.* Editor's Introduction, pp. xxii–xxxii.

the Valley of Jehoshaphat: *v. Joel* iii. 1–14.

cure their spirit: ed. 1 reads "cure them of Hebraising and omits "Ousted they will not be, but transformed. Ousted they do not deserve to be, and will not be." "Ousted" is the reading of ed. 3; the text of 1875 reads "Expelled."

the days of Israel, etc.: *Ecclesiasticus* xxxvii. 25.

the first rank to-morrow: ed. 1 makes no new paragraph here and omits "Let us conclude by marking this distinctly."

p. 38. **Sophocles and Plato...larger than his**: ed. 2 omits this. Arnold's views on Sophocles as a religious thinker may be found in *Ess. Crit.* 1, pp. 221–2.

holiness...scope of: ed. 2 omits.

Lo, thy sons...of God: *Baruch*, iv. 37.

INTRODUCTION

p. 39. **Mr. Frederic Harrison**: v. Editor's Introduction, p. **xxv**. Arnold quotes from an article on "Our Venetian Constitution" (*Fortnightly*, March, 1867), reprinted as "Parliament before Reform" in *Order and Progress*, 1875.

professor: ed. 1 reads "possessor," a misprint corrected in ed. 2.

p. 40. *Daily Telegraph*: v. note on "Mr G. A. Sala," p. 8.

p. 41. **experience, reflection, and renouncement**: a glance at the Liberal party-cry "Peace, retrenchment, reform."

I. SWEETNESS AND LIGHT

p. 43. **I have before now pointed out, etc.**: v. *Ess. Crit.* 1, p. 16. In the *Quarterly Review* some time ago: i.e. Jan. 1866.

M. Sainte-Beuve (1804–69): v. Editor's Introduction, p. **xix**.

p. 44. **Montesquieu** (1689–1755): the French political philosopher, author of *De L'Esprit des Lois*.

p. 47. **As I have said on a former occasion**: v. *A French Eton* (ed. 1892), pp. 116–17.

p. 50. **Mr. Roebuck's stock argument**: J. A. Roebuck (1801–79), a prominent radical politician of the Benthamite school. Arnold often refers to him, since his utterances provided useful examples of Benthamite extravagance. Cf. *Ess. Crit.* 1, p. 21 and *A French Eton* (ed. 1895), p. 102. The quotation comes from a speech made at Sheffield. Cf. p. 121.

p. 52. **the Philistines**: v. note, p. 100.

p. 53. **the utilitarian Franklin**: Benjamin Franklin (1706–90), the American politician, scientist and philosophical writer. Arnold is quoting from the *Autobiography* (1817), his best known work.

Epictetus: Stoic philosopher, born c. A.D. 60, v. essay on Marcus Aurelius in *Ess. Crit.* 1.

p. 54. *Battle of the Books...sweetness and light*: Arnold borrows more than the phrase "sweetness and light" from Swift. In the story Swift tells of the Bee and the Spider may be found the origin of Arnold's distinction between the man of culture and the Philistine. The spider boasts of his web, for all the world like Bright boasting of the industrial prowess of England, "I am a domestic

animal, furnished with a native stock within myself. This large castle
(to show my improvements in the mathematics) is all built with my
own hands, and the materials extracted altogether out of my own
person." Whereupon the Bee asks "Whether is the nobler of the
two, that which by a lazy contemplation of four inches round, by
an overweening pride, feeding and engendering on itself, turns
all into excrement and venom, producing nothing at all but fly-
bane and cobweb; or that which by a universal range, with long
search, much study, true judgment and distinction of things,
brings home honey and wax." The Spider, as Aesop then points
out, is the type of the moderns, the Bee of the ancients, who have
"by infinite labour and search, and ranging through every corner
of nature" filled their "hives with honey and wax, thus furnishing
mankind with the two noblest of things, which are sweetness and
light."

Far more...to save us: omitted in ed.1.

p. 56. **And very freely...yet it:** omitted in ed. 1, which
reads "which" instead.

language too...every day: omitted in ed. 1.

Independents: i.e. Congregationalists.

the *Nonconformist*: a weekly Congregational paper founded
in 1841 and edited by Edward Miall, v. note, p. 87.

p. 58. **Prof. Huxley:** T. H. Huxley (1825–95), scientist
and agnostic. A friend of Arnold, though they differed on many
points. He criticized Arnold in an address on "Science and
Culture" (1880) delivered at Birmingham (v. *Science and
Education*, no. vi) and Arnold replied in "Literature and Science"
printed in *Nineteenth Century*, April, 1884 (v. *Discourses in
America*, no. ii). The personal relations between the two men are
well illustrated by the following letter from Huxley, dated July 8,
1869:

My dear Arnold—Look at Bishop Wilson on the sin of covetousness
and then inspect your umbrella stand. You will there see a beautiful
brown smooth-handled umbrella which is *not* your property. Think
of what the excellent prelate would have advised and bring it with you
next time you come to the Club. The porter will take care of it for
me.—Ever yours faithfully, T. H. Huxley.

so incomplete: ed. 1 omits this.

p. 59. *publicè egestas, privatim opulentia:* cf. *A French*

Eton (p. 20), "With us it is always the individual that is filled, and the public that is sent empty away."

the largest circulation in the whole world: v. note, p. 8 "Mr. G. A. Sala."

muscular Christianity: a reference to Charles Kingsley who was said to preach this type of religion.

p. 60. complete, a harmonious perfection: ed. 1 reads "complete perfection."

Mr. Gladstone...at Paris: probably in connexion with the great Industrial Exhibition of 1867.

p. 61. Puritanism was perhaps necessary: ed. 1 reads "Puritanism was necessary."

Mr. Beales and Mr. Bradlaugh: v. Editor's Introduction, pp. xxv–xxvi.

p. 62. The Oxford movement was broken, it failed: v. Editor's Introduction, p. xiii. In 1869 Liberal Churchmanship seemed everywhere triumphant. *Essays and Reviews* had appeared in 1860 and its authors escaped official condemnation as heretics; Bishop Colenso (v. note, p. 181) published a still more startling book in 1862 and likewise survived. Meanwhile Wilberforce, the leader of the High Church party, was twice disappointed of a hoped for succession to the archiepiscopal throne and in 1863 the latitudinarian Stanley was appointed Dean of Westminster (v. note, p. 8).

Quæ regio in terris nostri non plena laboris? What part of the world is not full of our calamities? *Aeneid*, 1, 460.

p. 63. Mr. Lowe: Robert Lowe (1811–92), Viscount Sherbrooke, v. Editor's Introduction, pp. xiv, xxiii.

It is thrust into the second rank...the future: referring to the Reform Act of 1867 which first gave the vote to the working classes, v. Editor's Introduction, pp. xxiii–xxviii.

pp. 64–65. See what you have done, etc. From a speech of Dec. 4, 1866, v. *Public Addresses*, ed. T. Rogers, p. 373.

p. 65. the bigness of the tabernacle: a reference to Spurgeon, v. note, p. 20.

the *Journeyman Engineer*: v. p. 238.

p. 66. Jacobinism: i.e. revolutionary principles.

abstract system: Arnold is here drawing freely upon Burke's *Reflections on the Revolution*.

Comte, Auguste (1789–1857), founder of Positivism, at once a philosophy aiming at a unification of all knowledge and a religion based upon the worship of Humanity.

Mr. Congreve: Richard Congreve (1818–99), founder of the Positivist community in London; educated at Rugby with Arnold, who calls him "acquaintance" in ed. 1 and ed. 2, but alters it to "friend" in ed. 3.

Bentham: Jeremy Bentham (1748–1832), the founder of Utilitarianism, the reformer of the criminal code, the leader of philosophic radicalism which inspired the Liberalism of the age. Cf. p. 67 and the preface to *Ess. Crit.* 1. It is easy to make fun of Bentham's notions about Plato, of his style, and of his crotchets, but no other single man has exercised a more profound influence upon modern England (v. Dicey, *Law and Opinion in England*). The worse, Arnold would reply, for England! For to him Benthamism was the philosophic expression of the Englishman's "worship of machinery."

p. 67. Benjamin Franklin: v. note, p. 53.

Deontology or *Science of Morality*: published after Bentham's death in 1834 in 2 vols.

p. 68. Mr. Buckle: Henry Thomas Buckle (1821–62), author of *A History of Civilisation in England* (1857–61), which had an immense and world-wide circulation, and was an attempt to trace historic factors to geographical causes.

Be not ye called Rabbi! *Matth.* xxiii. 8.

Mr. Mill: John Stuart Mill (1806–73), economist, philosopher, radical, a disciple of Bentham (v. above), whose Utilitarianism he softened and humanised. Cf. *James and John Stuart Mill on Education*, another volume in the present series. Arnold describes him in *A French Eton* (p. 156) as "not perhaps the great spirit that some of his admirers suppose, but. . .a singularly acute, ardent, and interesting man. . .capable of following lights that led him away from the regular doctrine of philosophical radicalism." Cf. *Ess. Crit.* 1, 348.

p. 69. He who works for sweetness. . .sweetness and light united: ed. 2 substitutes the single "He who works for sweetness and light."

p. 70. It seeks to do away with classes. . .bound by them: I follow the ed. 2 text here, Arnold in 1869 omitting the words "to make the best . . . current everywhere" and reading "where they may use" for "and use."

Abelard (1079–1142): the great scholastic philosopher, who was for a time the centre of extraordinary intellectual ferment at the University of Paris.

Lessing (1729–81): the great German critic.

Herder (1744–1803): a writer of inferior merit to Lessing, but with a considerable reputation in his own and Arnold's time. His ideas were of a sort to interest Arnold, and were not unlike those which form the staple of *Culture and Anarchy*.

p. 71. And why? omitted in ed. 1.

II. DOING AS ONE LIKES

p. 72. a religion proposing parmaceti: Parmaceti was the remedy "for an inward bruise" proposed by the foppish courtier to Hotspur in 1 *Henry IV*, 1, iii, 58, v. notes, p. 73 below.

Alcibiades: v. next note. The comparison of the narrow-minded and smug puritan editor of a "raucous" Nonconformist journal with the type of all that was luxurious, cosmopolitan, brilliant, accomplished, fascinating and unprincipled in the Athens of Socrates is a good example of Arnold's irony.

Morning Star: a penny paper, organ of advanced radicalism, started 1856, edited by Samuel Lucas, Bright's brother-in-law. Arnold called it "that true reflexion of the rancour of Protestant Dissent in alliance with all the vulgarity, meddlesomeness, and grossness of the British multitude" (*Letters*, 1, 204), and Disraeli jestingly told Bright that "he read the *Star* more than any other paper, it was the best paper published" (Trevelyan, *Bright*, p. 290).

p. 73. Mr. Frederic Harrison, in a very good-tempered and witty satire: i.e. an article published in *The Fortnightly Review* (Nov. 1867) entitled "Culture: a dialogue," the speakers being the writer and "Arminius," the Prussian savant of Arnold's *Friendship's Garland*. The article is headed with the passage from Shakespeare's 1 *Henry IV*, about parmaceti referred to above. Arnold found the satire "scarcely the least vicious, and in parts so amusing that I laughed till I cried" (*Letters*, 1, 372). For F. Harrison v. Editor's Introduction, p. xxv.

pouncet-box:

"And 'twixt his finger and his thumb he held
A pouncet-box."   1 *Henry IV*, I, iii, 37.

p. 75. *posse comitatûs*: the body of men entitled to be called out by the Sheriff to aid in enforcing the law.

M. Michelet: v. note, p. 4.

p. 77. breaks down the park railings: reference to the Hyde Park riots, v. Editor's Introduction, p. xxvi.

invades a Secretary of State's office: v. Editor's Introduction, p. xxviii.

Mr. Murphy: v. Editor's Introduction, p. xxix.

the Home Secretary, Mr. Hardy: ed. 1 reads "Mr. Hardy," ed. 2 reads "the Home Secretary."

p. 78. The views were not...and the bequest: I follow ed. 2; ed. 1 reads simply "This bequest."

p. 79. Fenianism: v. Editor's Introduction, p. xxviii.

p. 80. Truss Manufactory: a hideous building in Trafalgar Square for the manufacture of Cole's trusses. Arnold makes play with it in *Friendship's Garland*, p. 13.

Sir Daniel Gooch (1816–89): railway engineer and inventor, Chairman of the G.W. Railway, 1865–87. Swindon is, of course, the G.W.R. headquarters.

p. 82. the brightest powers...action: the words are from F. Harrison's article "Our Venetian Constitution" referred to in the note on p. 39. The context runs: "So far from being the least fit for political influence of all classes in the community, the best part of the working class forms the most fit of all others....Theirs are the brightest powers," etc.

p. 83. Mr. Carlyle...rule to the aristocracy: referring to *Shooting Niagara*, v. Editor's Introduction, p. xxiv.

epochs of concentration: such as the 18th century, v. *Ess. Crit.* I, p. 13.

Now is the judgment, etc. *John* xii. 31.

p. 84. From such an ignoble...preserve us: omitted in ed. 2.

poor Mrs. Lincoln: I cannot trace the precise incident alluded to here, but the widow of the great American president was always an impossible sort of person, whose mind became unhinged after the assassination of her husband in 1865.

p. 85. sadly to seek...in "a philosophy with coherent... principles": the criticism comes from F. Harrison's *Culture: a dialogue*, v. note, p. 73.

Oxford in the bad old times: i.e. before the Oxford University Act of 1854 which reformed the constitution of the university and opened the door to salutary changes in the curriculum; v. J. W. Adamson, *English Education*, 1789–1902, ch. vii, and Newman, *Idea of a University*, pp. 69–70 (ed. in this series).

p. 86. by the study of modern languages: omitted in ed. 1.

Mr. Lowe's great speech at Edinburgh: i.e. an address on Primary and Classical Education at the Philosophical Institute of Edinburgh, Nov. 1, 1867, in which Lowe propounded a scheme of education for all classes of English society, upper, middle and lower, compelled after 1867 to live under a democracy, and attacked the study of dead languages, declaring that instead of Latin and Greek it would be better to master English and French. Cf. Editor's Introduction, p. xiv.

the waiters...hotels: ed. 1 reads "the German waiters."

Aristotle...virtue being in a mean, etc.: Aristotle thought that a virtue or excellence is the golden mean between two extremes: thus courage is the "mean" between the "excess" rashness and the "defect" cowardice, and so on.

Lord Elcho and Sir Thomas Bateson: ed. 2 reads "a well-known lord and a well-known baronet." Lord Elcho, afterwards Earl of Wemyss, was a Liberal Conservative who followed Robert Lowe in resisting the Reform Bill. Arnold describes him in *Friendship's Garland* as "a dashing nobleman" and writes (p. 22): "Everybody knows Lord Elcho's appearance, and how admirably he looks the part of our governing classes; to my mind, indeed, the mere cock of his lordship's hat is one of the finest and most aristocratic things we have." Sir Thomas Bateson was M.P. in 1865 for Devizes. The speech to which Arnold listened was delivered on June 4, 1867, and does not appear to have excited comment in any way. Arnold quotes from it on p. 115.

p. 87. Mr. Miall: Edward Miall (1809–81), politician and Congregational minister, first editor of the *Nonconformist* (v. p. 56), founded in 1844 the British Anti-State Church Association which became later the Liberation Society (v. p. 170). "The primary object of the *Nonconformist*," he wrote, "is to show that a national establishment of religion is essentially vicious in its constitution, philosophically, politically, and religiously" (v. *Life of Ed. Miall*, by Arthur Miall, 1884, p. 51). The early writings of Herbert Spencer appeared in this paper.

p. 88. **abolition of church-rates:** referring to the Act of July, 1868, due to Gladstone's initiative, which relieved Nonconformists of the necessity of paying rates for the upkeep of parish churches, an injustice of which they had long struggled to rid themselves (v. Spencer Walpole, *History of Twenty-Five Years*, II, 334–8).

p. 89. **Mr. Bright's brother...very well in himself:** ed. 2 reads "Some more ordinary man would be more to the purpose— would sum up better in himself," and omits Mr. Bazley's name where it occurs below.

Mr. Jacob Bright (1821–99): M.P. for Manchester, 1867–74.

p. 90. **voluntaryism:** i.e. the principle of leaving religion and education to voluntary effort rather than to establishments or state action; another word for "Mialism," v. notes, pp. 87, 117, 207.

Now it is clear...a famous sentence: ed. 2 reads "Now it happens that a typical middle-class man, the member for one of our chief industrial cities, has given us a famous sentence."

Mr. Bazley: created Sir Thomas Bazley, 1869, a Manchester cotton-spinner and for a time chairman of the Manchester Chamber of Commerce.

p. 91. **Mr. Murphy:** v. Editor's Introduction, p. xxix.

the Rev. W. Cattle: ed. 2 omits this name wherever it occurs, substituting some phrase like "this Walsall gentleman." Cattle was a Wesleyan minister who took the chair for Murphy at Birmingham.

Sir Thomas Bateson: ed. 2 reads "our aristocratical baronet."
hauled: ed. 1 misprints "handed."

p. 92. **Alderman Wilson:** ed. 2 omits these two words, v. Editor's Preface, pp. ix–x and Editor's Introduction, p. xxx.

p. 93. **men like the chiefs of the Hyde Park demonstration:** omitted in ed. 1, v. Editor's Introduction, p. xxvi.

p. 94. **Mr. Odger:** i.e. George Odger (1820–77), v. Editor's Introduction, p. xxv.

as in Lord Elcho: omitted in ed. 2.

p. 95. **Sir Thomas Bateson...Rev. W. Cattle...Mr. Bradlaugh:** ed. 1 reads these names alone, ed. 2 suppresses the first two and reads instead, "our fierce aristocratic baronet...our truculent middle-class Dissenting minister...its notorious tribune, Mr. Bradlaugh." The names "Elcho," "Bateson" and "Cattle" are similarly suppressed in later passages of the book, and it is unnecessary to record instances. For "Bradlaugh," v. Editor's Introduction, p. xxv. "Iconoclast" was a pen-name of Bradlaugh's.

p. 96. **the Rev. W. Cattle...rest of us:** omitted by ed. 2.

p. 97. **with Sir Thomas...of his children:** ed. 2 reads "with our baronet's aristocratical prejudices or with the fanaticism of our middle-class Dissenter."

III. BARBARIANS, PHILISTINES, POPULACE

p. 98. **a man without a philosophy:** cf. note, p. 85.

mean...excess...defect: v. note "Aristotle," p. 86.

p. 99. **"refuse to lend a hand to...evils":** the words come from F. Harrison's article "Culture: a dialogue," v. p. 73 and note.

p. 100. **"bright powers...of action":** v. note, p. 82.

Canning's "Needy Knife-Grinder": George Canning (1770–1827), the orator and politician, contributed to the *Anti-Jacobin* this famous skit upon Southey which narrates in Sapphic rhyme a conversation between a Friend of Humanity and a knife-grinder in which the latter refuses to be worked up into a fury of resentment at "rich tyrants" or to show any consciousness of his "wrongs."

Zephaniah Diggs: an imaginary person in *Friendship's Garland* representing the seamy side of English peasant life.

Mr. Bazley...Dissenter: ed. 1 gives the names only; ed. 2 omits the names and substitutes the descriptions.

p. 101. **Philistines:** The word "Philistine" as a term of contempt comes from Germany, "Philister" being originally applied by students to the townsman who was not a member of the university. Arnold himself first used it in his essay on Heine (*Ess. Crit.* 1, 162–3) "Philistinism!—we have not the expression in English. Perhaps we have not the word because we have so much of the thing. At Soli, I imagine, they did not talk of solecisms; and here, at the very headquarters of Goliath, nobody talks of Philistinism.... Philistine must have originally meant, in the mind of those who invented the nickname, a strong, dogged, unenlightened opponent of the chosen people, of the children of light."

our chivalrous...Bateson: here again we combine the readings of edd. 1 and 2.

which Mr. Carlyle proposes: i.e. in *Shooting Niagara*, v. Editor's Introduction, p. xxiv.

p. 102. **lured off:** the reading of 1882, edd. 1 and 2, read "seduced."

in a way: ed. 1 omits.

employing, in order to designate...name: ed. 1 reads "putting side by side with the idea of...idea."

p. 104. **and of even...feminine half:** ed. 1 omits.

Mrs. Gooch's Golden Rule: cf. p. 80.

which so much occupies the attention of philanthropists at present: a reference to the Royal Commission on Trades' Unions (1867–69), v. Editor's Introduction, p. xxv.

p. 105. **Plato's subtle expression:** perhaps a reference to *Charmides*, 170, etc.

p. 106. **Mr. Swinburne would add,** etc.: A. C. Swinburne (1837–1909), the poet, in an article entitled "Mr. Arnold's New Poems" published in the *Fortnightly Review* for Oct. 1867, referring to Wordsworth's influence upon Arnold, writes (p. 425):

It will be a curious problem for the critics of another age to work at, and, if they can, to work out, this influence of men more or less imbued with the savour and spirit of Philistia upon the moral Samson who has played for our behoof the part of Agonistes or protagonist in the new Gaza where we live. From the son of his father and the pupil of his teacher [Wordsworth] none would have looked for such efficient assault and battery of the Philistine outworks...A profane alien in my hearing once defined him as "David, the son of Goliath."

p. 108. **rattening:** ed. 1 reads "trades' unions"; "rattening" means "abstracting tools, destroying machinery or appliances, etc., as a means of enforcing compliance with the rules of a trade-union" (chiefly associated with Sheffield), *N.E.D.*; v. Editor's Introduction, p. xxviii. For the Sheffield outrages v. *Annual Register*, June 12, 1867.

p. 110. **Martinus Scriblerus**: "The Memoirs of Martinus Scriblerus" (1741), an elaborate satire upon the extravagancies of learning, by John Arbuthnot (1667–1735), the friend of Pope and Swift.

I have formerly...like an Academy: cf. "The Literary influences of Academies" (*Ess. Crit.* 1).

the *Saturday Review*: v. Editor's Introduction, pp. xx–xxi.

p. 111. **the *British Banner***: a weekly Nonconformist paper founded in 1847.

Mr. Hepworth Dixon (1821–79): editor of *The Athenæum* (1853–68), a journalist and writer of travel books and historical biographies. His book on Mormonism, etc., the real title of which is *Spiritual Wives*, was published in 1868; v. below, pp. 181–2.

Smith...Young: the founder of the Mormons and his successor.

p. 112. **Shakerism**: an offshoot of the Society of Friends which springing up in Manchester about 1750 obtained a considerable following in the U.S.A. Its founders were two women, one of whom claimed to be a reincarnation of Christ.

p. 113. **or the imaginative**: omitted in ed. 1.

p. 114. **he that trusteth**, etc.: *Prov.* xxviii. 26.

Mr. Tennyson: Arnold, who considered Tennyson "deficient in intellectual power" (*Letters*, 1, 127), quotes from *The Princess* (Conclusion, ll. 66–85), pub. 1847; "a schoolboy's barring out" refers to rebellions at public schools, not infrequent in the 18th and early 19th century, the common tradition of which was to shut out the master until he granted the demands of the boys.

all the world knows that the great middle class, etc.: a quotation I have not traced, probably from a speech by Lowe.

p. 115. **"theirs are the brightest powers,"** etc.: cf. note, p. 82.

Reform League: v. Editor's Introduction, pp. xxv–xxvi.

Mr. Lowe calls the Populace drunken and venal: v. Editor's Introduction, pp. xxiii–xxiv.

p. 116. **Figaro**: the hero of the *Barber of Seville* (1775) and *The Marriage of Figaro* (1784), two plays by Beaumarchais.

Daily News: the organ of moderate Liberalism, with a very wide circulation. The paper was founded in 1846 by Charles Dickens, who, however, retired after a few months.

p. 117. **Sir James Graham's useful Education Clauses
in 1843**: i.e. the Clauses in the Factory Act of that year, introduced by the Home Secretary in Peel's Second Ministry, which
provided for the instruction of children employed in factories,
including religious instruction according to the tenets of the
Church of England. Though a conscience clause was added,
the Nonconformists opposed the clauses so vigorously that
they were withdrawn. v. J. W. Adamson, *English Education,
1789–1902*, p. 133, and note "voluntaryism in education,"
p. 207 below.

p. 118. **when I was in North Germany**: i.e. for the
Taunton Commission, v. Editor's Introduction, p. xix.

Licensed Victuallers or the Commercial Travellers: on
June 18th, 1866, the Prince of Wales opened the Warehousemen,
Clerks and Drapers School at Russell Hill, Purley, an incident to
which Arnold is no doubt referring in his oblique fashion. The
Princess Louise opened a new wing in 1878 and the King is still
a Patron of the School.

p. 119. **Wilhelm von Humboldt** (1767–1835): the first
Prussian minister of Public Instruction and the architect of the
modern German educational system. Cf. pp. 126–7.

Schleiermacher (1768–1834): German theologian and
educationalist, friend of von Humboldt, whom he helped in
founding the Frederick-William University of Berlin.

p. 121. **"It is of no use," says the *Times*, etc.**: clearly a
quotation from some article written in reply to Chapter II ("Doing
as one likes") which appeared in the *Cornhill* in Jan. 1868.

Mr. Roebuck's celebrated definition of happiness: v.
note, p. 50.

p. 122. **our other philosophical teacher, the *Daily News*,
etc.**: cf. note, p. 116. Once again Arnold seems to be answering an
article written in reply to himself: cf. below, p. 125: "the *Daily
News* says, I observe, that all my argument for authority," etc.

in my last paper: i.e. chap. II, *supra*, pp. 77–9, 92.

p. 124. **because...discovered**: omitted in ed. 2.

and it will...operation: also omitted in ed. 2.

the Rev. W. Cattle: ed. 2 reads "Mr. Murphy."

p. 126. **an able writer**: v. the *Westminster Review*, Jan.
1868, "Dangers of Democracy," an anonymous review of

Carlyle's *Shooting Niagara* and von Humboldt's *Sphere and Duties of Government.*

p. 127. M. Renan on State action: v. note, p. 17. Arnold quotes from p. 73, *Questions Contemporaines,* 1868.

IV. HEBRAISM AND HELLENISM

p. 130. partakers of the divine nature: 2 *Pet.* i. 4.

Frederick Robertson (1816–53): the well-known popular preacher of Trinity Chapel, Brighton, deeply sympathetic with working class movements. Arnold first read his life by Stopford Brooke "by accident" in 1865 and became greatly interested in him (*Letters,* 1, 311).

p. 131. Heinrich Heine (1797–1856): the great German poet, who lived in Paris, and a Jew by birth who worshipped the Greeks. Cf. *Heine's Grave* and the essay on him in *Ess. Crit.* 1.

"He that...is he": *Prov.* xxix. 18.

"Blessed is the man...commandments": *Ps.* cxii. 1; ed. 1 reads "There is nothing sweeter than to take heed unto the commandments of the Lord" (*Eccl.* xxiii. 27). The change is perhaps connected with Arnold's writing of *Literature and Dogma.*

words of a great French moralist: I have not traced these words.

p. 133. Zechariah: ix. 13.

"Understanding...hath it": *Prov.* xvi. 22.

Aristotle: quoting from the *Nic. Ethics,* bk. 11, p. 4 (v. trans. W. D. Ross).

Epictetus: v. note, p. 53.

Plato...calls life a learning to die: v. *Phaedo,* 63.

p. 134. Plato expressly denies...$\phi\iota\lambda o\mu\alpha\theta\dot{\eta}\varsigma$: v. *Republic,* v, 475 D–480.

To St. Paul...judged impossible: ed. 2 omits.

Memorabilia: by Xenophon; written to defend the reputation of Socrates. Not all would now agree that it gives us "the true Socrates" (cf. G. C. Field, *Plato and his Contemporaries,* pp. 137–45).

p. 135. "Socrates is terribly *at ease in Zion*": I have not been able to trace this in Carlyle.

Dr. Pusey (1800–82): Regius Professor of Hebrew at

Oxford, one of the founders of the Oxford Movement in the Church of England.

p. 136. **with groanings...body of this death:** combining viii. 26 with vii. 24 *Romans*.

Zechariah: viii. 23.

p. 137. **George Herbert** (1593–1633): the well-known religious poet.

alma Venus: v. Lucretius, *De rerum natura*, prol.

p. 141. **Science has now made visible,** etc.: cf. Arnold's *Celtic Literature*, passim. He is here probably thinking chiefly of Renan's *Histoire des Langues Sémitiques*.

p. 143. **habitual courses of action:** misprinted "habitual causes of action" in the popular edition.

V. PORRO UNUM EST NECESSARIUM

The title is taken from the Vulgate; cf. *Luke* x. 41–2: "But one thing is needful."

p. 146. **his intellectual side:** ed. 1 prints "his moral side," an error corrected in ed. 2.

p. 147. **the world by wisdom,** etc.: v. 1 *Cor*. i. 22.

p. 148. **Mr. Sidgwick:** Henry Sidgwick (1838–1900), the Cambridge philosopher: by "somewhat rigid" Arnold probably meant that Sidgwick was too closely allied to the utilitarian school for his liking. In Aug. 1867, Sidgwick published in *Macmillan's Magazine* an article on "The prophet of culture," replying to the earlier chapters of *Culture and Anarchy* in the July *Cornhill*, v. Editor's Introduction, pp. xxi, xxxv.

Mr. Buckle: v. note, p. 68.

p. 150. **Mr. Murphy:** v. Editor's Introduction, p. xxix.

p. 155. **The characteristic...as beautiful:** some confusion has clearly impaired the sense of ed. 1 which, following straight on without a break from "take their chance," reads "because the characteristic bent of Hellenism, as has been said, is to find the intelligible law of things, and there is no intelligible law of things, things cannot really appear intelligible unless they are also beautiful. The body...is not intelligible, is not seen in its true nature and as it really is, unless it is seen as beautiful."

Faraday (1791–1867): the great chemist and electrical

scientist. The Sandemanians or Glassites are a Scotch sect founded c. 1730 by John Glas and Robert Sandeman; their doctrines are founded upon a literal interpretation of Scripture. For a different view of Faraday's religion v. *Sanderson of Oundle*, pp. 203–8.

p. 156. **the desire which, as Plato says,** etc.: v. *Symposium*, 210, 211.

p. 159. **"Thou that sayest,"** etc.: *Rom.* ii. 22.

p. 160. **whereas he well-nigh exhausted**: ed. 1 reads "whereas he exhausted."

p. 163. **Proceeding...no real aim at perfection**: ed. 2 omits.

enabling ourselves...to come as near, etc.: ed. 2 reads "enabling ourselves by getting to know, whether through reading, observing, or thinking, the best that can at present be known in the world, to come as near," etc.

when we are accused, etc.: cf. pp. 72–3.

VI. OUR LIBERAL PRACTITIONERS

p. 165. **an unpretending writer...coherent principles:** cf. note, p. 85.

Therefore, since...have advanced: Arnold arranges this sentence somewhat differently in ed. 1.

the disestablishment of the Irish Church: the election of 1868 was largely fought upon this issue; v. Editor's Introduction, p. xxxi.

delicate...scepticism and cultivated inaction: cf. notes, pp. 73, 99.

p. 166. **But the apportionment...made:** omitted in ed. 1.

that maxim...more than once used: cf. "this favourite old stock maxim of theirs [the Liberals]: 'The State (that is the nation in its collective and corporate capacity) is of no religion' is quite unsound. In exchange we ought to solicit them, with a persistency which never tires, to take a better: 'It is false to say the State is of no religion; the State is of the religion of all its citizens without the fanaticism of any of them'" (Preface written for 1874 ed. of *Schools and Universities on the Continent,* v. *A French Eton,* ed. 1892, pp. 201–2), and *Popular Education in France* (1861), p. 220.

either of the State or of religion: ed. 1 continues the next paragraph straight on from this, reading a comma after "religion" and "and" before "our statesmen."

p. 167. like Mr. Baxter and Mr. Charles Buxton: ed. 2 omits; v. note, p. 12.

p. 168. Mr. Spurgeon: v. note, p. 20; "eloquent and memorable" is, of course, ironical.

p. 170. the Liberation Society: i.e. "the Society for Liberating Religion from State patronage and control," founded in 1845 by Edward Miall and others; v. note, p. 87.

Miss Cobbe and the British College of Health: Frances Power Cobbe (1822–1904) was a philosophical and religious writer. Her book *Religious Duty*, which attempts to construct a new religion for the future of mankind, is referred to by Arnold in *Ess. Crit.* i, pp. 32–3, and compared with a pretentious building in the New Road "with the lion and the Statue of the Goddess Hygiene before it" erected by a certain Dr. Morrison and arrogating to itself the title of "The British College of Health"— "the grand name without the grand thing."

p. 171. Joubert: v. note, p. 4.

Mr. Spurgeon's great Tabernacle: v. note, p. 20.

p. 174. the effeminate horror which, etc.: v. note, p. 73.

the Real Estate Intestacy Bill: introduced in 1869 by Locke King; for the assimilation of real estate to personality in cases of intestacy.

p. 178. As he who putteth a stone in a sling, etc.; *Prov.* xxvi. 8.

p. 179. in the endeavour...known: ed. 1 omits this.

p. 180. Mr. Lowe when he called, or was supposed to call, etc.: v. Editor's Introduction, p. xxiii.

deceased wife's sister: v. Editor's Introduction, pp. xxxi–xxxii, and *Friendship's Garland*, Letter viii. Thomas Chambers (1814–91), Liberal M.P. for Marylebone, introduced the bill in 1866.

p. 181. Hepworth Dixon: v. note, p. 111.

Dr Colenso (1814–1883): bishop of Natal, attained notoriety in England by publishing *A Critical Examination of the Pentateuch* (1862–79) which argued that these books were post-exilic forgeries. He was deposed and excommunicated by the bishop of Cape Town, but the decision was negatived by the courts of law in 1866. In Jan. 1863, Arnold published an article in *Macmillan's Magazine* entitled "The Bishop and the Philosopher," the former being Colenso and the latter Spinoza, an article later published in a revised form as "Spinoza and the Bible" in *Ess. Crit.* 1.

p. 182. lithe and sinewy: v. next note. The newspaper referred to is the *Daily Telegraph*: v. notes pp. 7–8 (Mr G. A. Sala) and *Friendship's Garland*, p. 68.

delicacy of perception: cf. *Friendship's Garland*, pp. 66–7: "'Will any one dare to call Bottles, if he contracts a marriage of this kind, a profligate man?' Poor Mr. Matthew Arnold, upon this, emerged suddenly from his corner, and asked hesitatingly: 'But will any one dare call him a man of delicacy?'...My friend Nick, who has all the sensitive temperament of genius, seemed inexplicably struck by this word delicacy, which he kept repeating to himself. 'Delicacy,' said he, 'delicacy—surely I have heard that word before! Yes, in other days,' he went on dreamily, 'in my fresh, enthusiastic youth; before I knew Sala, before I wrote for that infernal paper [the *Daily Telegraph*], before I called Dixon's style lithe and sinewy.'"

p. 184. free-trade: this was effected by the repeal of the Corn Laws in 1846, a measure chiefly due to the agitation in the country by Bright and his friend Cobden.

p. 186. Mr. Bright...tells it...built: cf. pp. 64–5, note.

p. 188. Bastiat (1801–50): eminent French economist; an ardent free trader who made a special study of the English movement for the repeal of the corn laws.

p. 189. East of London, whither my avocations often lead me: i.e. as an inspector of schools.

p. 190. Mr. Robert Buchanan (1841–1901): a minor poet and journalist, chiefly noted for his attack on Rossetti in the *Contemporary Review*, Oct. 1871, entitled "The Fleshly School of Poetry." Arnold quotes from "The Student and his vocation" a comment upon the early "Culture and Anarchy" articles (v. *David Gray and other Essays*, 1868, pp. 198–200).

p. 192. "The *multitude*...world": v. *Wisd.* vi, 24.

p. 193. one pauper...nineteen of us: ed. 2 omits this parenthesis.

And though Hebraism...teaching; yet: ed. 2 omits.

p. 194. *The poor shall never cease,* etc.: *Deut.* xv. 11.

p. 196. the psalm-verse: i.e. *Psa.* cxxvii. 3–5.

that is to say...as infallible: not in ed. 1.

p. 197. and to diminish...nineteen of us: ed. 2 omits; cf. note, p. 193.

pp. 199–200. Thus we may often, perhaps...development would be baneful: ed. 2 omits this whole paragraph.

p. 199. New Road forms of religious institution: i.e. "the grand names without the grand thing," like the British College of Health in New Road, v. note, p. 170.

Archdeacon Denison (1805–96): prominent high churchman of an extreme and controversial type. Created many difficulties with the Education Department over Church Schools; v. Frank Smith, *History of English Elementary Education,* 1760–1902, pp. 172–3, 208–9. In 1885 he published a violent diatribe against Gladstone.

pp. 200–1. For example...producible and possible: ed. 2 omits.

p. 201. Sir Henry Hoare: M.P. for New Windsor in 1865.

p. 203. With me, indeed...Tarpeian Rock! ed. 2 omits; v. Editor's Preface, p. viii.

p. 205. Barbarian Secretaries of State: referring to Spencer Walpole, Home Secretary in Lord Derby's government at the time of the Hyde Park Riots, v. Editor's Introduction, pp. xxix–xxx.

Philistine Alderman-Colonels: i.e. Ald. Samuel Wilson, v. Editor's Preface, pp. ix–x and Editor's Introduction, p. xxx.

fire and strength: a quotation from Sidgwick, v. p. 148.

p. 206. Aristotle says: cf. *Nic. Ethics,* x, 9, trans. W. D. Ross.

p. 207. church-establishments: ed. 1 reads "Church-rates."

than Churchmen have: ed. 2 omits.

voluntaryism in education: a Nonconformist movement led by Edward Miall (v. note, pp. 87, 90, 117) and Edward Baines, and arising out of the opposition to Sir James Graham's Education Clauses, to free education entirely from State connexion; v. Birchenough, *History of Elementary Education,* pp. 84–8.

p. 208. Mr. Sidgwick: v. note, p. 148.

ourselves through finding: added in ed. 2.

pp. 208–9. And even in education...hands ever so fully:

ed. 2 omits this passage. It was out of date after the Education Bill of 1870.

p. 209. **Mr. Samuel Morley**: a prominent Nonconformist who became a convert to State education. M.P. for Nottingham in 1865.

p. 210. **Thyesteän banquet**: i.e. a feast of an abominable and barbarous character, Thyestes unwittingly feeding upon the flesh of his own son at a feast prepared out of revenge by his brother Atreus. Cf. *Friendship's Garland*, p. xiv.

p. 211. **has drunk his hemlock and is dead**: I follow ed. 3 (1882) here; edd. 1 and 2 read, "is poisoned and dead."

p. 212. **the human race**: ed. 1 reads "the world."

Addendum

p. 65. **the *Journeyman Engineer***: i.e. Thomas Wright, author of *The Great Unwashed* (1868), *Some Habits and Customs of the Working Classes* (1867), etc., who attempted to interpret the ideas and habits of the working classes to the rest of the community. [I owe this note to Mr H. L. Beales.]

BIBLIOGRAPHY

I. GENERAL

For the historical background of *Culture and Anarchy* the student should consult Spencer Walpole's *A History of Twenty-Five Years*, vol. II of which deals with the years 1865–70, Herbert Paul's *History of Modern England*, G. M. Trevelyan's *Life of John Bright* and where these fail, *The Annual Register* and *The Times*. For educational history J. W. Adamson's *English Education, 1789–1902*, R. L. Archer's *Secondary Education in the XIXth Century*, Frank Smith's *History of Elementary Education, 1760–1902*, and C. Birchenough's *History of Elementary Education in England and Wales from 1800 to the present day* are the standard authorities, while Arnold's own educational writings are indispensable.

II. BIOGRAPHICAL AND CRITICAL MATERIAL

Arnold's *Letters*, edited by his friend G. W. E. Russell (2 vols., 1895), are of capital importance, and of the lives the same friend's *Matthew Arnold* (1904) is the best. Herbert Paul's volume in the "English Men of Letters" series and Professor Saintsbury's in the "Modern English Writers" series are both too purely literary in outlook and too wayward in judgment to be altogether satisfactory. Suggestive books are W. H. Dawson's *Matthew Arnold and his relation to the thought of our time* (1904) and J. G. Fitch's *Thomas and Matthew Arnold and their influence on English Education* (1897), while no better introduction for a beginner could be found than *Selections from Matthew Arnold's Prose* by D. C. Somervell (1924). Leonard Woolf, *After the Deluge* (1931), i, 281–7, criticizes Arnold severely. R. H. Tawney, *Equality* (1931), esp. ch. ii, is on the other hand appreciative.

III. ARNOLD'S PRINCIPAL PUBLICATIONS

(a) Verse

The Strayed Reveller, 1849.
Empedocles on Etna, 1852.
Poems, 2 vols., 1869. The only poem of note written after this date is *Westminster Abbey* (v. note on Dean of Westminster, A. P. Stanley, p. 8).

(b) Educational writings

Popular Education in France, etc., 1861 (Arnold's report as foreign assistant-commissioner to the Newcastle Commission, reprinted with a special Introduction on the relation between popular education and the State).

A French Eton, or Middle-class Education and the State, 1864.

Schools and Universities on the Continent, 1868 (a reprint of Arnold's report as foreign assistant-commissioner to the Taunton Commission, otherwise known as the Schools Enquiry Commission).

Special Report on Elementary Education abroad, 1886 (issued by the Education Department).

Reports on Elementary Schools, 1852–1882, edited by F. S. Marvin (1910) (containing the annual reports made by Arnold as H.M. Inspector to the Education Department).

Thoughts on Education from Matthew Arnold, ed. Leonard Huxley, 1912.

(c) Religious writings

St Paul and Protestantism, with an Introduction on Puritanism and the Church of England, 1870.

Literature and Dogma, an essay towards a better apprehension of the Bible, 1873.

God and the Bible, a review of objections to "Literature and Dogma," 1875.

Last Essays on Church and Religion, 1877.

(d) Literary, social and political

On translating Homer, 1861.

Essays in Criticism, 1865 (1st series).

On the Study of Celtic Literature, 1867.

Culture and Anarchy, 1869, 2nd ed. 1875, 3rd ed. 1882, Pop. ed. 1889.

Friendship's Garland, 1871.

Mixed Essays, 1879.

Irish Essays and others, 1882.

Discourses in America, 1885.

Essays in Criticism, 1888 (2nd series).

A useful bibliography of Arnold's writings was compiled in 1892 by T. B. Smart.

IV. SOME CONTEMPORARY ARTICLES ILLUS-TRATING *CULTURE AND ANARCHY*

The Saturday Review, Feb. 1865, "Mr Arnold and his Countrymen" (a review of *Essays in Criticism*).

The Cornhill Magazine, Feb. 1866, "My Countrymen" by M. Arnold (a reply to the *Saturday Review*; reprinted in *Friendship's Garland*).

Macmillan's Magazine, Aug. 1867, "The prophet of Culture" by Henry Sidgwick (referred to on pp. 148, 208).

The Fortnightly Review, Oct. 1867, "Mr Arnold's New Poems" by A. C. Swinburne (referred to on p. 106).

The Fortnightly Review, Nov. 1867, "Culture: a Dialogue" by Frederic Harrison (referred to on p. 73).

The Quarterly Review, Oct. 1868, "Mr Matthew Arnold's Report on French Education" (a review by Oscar Browning of *Schools and Universities on the Continent*; referred to on p. 8).